Effective Collective Bargaining in Public Education

Effective Collective Bargaining in Public Education

WILLIAM G. WEBSTER, SR.

IOWA STATE UNIVERSITY PRESS, AMES

LB
2844.59
U6
W43
1985

Composed and printed by The Iowa State University Press
Ames, Iowa 50010

First edition, 1985

Library of Congress Cataloging in Publication Data

Webster, William G. (William Gerald)
    Effective collective bargaining in public education.

    Bibliography: p.
    Includes index.
    1. Collective bargaining — Teachers — United States.
I. Title.
BL2844.59.U6W43   1985   331.89′0413711′00973   85–2516
ISBN 0–8138–0526–0

This book is dedicated to my parents,

Arthur M. Webster (1900–1982) **and Della G. Webster** (1910–1973),

who persisted in the belief that there was hope for
two little black boys born in the depression-era South—
and worked hard to fulfill their dream.

CONTENTS

PREFACE

COLLECTIVE BARGAINING in public education has developed to an extent not considered possible a few years ago. Combinations of events like the women's movement, the civil rights movement, and others have accelerated the shift to legalized bargaining. Almost every state in the nation has enacted laws to insure that the teacher viewpoint will be heard. These laws range from "meet and confer" arrangements to collective bargaining outright.

Despite these legislative changes, the bargaining skill of educators has not kept pace. It is easier, perhaps, to organize and train bargainers from private or other public sector fields, for apart from problems of role confusion that derive from former working relationships with administrators, teacher organizations face certain other problems related to the nature of the profession itself. These organizational problems involve (1) internal political frictions, (2) competing teacher organizations, (3) provincialism, and (4) general distaste for activities considered blue-collar activities.

Certain administrators, too, have faced problems in adjusting to the mind-sets and attitudes necessary for effective bargaining. These problems may be summed up as (1) those incidental to "changing hats" between the school site and the bargaining table; (2) those that derive from the threat value of collective bargaining as a device for increased teacher power; and (3) those that result from the ambiguous position some school site administrators are in as a result of collective bargaining.

To illustrate the time lag between the onrush of collective bargaining legislation and preparation of the parties to bargaining, one only has to observe what happened in California after the passage of their collective bargaining law. In less than one year after the Rodda Act was passed, the state employment relations agency was deluged with hundreds of cases of impasse from school districts statewide. Many cases were simply the result of "muscle flexing" by teacher organizations in response to the new legislation, but others reflected misconceptions about the basic nature of collective bargaining. Thus in many instances teacher organizations interpreted the legislation as an entree to teacher takeover of school districts, and school boards stiffened in opposition to such teacher perceptions.

The content and format of this book were conceptualized during those early months of confusion. The need for a book such as this was obvious. Members of various factions of the public education community, teacher organization leaders, administrators, school board members, and professors of education were very interested in the philosophies, strategies, tactics, and dynamics of collective bargaining in public education. Surveys of the literature of collective bargaining in public education revealed very few comprehensive works on the subject. Also, those works available were in large part dated and in desperate need of editorial update.

One additional nagging concern gave rise to this book. That concern came out of the observation that most of the available books on collective bargaining in education were heavily oriented to the classical topics of bargaining, like the history of bargaining in general, the development of teacher unionism, and — when possible — certain theoretical models and other formulations borrowed mainly from the literature of public sector bargaining, private sector bargaining, and public school administration.

In the behavioral sciences there is always a need for classical approaches to literature because they promise broader conceptualizations and better generalizations. But there is also an ongoing need for practical books in certain areas of the behavioral sciences, and collective bargaining in public education is one such area.

This book was intended as a *practical reference* for those interested in public education collective bargaining. Because of this, certain topics were omitted and others were included. Four broad aspects of bargaining were selected as its framework: (1) the fundamentals of collective bargaining in education; (2) the struggle for bargaining position; (3) preparing for bargaining; and (4) the procedures, tactics, dynamics, and other dimensions of the confrontation.

Part 1 seeks to prepare the reader for understanding bargaining. Chapters 1 and 2 introduce the fundamental concepts of collective bargaining and certain generalizations about the perceptions of the parties typically interested in the dynamics and outcomes of public education bargaining. Part 2 is focused on an aspect that is sadly overlooked in many if not most education bargaining books: preparation of the support elements of bargaining. Unfortunately, the adoption of the private sector model of bargaining by educators and other employees has encouraged certain philosophies and attitudes wherein public opinion is not perceived as important as it actually is in influencing the outcomes of bargaining. Parts 3 and 4 focus on bargaining team preparation and at-the-table dynamics, respectively. In these parts as well as the first two, certain basic themes are repeated: (1) there is no mystique involved in effective bargaining; (2) public opinion is the key to effective bargaining; and (3) in effective bargaining, both sides "win." Part 5 is dedicated to the implementation of bargained contracts.

Throughout, an attempt is made to explain various aspects through examples that might be meaningful to practicing administrators and teachers. While some examples might be more applicable to some districts than others because of local variations in school practices and state-to-state fluctuations in collective bargaining legalities, many examples will apply.

Grievance arbitration is given comprehensive treatment for two reasons. The first reason derives from the importance of the area for scope-widening tactics and strategies by teacher organizations; that is, much of teacher organization energies aimed at enlarging the scope of bargaining will necessarily be focused on grievances and the potential of arbitration awards for broadening or otherwise changing contract interpretations. The second reason is that of administrator need. Administrators need a clear grasp of what grievance arbitration is about and what is to be expected from arbitration proceedings.

No one can write a book without the exchange of ideas with others, especially those who are or have been practitioners in the field of collective bargaining in public education. There are several persons who helped along the way. First, I thank my wife Peggy Webster (Hilma Hagberg Webster), a recent doctoral graduate in Curriculum and Instruction (Stanford University, 1982), for her encouragement at every phase in the book's development. Second, I would like to thank four former students and co-workers: Paula Crawford, Ken Dotson, Bonnie Emerson, and James C. Johnston (a former teacher-bargainer turned principal). For general encouragement and support, I am grateful to Dr. Charles R. Farrar, my closest colleague at California State College, Stanislaus, for spending considerable time reading the manuscript in its early stages and giving feedback and encouragement about the project.

It is my hope that the practical design and orientation of this book fit the needs of the various factions for which it was intended—from school board members to teacher-bargainers to practicing administrators to graduate students. I also hope that it conveys the notion that in effective bargaining, both sides win.

PART 1

Some Fundamentals of Collective Bargaining in Education

CHAPTER 1

A Workable Concept
of Collective Bargaining

MANY IF NOT MOST OBSERVERS of the changing panorama of American sociology have developed general notions of what collective bargaining is. The well-publicized strikes, job actions, and other activities of giant labor unions and other organizations tend to encourage conceptualization about the basic nature and processes of collective bargaining.

Such conceptualizations invite the tendency to equate the dynamics of collective bargaining in private industry to those in public service occupations. The generalizations often fail for many reasons, among them: (1) the highly visible character of public sector collective bargaining forces modification of tactics used by private sector labor and management; (2) the public attitudes about public servants that often tend to limit the bargaining aspirations of public employees; and (3) the difficulty of measuring many public service jobs with the same accuracy as the work of, say, a plasterer.

The generalization is confounded even more when collective bargaining in public education is considered. In addition to the problems cited above, one concern of paramount importance to all Americans must be included in bargaining: quality education for children. And the pursuit of quality education in the face of declining enrollments and severe budgetary crises must catalyze a greater spirit of cooperation than ever before (Levin 1982, 34, 37–38).

Quality education is extremely hard to measure. Along with the quantification of child achievement, teachers and administrators and their school boards must deal with certain qualitative aspects of education: even when Johnny is a good reader, what of his character? Is his self-concept adequately developed?

Education bargaining, like bargaining in other quarters, involves a quid pro quo, an exchange wherein both sides win. But because of the nature of the "product"—the child—it is often extremely difficult to get agreement on the adequacy of both sides of the exchange.

Understanding the full range of considerations in collective bargaining demands a look at several aspects of the process that cover much more than the legalities and economics commonly thought of as central to the endeavor.

Many things occur simultaneously during collective bargaining, and the successful student of the process must be aware of all of them. Because of this, the content of this chapter is devoted to helping the reader develop a comprehensive basic mind-set about collective bargaining. It involves the following topics:

Collective Bargaining Defined
Why a Concept of Bargaining is Needed
Bargaining as a Rational Activity
Bargaining as a Dynamic Activity
Process as an End in Bargaining
Bargaining as a Struggle for Equality
Bargaining as Emotional Expression
Bargaining as Political Activity
Bargaining as Compromise
Bargaining as Attitude Restructuring
Bargaining as Problem Solving
Bargaining as a Legal Requirement

□ Collective Bargaining Defined

The exchange of toys between children a few days after Christmas is a simple but perfect example of negotiating or bargaining. Each child makes decisions about which toys he or she would part with in order to own others. Each child seeks a *bargain* or advantage in the exchange, irrespective of how she or he defines that bargain. In such innocent contexts, it is not likely that bargains are defined strictly in material (price) terms; rather, they were probably defined in terms of how each child perceives his or her possible enjoyment of toys owned by other children.

Negotiating and bargaining are synonymous with both the decisions made prior to the exchanges and the mechanics of the exchanges. However, negotiations is a much broader term than bargaining as it is typically used. Neutral third parties who put two parties together in, say, real estate transactions or exchanges of securities are negotiators; lawyers who resolve probate disputes out of court are negotiators; and others who represent one or more clients in exchanges of something for something are also negotiators — even police who attempt to convince downtown snipers to surrender their weapons.

Bargaining as used in the term *collective bargaining* is not synonymous with negotiating. In one sense, it is a narrower term, bound by legal context. While the behaviors of negotiators as described above are not controlled by laws or other criteria except successful completion of their tasks, bargainers in collective bargaining situations are governed by laws that define legal and illegal behaviors. In another sense, bargaining means more than negotiating because it includes several other dimensions, the more important of which are: (1) bargaining is ongoing, without closure at any time point; (2) the bargaining process in both private and public sectors is legally controlled by the degree of public interest involved; and (3) bargaining has inherent potential for displacement of power relationships within the institution or corporation where it occurs. These three aspects deserve elaboration.

☐ **BARGAINING IS ONGOING**   On the surface it appears as though finalization of a written contract closes the bargaining process until time for contract renewal. This is not true. Almost all bargained contracts—in private or public sectors—contain provisions for grievance procedures if there are contractual violations. The existence of such grievance machinery insures ongoing modifications of contract interpretations due to the "watchdog" activities of labor organizations. This means there is constant communication between both parties throughout the life of the contract.

☐ **BARGAINING PROCESS IS LEGALLY CONTROLLED**   Federal laws control collective bargaining to the extent that the public interest is threatened. The same is true of state bargaining statutes. It is perhaps logical that there are more state statutory controls on the scope and process of collective bargaining in the public sector simply because the teachers, police, and fire safety workers have an immediate, direct impact on the public interest whenever they withdraw or threaten to withdraw their services. This means that collective bargaining must be considered in a legal context at all times.

☐ **BARGAINING POTENTIAL FOR POWER RELATIONSHIPS DISPLACEMENTS**   Although collective bargaining differs considerably in private and public sector contexts, it has alteration of power relationships as one of its prime motivations in both. Even the singular focus on salaries and fringe benefits by some labor unions in the private sector involves displacement of power, for management does not usually volunteer increased salaries and benefits. Such salaries and other perquisites must be fought for.

The battle for power through collective bargaining is more clearly evident where working conditions are at issue. Here, management rights and prerogatives are often attacked directly. In education bargaining, for example, teachers are now seeking to participate in formulating the procedures that govern their job evaluations in those states where such participation is not presently included in the scope of bargaining.

A distinction should be made between procedures and criteria for teacher evaluations. This distinction is important because of its potential for displacement of power relationships. On the one hand, school boards insist that it is their legal responsibility to make curriculum decisions. On the other hand, *fair* evaluations of teachers are virtually impossible without references to how teachers have performed instruction, the operational manifestation of curriculum. A question that arises is: how can teachers be limited strictly to decisions about procedures for their evaluations with no references to the criteria on which such procedures are based?

The laws of collective bargaining are written around two basic definitions. Although they are included in the Glossary and are referred to elsewhere, they deserve further explanation. Those terms are: "good faith bargaining" and "unfair labor practices."

One way of clarifying good faith bargaining is earnest bargaining, aimed at a solution. The solution does not have to be mutually beneficial. The only requirement of good faith bargaining is that the intentions of the bargainers are sincere and oriented to a solution of the issues.

Failure to bargain in good faith is difficult to prove because intentions of the parties are hard to discern and because the term is subjective and open to various interpretations. Most collective bargaining laws attempt to define bargaining in good faith by offering certain circumstances under which the behavior of the parties can be interpreted as violative of the requirement. For example, California's Collective Bargaining Act (Govt. Code, Division 4, Title 1, Chap. 10.7, Sec. 3543.5c, 3543.5e, 3543.6c, and 3543.6d) sets forth conditions under which employers or employees can be charged with failure to bargain in good faith:

> The duty to meet and negotiate in good faith requires the parties to begin negotiations prior to the adoption of the final budget for the ensuing year sufficiently in advance of such adoption date so that there is adequate time for agreement to be reached, or for the resolution of impasse. (3543.7)

The law then uses the term in good faith to describe conditions under which the parties can be charged with unfair labor practices:

> The employer or employee organization refuses to meet and negotiate in good faith. (3543.5c and 3543.6c)

or,

> The employer or employee organization refuses to participate in good faith in the impasse procedure set forth in. . . . . (3543.5e and 3543.6d)

"In good faith" is also used loosely in collective bargaining contracts or even in reference to such contracts. Fortunately, unfair labor practices lend themselves to more concrete interpretations. Most collective bargaining laws simply list practices which are considered unfair labor practices. Many are expanded variations of those listed in Section 8 of the National Labor Relations Act. Typically, these laws hold employers can be charged with unfair labor practices if they:

1. Interfere with school employees joining and participating in the activities of employee organizations
2. Refuse to permit individual employees the right to represent themselves individually before selection of an exclusive representative
3. Let an employee represent himself/herself even though that employee is a member of the exclusive bargaining organization
4. Refuse to receive, review, and adjust grievances according to procedures established in the agreement
5. Fail to involve the exclusive representative in the grievance process under the terms of the agreement or upon a grievance going to arbitration
6. Prevent or interfere with the right of employee organizations to establish reasonable restrictions as to who may join or who may be dismissed from membership
7. Prevent or interfere with the rights of employee organizations to:
   a) Reasonable access to employee work areas
   b) Use of bulletin boards, mailboxes, and other reasonable means of communication
   c) Use of institutional facilities at reasonable times
   d) Release time without loss of compensation for meeting and negotiating and processing grievances
   e) Have dues deducted for employee members
8. Interfere with the formation or administration of any employee organization; contribute support to it, or encourage employees to join any organization in preference to another

States vary slightly in their definitions of unfair labor practrices by employers. The same is true for unfair labor practices by employees. Usually, however, employee organizations can be charged with unfair labor practices if those organizations: (1) impose reprisals on employees or threaten such reprisals; (2) discriminate or threaten to discriminate against employees; (3) interfere with, restrain, or coerce employees because they exercise their individual rights under collective bargaining laws.

Because of certain tactics available to and sometimes used by employee organizations, the following broad unfair labor practices provision is often found in collective bargaining laws:

> An employee organization may be charged with unfair labor practices if that organization causes or attempts to cause a public school employer to violate legalities related to unfair labor practices.

Of course, allegations of unfair labor practices must be supported with documentation, witnesses, and other forms of evidence. Certain aspects of collective bargaining laws in public education are sometimes nebulous simply because the words and terms used in those laws lend themselves to various interpretations. Like other rules by which humans govern themselves, the laws of collective bargaining evolve – and they evolve slowly. Much of the evolution centers on selection of better language after a series of negative experiences with the legal language. The problem is much the same as that involving the language of collective bargaining contracts: ambiguity. How often is "sometimes?" And consider the word "reasonable"; reasonable to whom? To the parties to the contract? To laymen? Or to the average reasonable person?

General. A neat, precise definition of collective bargaining is difficult if not impossible. A definition must be acquired by individuals through their grasp of several related perspectives, all of which merge to provide a conceptual grasp. Such a conceptual grasp is very important.

☐ Why a Concept of Collective Bargaining is Needed

The definition of *theory* advanced by Kerlinger (1973, 9) involves the dual dimensions of explanation and prediction. Behavioral phenomena can often be grasped and explained after theories are formulated. Similarly, well-formulated theories offer the potential for predictions of future behavior. The ongoing search for theories that unify behavioral phenomena is justified and should continue. At this time, however, there are no established theories of or for collective bargaining.

In the absence of well-formulated theories of bargaining, something else is needed to promote the unification of thought about collective bargaining. Models of varying degrees of abstraction help to portray relationships and other dynamics of bargaining, but they often fall short for several reasons: (1) they only portray isolated aspects of bargaining, usually procedural; (2) so many variables impact on the bargaining endeavor at any single instant that they are impossible to capture in a model that has as its strong point the neat summation of ideas; and (3) models offer the temptation to oversimplify. Needed, then, is an overall concept, held by each observer.

As previously stated, such an overall concept cannot be a neat one. In addition to drawing from most of the behavioral sciences, collective bargaining must be thought of from many standpoints. These standpoints – or perspectives – constitute the remainder of this chapter.

☐ Bargaining as a Rational Activity

Stated simply, the idea of collective bargaining in education as a rational activity means that both parties will use common sense to achieve their bargaining goals. This implies it is not likely that members of either side will "go crazy" and act irrationally in the overall bargaining.

But the rational aspect of collective bargaining in education must be considered as much more than behavior during the discussions and exchanges of proposals and counterproposals. Of major importance are dimensions of *goal setting* and *retention of power.*

For school boards, goal setting means achieving the desired ends of quality education within the framework of fixed, publicly approved operational budgets. It is possible that in any school year the average school board could reduce its budget to a bare minimum and save many tax dollars. But it is equally possible that such reductions would lead to an exodus of good teachers and a possible drop in the quality of childrens' education in the district. Such a situation would (or could) in turn catalyze public dissatisfaction and lead to the recall of the board members.

From the standpoint of teacher organizations, goals are also closely related to the retention of power. Goal-setting activity must accomplish several simultaneous ends: (1) goals must be achievable; (2) organization goals must be credible to both the teacher membership and the general public; (3) organization goals must not appear to counter the best interests of children; (4) goals must not overreach the will of the public to support effective teachers; and (5) goals must not generate backlash within the teacher organization. All five criteria for goal setting are rational and they govern much of the behavior of teacher organization leaders. An example may illustrate what happens when teacher organization leaders fail to use rational, balanced criteria in goal setting.

In 1977 a fiery, energetic young man became president of the "certified" organization (exclusive bargaining agent) of teachers of a small West Coast school district. Teachers were supportive of his direct, abrasive manner in dealing with the school board and administration because they felt the board had failed to be responsive to their pleas for fringe benefits (hospitalization, dental, income protection plans, and others) comparable to those of other similar districts in the state. Desperate for a device that could put direct pressure on the school board, the young leader obtained permission from his teacher executive board and sought an alliance with the local chapter of the teamsters union, an alliance that would mean that teachers would be organized as teamsters. The proposed alliance was voted on by the total teacher membership and failed by a great margin. The failure was followed by a recall movement within the teacher organization. The young president was unseated. While the potential alliance met the criteria offered in (1), (3), and (4) above, it did not agree with (2) and (5). These two are related: the proposed alliance with teamsters did not appear credible to the teachers, and that lack of credibility generated a backlash within the teacher organization.

Even the resort to impasse during bargaining must be rational to most observers. Simply walking out and declaring impasse is irrational behavior unless it can be shown that all avenues to effective bargaining are blocked and the issue is *worth* the declaration of impasse.

Thus goal setting is inextricably woven with retention of power. Goals for school boards must be optimal, not maximal; maximizing can sometimes upset the delicate balance between process and outcome, which can (in turn) make the retention of power extremely difficult.

Implied is the notion that collective bargaining is always in a state of flux. Variables that impact on bargaining success or failure are always changing, often without the efforts of either party. Words are important. "Fluctuating?" "Mercurial?" Perhaps "dynamic" is best because it suggests that collective bargaining relationships are always changing, whether the bargainers want them to or not.

☐ Bargaining as a Dynamic Activity

Dynamic means herein that whenever an event relevant to the bargaining context occurs, the entire balance of bargaining power is likely to be changed. The school board that seems to acquiesce to *all* demands of its teacher organization flirts with recall possibilities because of the active politics of the portion of its constituency opposed to collective bargaining in education. Similarly, failure to achieve certain desirable bargaining ends often results in the creation of platform "fodder" for other would-be officers of teacher organizations.

At any time in the collective bargaining situation, both school boards and teacher organizations have (1) certain support systems composed of their constituents and (2) a certain amount of latitude or position credibility to perform tasks for which their positions exist. The relative bargaining power of either party depends to a great extent on the amount of each attribute possessed.

A minor event (a justifiable teacher grievance not backed by the teacher organization, for example) can spend some of the position credibility enjoyed by the teacher organization leadership. A second, subsequent event (a free-flying rumor about the teacher organization's failure to support the aggrieved teacher) might result in the expenditure of much of the organization's remaining position credibility, rendering it ineffective in convincing school board representatives about teachers' unity. The same goes for school boards. Many things can erode the position credibility of school boards: angry, impulsive statements released to the press after riots that occurred during a football game; suggested conflict of interest generated by a car salesman-school board member during bid letting for vehicle purchases; or a one-word slip during board meetings.

Conversely, positive events *increase* position credibility for each side. The relative bargaining power of a teacher organization can be increased by many things: an announced merger of two teacher organizations, victories of teacher-supported politicians, or parent support of teacher organization positions are but a few examples. Similarly, the exposure of illegal doings within teacher organizations (evidence of dishonest election practices, for example) can strengthen the relative bargaining power of the school board with which that teacher organization is dealing.

☐ Process as an End in Bargaining

In the 1970s, shortly after collective bargaining was legalized in California, a simple but strange sequence of events occurred in a small school district. The district superintendent and president of the teachers' association sat down in a friendly, informal session and worked out what appeared to be an excellent contract for their district teachers — especially when compared to contracts in nearby school districts.

Coming to terms was easy; after all, the two men had worked together for years when the superintendent was a principal and the organization president was a teacher. Also, the superintendent believed in collective bargaining, a limited but adequate sum of money was available, and — generally — the time was ripe. The district teachers gained higher salaries and more progressive personnel policies than teachers in other nearby districts without the expenditure of time and effort usually required.

But less than four months later, a recall movement started inside the teacher organization. Leaders of that movement organized against the contract *and* the president. Why? Why did opposition congeal around such a desirable contract? Why would the president of the teachers' association be vulnerable to attack so soon after he had bargained such a good contract?

The easy, informal process had failed to satisfy some very important aspects of the collective bargaining process. As previously mentioned, bargaining must be considered from many perspectives. It is more than legalities and economics; it is human, social, emotional, and political, involving more than camaraderie between the president and superintendent of schools. What about the politics within the teachers' association? What about the emotional release needed by the hotheads within the association? Wasn't the newly enacted legislation the perfect entree for humbling the superintendent and the board of education? Besides, why would the superintendnt give in so easily? Had the president demanded enough? Were the gains worth having?

This example illustrates an extremely powerful idea, one that is at the very core of the reason for the existence of collective bargaining in education; the *process* involved may be as important if not more important than the *outcome*. The right to bargain is important to the egalitarian principles on which this nation was founded, and this struggle for equality merits consideration.

☐ Bargaining as a Struggle for Equality

The struggle for equality in bargaining occurs because of the egalitarian expectations of Americans. Put another way, the bargaining scenario highlights American desires for perceived equality.

The focus of the struggle for equality between bargainers is in two broad areas: (1) perceived socioeconomic differences and (2) the vested interests and responsibilities commensurate with jobs in school systems.

It is likely that in most communities the superintendent and other high-ranking officials of school districts, as well as the board members, do not live in the same neighborhoods as most teachers. It is equally likely that some of these officials, because of their significantly higher incomes, will belong to different clubs, political organizations, and social circles from most teachers. Given such differences in incomes and life-styles, it is natural to expect some friction at the bargaining table because the bargaining situation can sometimes highlight those socioeconomic differences.

However, the struggle for equality is likely to be centered on job-related inequalities. The teachers and their representatives want more power in the day-to-day operation of the schools, and the administrators at the bargaining table are interested in the retention of the power they possess.

Teacher-bargainers often react vigorously to administrator's remarks that point to such socioeconomic and power differences during bargaining discussions. Remember that many teacher organization leaders were selected *because* of their outspoken positions against school boards and their administrators. Also, some classroom teachers, acting as bargainers for the first time, will experience—perhaps for the only time in their careers—chances to sit across from their "superiors" as equals. For some, the situation represents a great opportunity to be outspoken.

While the struggle for equality is basic to the teacher viewpoint toward collective bargaining, there are implications for all persons concerned. For school board members and administrators, it means that teachers and their representatives must be treated as equals in the bargaining process, despite the temporary nature of the bargaining encounter. For teachers and their bargainers it means that aggressiveness must be controlled during bargaining so that the time spent is productive.

The teachers' need for a feeling of equivalent status with administrators and board members constitutes much of the motivation to continued bargaining. Administrators, sensitized to this desire for equivalent status, can do much to enhance the climate of the bargaining encounter so that it is maximally productive in relatively short time periods. Likewise, teacher-leaders must bear in mind the symbolic equivalence represented by collective bargaining. Failure to do so can generate many internal problems for those teacher organizations.

□ Bargaining as Emotional Expression

The collective bargaining context is a natural arena for emotional displays by teachers. This happens because in some school districts—smaller ones, usually—certain administrators are forced to wear two "hats": school site administrator and bargaining team member representing the school board.

In such situations the potential for emotional outbursts is great because discussions often lapse into fiery accusations from one side or the other, related to school site concerns that have little or nothing to do with the substance of the bargaining. Both sides—administrators and teachers—often have difficulty with the role switches involved.

Whether or not a visible problem exists, the leader of each bargaining team should always be aware of the potential for emotional expression in collective bargaining. While *all* emotional expression at the table is not necessarily negative, awareness of its operation can do much to prevent breakdowns in a positive climate and avert needless blowups. A sensitivity to the potential for emotional expression can give each team leader an important tool for protecting team members from manipulation by shrewd members of the opposing team.

A prime theme of this book is: public opinion is the ticket to successful bargaining. This point will be elaborated in later chapters. The potential for emotional expression in the bargaining encounter is particularly important in states that require public access to the collective bargaining process (Downey and Mullins 1976). Such "sunshine" laws change the basic nature of the bargaining encounter, simply because they change the acceptable overt behavior of both parties to the bargaining endeavor.

Even to the extent of favoring compulsory arbitration as a way of settling teacher strikes (Gallup 1982, 44), the public appears positive about collective bargaining in public education (Gallup 1976). But the general public still holds dear certain basic qualities in educators. Those qualities are (1) the ability to communicate, (2) the ability to understand, (3) the ability to relate to others, (4) the ability to discipline, (5) the ability to inspire and motivate, (6) high moral character, (7) love of children, and (8) ability to provide model behavior for children (Gallup 1976, 195).

Control of emotions is of greater importance when the public is present. The public must be convinced of the importance of the missions of both sides at the bargaining table. When public support is lost, bargaining power is lost. This suggests that the bargaining process is also political.

□ Bargaining as Political Activity

Simple logic can verify the political nature of collective bargaining in education. Such logic could follow in sequence: (1) if "the essence of the political act is the struggle of men to secure authoritative support of government for their values" (Wirt and Kirst 1975, 5–11); (2) if the function of elected school boards is determination of the aims, goals, and objectives of the curriculum; and (3) if collective negotiations are basically a set of interactions among groups or their representatives, the intent of which is to foster an unequal power relationship designed to reap the greatest possible benefits for the groups' constituencies (Carlton and Goodwin 1969); then both school boards and teacher organizations are political in nature.

The political nature of school boards was suggested as far back as 1927 by Counts. Despite ongoing efforts of professional educators to appear apolitical, there is little doubt about the political nature of many — if not most — school board members, at least in their alliances and other relationships to middle-class entrepreneurial and other special interests.

Teacher organizations are relative newcomers to the world of overt political participation. Until recently they limited their political participation in school district affairs to salary and conditions of employment. Teacher zeal in those areas of immediate payoff had been so great that they had accepted those limitations.

By even simpler logic than that of its political nature, collective bargaining can be explained as political activity because of its intent and the context in which it occurs. The intent of fostering unequal relationships may manifest itself in any broad area within the permissible scope of bargaining. If politics is basically the ability to influence others, then collective bargaining is political in that the unequal power relationships generated put influence at the disposal of one group or the other.

The second aspect that makes collective bargaining political is the context in which it operates. Almost all states have legislation requiring public input or information at key points in the bargaining process (Pisapia 1979, 424–27). It is interesting to watch school board dynamics in the light of public information requirements for collective bargaining: whenever those boards sense that public opinion favors teacher organizations, they stop resisting teacher organization demands immediately. Conversely, when they sense public opposition to teacher demands, they resist those demands, often without further explanation or discussion.

It is clear that teacher organizations and their members are aware of the political nature of collective bargaining. Both the National Education Association (NEA) and the American Federation of Teachers (AFT) are overt political entities actively seeking to influence legislation and decisions in many areas, even those that do not appear to bear directly on the quality of public education (Clark 1981, 365–72).

The advantage of maintaining a proper perspective on bargaining as political activity is simple. From the standpoint of administrators seeking to predict the bargaining behavior of teacher organizations, viewing those organizations as political entities forces inclusion of many additional considerations in the prediction model used. Similarly, teacher organizations attempting to anticipate counterproposals from their school districts must remember the political nature of collective bargaining. Doing so will avoid many surprises and keep leaders and members able to maintain public postures that permit the most effective bargaining possible.

□ Bargaining as Compromise

The compromise aspect of collective bargaining is central to the very definition of bargaining; that is, compromise is a necessary condition to successful bargaining wherein *both* sides gain. A typical example in the current era of severe fiscal limits is one in which school boards agree to restrict layoffs of teachers in return for the understanding that teacher organizations will not file grievances if and when those boards reduce or eliminate teacher preparation periods (Levin 1980, 37).

Another example of compromise is the situation wherein the certified teacher organization is under pressure because of stiff competition from a smaller, more outspoken teacher organization. It is often the case that the school administration would like to see the smaller teacher organization "defanged" if possible, because the larger organization is (perhaps) easier to deal with. The compromise results when the school board representatives give enough to the larger organization to help that organization improve its image. The gains help the larger organization of teachers enroll new members, thereby increasing its strength relative to the smaller organization.

Compromise occurs in collective bargaining in many other instances. It occurs in grievance resolution during contract administration; in mutual endorsements of new programs previously considered too daring; in decisions about extra-duty pay and many other situations.

□ Bargaining as Attitude Restructuring

The usual focus on legally permissible topics during collective bargaining tends to divert the casual observer's attention from one vital process that occurs at the same time: attitude restructuring. Used by both parties, it is ongoing, sometimes overt, sometimes subtle, and often occurs without references to specific demands or concessions. Attitude restructuring has several objectives:

1. Statement and restatement of the legitimacy of one's role in bargaining
2. Establishment of the belief that one will represent constituency interests at all times; even taking risks to do so
3. Introduction of futuristic issues, gradually and repeatedly, so that the other party gets accustomed to hearing them

The first objective referred to means that each party constantly lets the other party know that it is *supposed* to be at the table, that its role is proper, and that it is not "begging." This is particularly true of teacher organization bargainers who are trying to establish an image of the teacher organization as a partner in the operation of the school district. Similarly, administration bargainers try to establish the notion that they represent the school board — the legal representative of the general citizenry and its children.

Both sides are also interested in letting each other know they are committed to achieving the ends of their clients at any costs. Such a position is revealed when teacher organization representatives hint of possible future work stoppages or impasse in bargaining — despite legalities against job actions like the strike. Administration bargainers sometimes remind teacher-bargainers that impasse is a two-way street, that they are quite willing to permit third-party intervention if necessary.

But attitude restructuring is most evident when either side introduces a radically different, entirely new concept during casual, ongoing conversation during bargaining. An example is the issue of fully paid maternity leave for teachers with, say, ten years' or more service. Despite protests by administrator-bargainers, teacher-bargainers persist because they achieve several ends. In addition to projecting forward-looking and caring images, they prepare administrator-bargainers for other less daring proposals related to pregnant teachers, to be offered in upcoming bargaining sessions. Administrator-bargainers use this tactic also. An example is the ongoing mention of productivity bargaining wherein salary and fringe benefits improvements are tied to increased mean-student achievement on standardized test measures. Such a radical proposal by administrator-bargainers is an excellent method of getting teacher organizations ready for, say, merit pay plans or separate salary schedules for exceptional teachers, both aspects traditionally resisted by teacher organizations.

☐ Bargaining as Problem Solving

The concept of collective bargaining as problem-solving activity can be illustrated quite readily in the light of current federal, state, and local emphasis on quantifiable achievement, together with current parental interest in minimum competency standards. (See Haney and Madaus 1978, 462–68 for a critique of the minimum competency movement.) Teacher evaluation procedures, included in the scope of bargaining in many collective bargaining laws, are unavoidably tied to such government and parent interests. (McDonnell and Pascal 1979, 129–51). In such instances, it is imperative that compromise agreements be worked out between such externally mandated accountability requirements and fair teacher-evaluation procedures advocated by teacher organizations. Needed is agreement on (1) precise defining of outcome objectives based on student needs; (2) progress monitoring toward those objectives so that nonproductive trends can be rectified periodically; and (3) weighting factors that help with statistical adjustment caused by socioeconomic, psychological, physical, and other conditions for which teachers cannot be held accountable.

Another example of the problem-solving aspect of collective bargaining can be found in current federal, state, and local interest in vertical mobility programs for paraprofessionals who work in the public schools. In such cases, teacher organizations must work with school administrations in (1) meeting the overall affirmative action mandate; and (2) developing professional growth programs in conjunction with institutions of higher education.

Problem solving in collective bargaining is extremely important in situations like the ones above. Problem solving in collective bargaining is rooted in common sense. There are far more issues in which both sides have common interests than the reverse, and problems resolved via the bargaining process are far more likely to be implemented fully because of the commitment required of both sides.

☐ Bargaining as a Legal Requirement

Legal requirements that mandate collective bargaining are known to most participants in bargaining. However, reasons for maintaining perspectives on collective bargaining as a legal requirement revolve around permitted and/or prohibited behaviors of the parties to bargaining. The legal perspectives must be kept in view at all times because those laws (1) prohibit coercive actions by either party, (2) define methods of determining exclusive representatives, (3) define and demand good faith bargaining, (4) determine impasse resolution procedures, (5) define unfair labor practices, (6) define penalties for work stoppages and other violations, and (7) outline public notice provisions.

Because collective bargaining laws vary considerably from state to state, administrators and teacher-bargainers interested in effective bargaining should first of all learn the conditions under which collective bargaining is permitted in their jurisdictions.

Chapter 8 contains a section on the legal context of collective bargaining. It should be pointed out that this is intentionally general, and interested readers should research thoroughly the collective bargaining laws of their states.

☐ Summary

Although there are various models in the literature, all aimed at greater understanding of collective bargaining and its intricacies, some models invite overgeneralization. Human relationships, struggles, emotions, and other hard-to-quantify aspects of the collective bargaining endeavor are often overlooked or omitted in models.

Thus understanding collective bargaining from several independent but related perspectives can enhance overall understanding. Collective bargaining must be understood as (1) a rational activity, (2) a dynamic activity, (3) a process satisfying certain human power interests, (4) a struggle for equality, (5) emotional expression, (6) a political activity, (7) compromise, (8) attitude restructuring, (9) problem solving, and (10) a legal requirement.

CHAPTER 2

Some Basic Views of Collective Bargaining

BARGAINING IS AN ACTIVITY based on the assumption that the parties involved will act rationally (Andree 1971, 40). This means that the attitudes held by each party center on maximizing or, at worst, optimizing overall positions after bargaining.

Knowing the viewpoints of all parties related to collective bargaining in any given context can arm bargainers with the all-important tool of predicting strategies and tactics likely to be used by the other side. The parties related to bargaining here are the actual or perceived support groups, as well as the opposing groups, of both sides.

The bargaining parties' viewpoints must be studied through an examination of their fundamental mind-sets. While it is difficult to generalize about groups throughout the nation, there are some attitudes toward collective bargaining held by most school board members, superintendents, teachers, parents, and others concerned with the processes and outcomes of collective bargaining, irrespective of the specifics of a particular school year, financial picture, locality, or political situation.

Certain reasons not necessarily related to bargaining, per se, influence these mind-sets. Understanding these reasons can enhance the bargainers' ability to formulate effective tactics and strategies prior to and during bargaining. This chapter presents discussion of the following basic viewpoints:

School Boards
Superintendents
Principals
Noncertificated Employees
Teachers
Parents and Other Citizens

☐ School Boards

In any discussion of school board members' attitudes toward collective bargaining, their typical backgrounds should be considered. School boards are dominated by entrepreneurs and professionals. Citing earlier separate studies conducted in 1927 and again in 1958–1959, Wirt and Kirst (1975, 79–80) pointed out the distribution of the main occupational groups found on school boards:

> Although the most recent survey of the social characteristics of board members was taken in 1958–59, those findings had changed very little from a 1927 survey. More than three-fifths of the board members were either business owners, officials, and managers or they rendered professional technical services. Farmers ranked third, accounting for 12.4 percent, and then housewives for 7.2 percent. The main change between 1927 and 1958–59 was the decline in the number of farmers, reflecting the farm closures and rural-school consolidations. The proportion of women remained remarkably stable at around 10 percent. The income of board members was well above average for the nation, reflecting the fact that board members were drawn primarily from advantaged economic positions.

Both aspects, socioeconomic status and occupation, hold implications for the dominance of certain attitudes of school board members toward the collective bargaining process. Two additional aspects, political affiliation and political ambitions, also influence the attitudes and behavior of board members. Although all of these factors are interrelated, separate discussions of them are necessary.

□ **SOCIOECONOMIC STATUS**   Board members in all regions of the United States have median incomes far above average. While median family income in the United States is about $10,000 per year, 22.4 percent of school board members earn more than $40,000, 18.7 percent have family incomes between $20,000 and $29,000, and only 26.1 percent have incomes below $20,000 (Underwood et al. 1978a). Although it is hard to establish a causal relationship between income levels and attitudes toward collective bargaining, it is interesting to note that a National School Boards Association poll revealed that school board members in four of five regions in the United States listed collective bargaining as their prime worry. Respondents in the Northeast, Central, West, and Pacific regions, both men and women, identified collective bargaining as their prime concern. Only in the South did another issue (discipline) surface as the dominant concern of school board members (Underwood et al. 1978a).

Male and female board members alike are conservative in their viewpoints on most major issues faced by American schools today (Underwood et al. 1978b). But reasons for their conservatism about collective bargaining cannot be attributed solely to their levels of income, of course. Other dimensions must be looked at; and even after doing so, it is not likely that cause-effect relationships will be found. One dimension that appears to affect school board members' attitudes toward collective bargaining is their occupational interests.

☐ **OCCUPATIONS**   Collective bargaining brings together, in confrontation, representatives of two perspectives that may be vastly different: classroom teachers, hardly affluent types, and well-heeled school board members who hail from the upper strata of management in the private sector. If bargaining involves fostering unequal power relationships (see Carlton and Goodwin 1969), then the confrontation mentioned above is essentially one between power have-nots who are seeking power and power holders who are basically trying to insure retention of the power of the groups they represent. Observing such confrontations while knowing something of the backgrounds of board members in some measure serves to explain positions taken by board members during the bargaining encounter.

Another dimension is important: many school board members are entrepreneurs themselves. This means it is likely that at times they view the collective bargaining process as being antithetical to their best interests; that is, if the advantage sought by teacher organizations is, say, a salary increase and that salary increase involves increased taxes, these entrepreneur-type board members might immediately translate the teacher organization demand into a perceived future reduction in profits to the corporation or activity in which they have invested. The same would hold in the instance of school board members who are also high-level officials in corporations located in the same taxation jurisdiction as the school district.

Many corporations encourage "public service" by their employees, especially their middle- and high-level executives. It is likely that this public service incentive system is actually a system of rewards for those officials and executives who function as "gatekeepers," protecting the interests of the corporation wherever and whenever those interests are vulnerable to the actions of public bodies.

Political activity often carries rewards for participants, rewards that are not always immediately visible to the observer or school board watcher.

☐ **POLITICAL AMBITIONS**   School board membership represents an important, relatively easy, and relatively inexpensive access route to higher political office. In addition to projecting an unassailable image of service to the community, time spent on school board activity is actually quite moderate for the political visibility that results, especially for an aspiring politician who needs such visibility.

A distinction should be made here between the behavior of school board members with higher political ambitions and the actual attitudes of such board members. Behavior necessary to maintain vertical political mobility might be oriented to supporting many of the wishes of teacher organization memberships at times, particularly if that board member is counting on teacher support in future political plans. At the same time, actual attitudes may differ.

The support of teacher organizations in certain political campaigns can sometimes be a mixed blessing; that is, such support can actually damage other political relationships of candidates for school boards. "Teacher-owned" candidates can have their effectiveness impaired on many issues after the election simply because of the teacher support they enjoyed.

Politically ambitious board members can provide a chink in the armor for teacher organizations. Observation of such board members in action can indicate the proper time for offering trade-offs of political support in return for advocacy of issues dear to teacher organizations.

Unfortunately, many teacher organization leaders often make the mistake of assuming they should have total control of candidates they support. Not true. The relationship must necessarily be on an issue-by-issue basis. Otherwise, teacher-controlled board members can be rendered ineffective because of their vulnerability to attacks by other groups opposed to many teacher organization concerns.

There are implications here for administrators also. Representation of school boards composed of memberships partially committed to teacher organization interests is very difficult. One solution to such a problem is that counterproposals formulated in response to teacher organization proposals must be couched in terms of quality education for children whenever those counterproposals are not responsive to the specific content of the teacher organization proposals.

Prediction of the behavior of board members is of utmost importance to both teacher and administration bargainers. Three elements—socioeconomic status, occupation, and political ambitions—are keys to such prediction. A fourth element is the political affiliations of board members.

□ **POLITICAL AFFILIATIONS**   Although the three elements cited above are hard to separate from political affiliations of board members, such political affiliations must be discussed separately because they are not always easy to discover. Two aspects are important: (1) the manner in which political affiliations can influence the attitudes and behaviors of board members and (2) the kinds of relationships possible, however difficult they are to uncover or see.

The most obvious indicator of political affiliations of school board members is endorsement during political campaigns. Though not always true, endorsement often carries with it financial support. This financial support is not necessarily dishonest because financial disclosure laws force revelation of most support.

Less obvious, but perhaps more dangerous, are distant relationships in business or other connections. Family ties provide examples. Such relationships can lead board members into behaviors that operate against the best interests of children and confuse the strategies and tactics of both administrators and teachers in collective bargaining.

An example may help to clarify this point. A small food store chain is trying to compete with two or three much larger food chains in a city of 200,000 people. The three larger food chains are not local; that is, only their retail store outlets are located in the city. Warehouses and other facilities are located in unincorporated areas subject to much lower taxes. However, the small food chain has all of its facilities located within the city. The tax rate in the city is $11.50 per $100 assessed valuation, a rate the smaller food chain can live with and still realize enough profit for adequate returns to its stockholders. At the same time, teachers of the city school district are trying to pressure the school board into putting a $2.00 tax rate increase issue on the ballot for the next election. One member of the school board is an attorney who has the annual retainer for the small food store chain. It is a relatively large retainer. Although it does not necessarily follow, the potential for resistance to the $2.00 tax rate increase issue by that board member is obvious.

Relationships are not always as obvious as the one in the example, although even the obvious ones often escape the scrutiny of many board watchers. Uncovering such close relationships offers great advantages to teacher organizations because it puts them in commanding positions in the bargaining context. For administrators representing their school boards in such situations, it means that some teacher organization proposals must be weighed differently; the potential conflict of interest in this situation might force administrator-bargainers to "give" on certain other teacher organization proposals.

☐ **WILL THE SCHOOL BOARD MEMBER WHO IS INTERESTED IN CHILDREN PLEASE STAND?**   While the foregoing paints a picture of all-out socioeconomic and class interests dominating memberships on school boards, there are school board members who advocate quality education above all (Creswell and Murphy 1980, 208–9):

> In a given situation peaceful labor relations might be more important than holding down the price of a wage settlement. Public officials may even advocate a particular program or expenditure category and favor increased salaries and the allocation of other resources for that purpose. There are certainly school board members who see themselves as champions of education and favor expanding budgets and increasing salaries to attract the best teachers.

☐ **GENERAL**   There are no concrete rules to look for in revealing political relationships on school boards. Thorough knowledge of the backgrounds of board members, together with analyses of their current relationships with significant others in their communities, can help point to such relationships. Things to watch range from family relationships to discounts given on the purchase of commodities and services.

Reasons for participation on school boards are varied. Some persons are simply concerned about the tax impact of the schools; others are concerned about the curriculum; still others are nonpolitical laymen, honestly motivated about improvement of the quality of public education in their communities.

Attitudes of school board members toward collective bargaining are basically rational ones. Many school board members engage in collective bargaining on behalf of the corporations for which they work. Others are themselves members of trade unions or other labor organizations.

Generally, prediction of the collective responses of school boards should be done on an issue-by-issue basis. Much of the success at predicting depends on reasonably accurate analyses of the pecking order of school board membership. Specific things to look for are:

1. Whether *one* person runs the board.
2. Who that person is.
3. Why that person is able to run the board.
4. If no one person runs the board, does a coalition run it?
5. If so, why does that coalition exist?
6. If no visible coalition exists, what is the individual pecking order?
7. What is the overall feeling of uncertainty about decisions made?
8. Does any uncertainty exist? Why? Does it indicate vulnerability of one or more board members?
9. Is there a member who enjoys the respect of the others because of some kind of expertise? An accountant, perhaps?
10. What kind of voter mandate did each board member get during their campaigns?
11. When will each board member come up for reelection?

One more factor must be considered, quite apart from those mentioned above. That factor is the level of confidence the school board has in its superintendent of schools. The level of confidence enjoyed by the superintendent can be an important determinant of the attitudes of the school board toward collective bargaining. School boards with new superintendents or superintendents in whom they have recently expressed confidence through a vote or a new contract will usually leave bargaining up to the superintendent.

☐ Superintendents

Many variables influence the attitudes of superintendents of schools toward collective bargaining. Among these variables are:

1. Extent of school board support
2. Number of years in the superintendency
3. Whether promoted from within the district or hired from the outside
4. Salability of the superintendent in other districts
5. Ego needs
6. Former working relationships with teachers within the district
7. The real reason the superintendent was hired
8. Areas of expertise commanded by the superintendent

The extent of school board support is directly related to the perceived strength of the superintendent. Superintendents who feel that their boards are totally supportive of their administrations will act on the spot in many instances. Also, those superintendents will be unwavering in the face of teacher organization pressure when they have a strong opinion. On the other hand, those superintendents will not hesitate to sell the board on issues on which they agree with the teacher organization. Superintendents without unanimous board support or with doubtful support are likely to behave in unpredictable ways; that is, on an issue-by-issue basis they are likely to make decisions in terms of what is best for their professional survival.

The number of years in the superintendency is often closely related to the amount of board support superintendents enjoy. Once the "honeymoon" (the time period immediately following appointment) is over and superintendents begin to face challenges by board members on various issues, the superintendents' levels of uncertainty increase. Generally, as the level of uncertainty increases, independence decreases to the extent that superintendents are more likely to seek to please the collective school board or individual board members they perceive as powerful. This means that careful observation of reactions between superintendents and their school boards during board meetings can offer some pointers about what those superintendents are likely to do in the bargaining situation. Even when superintendents delegate bargaining tasks to assistants or to professional negotiators, the observations mentioned can still help to predict school board reactions to certain issues.

Backgrounds of superintendents are also important in predicting their behavior during collective bargaining. An "in-house" superintendent (one hired from within the district after coming up through the ranks) is likely to be closely tuned to the desires of board members, simply because *he or she was hired for that very reason:* in-house superintendents are often hired because of the board's belief that they will reflect the attitudes, beliefs, and political orientations of the board members. While superintendents hired from the outside are expected to reflect the values of the school board, they are also hired because the board believes that some changes are in order. If such changes include a new posture toward collective bargaining, the behavior of the new superintendent will show it.

The reputation and marketability of superintendents in other districts also bears on their attitudes toward collective bargaining. A superintendent with a national reputation — and its attendant salability — will operate more or less independently of the school board for a longer period of time. Moreover, these kinds of superintendents will often sell their boards on certain controversial issues and win.

It is important to observe manifestations of the ego-needs of superintendents. Much of the motivation of individuals who seek superintendencies derives from ego. Superintendencies are, more often than not, underpaid and underappreciated positions, considering the time they require and the stress that accompanies them. If observation of the behavior of the superintendent indicates strong, consistent ego needs in some professional situations, observers should incorporate that consideration into the variables they use to predict the probable responses of that superintendent to collective bargaining issues.

Former working relationships with teachers in the district can influence the attitudes of superintendents toward collective bargaining, especially in small school districts. Some in-house superintendents will often have trouble bargaining on equal bases with teachers they formerly supervised. This aspect is related to their ego-needs. Some in-house superintendents tend to be condescending in their interpersonal relationships with teachers during the bargaining process: "Why are you bringing this up *now*, Ellen? I remember when you came into this district and you told me that you thought this teacher union thing was ridiculous!"

The true reason superintendents are hired is also important in predicting probable responses in bargaining. For example, if superintendents are hired because of their reputations as cost cutters, it is likely that they will take hardline stances against increased costs of any kind or seek trade-offs that maintain certain maximum expenditure levels. Similarly, if superintendents are hired because of their reputations for dealing with student unrest, it is likely that they would be receptive to proposals dealing with student unrest to the extent of being willing to participate in meaningful trade-offs when possible.

Specific areas of expertise commanded by superintendents can also influence their reactions to aspects of collective bargaining. Often, teacher organization proposals in certain areas are challenged needlessly by superintendents with expertise in those areas. In some cases, administration counterproposals to teacher organization proposals might be so changed that they look as though the basic ideas originated with the superintendent — when they actually originated in the teacher organization.

☐ **GENERAL**   These observations (call them insights, if you will) are very general. They are offered as tools for predicting the behavior of school superintendents in certain bargaining contexts. They should not be interpreted to mean that all superintendents are predictable on the bases offered. Every possible factor must be considered. No "cookbook" formulas exist for predicting the probable attitudes of school superintendents. Inventive observers can uncover other aspects unique to their school districts.

Generally, successful superintendents are political creatures, although many of them exert considerable effort in trying to hide their political natures. Politics are a reality in the survival of present-day superintendents, whether urban, suburban, or rural.

Political creatures that they are, superintendents will often try to hide their basic opposition to collective bargaining. The reason many superintendents are opposed to bargaining is simple: the bargaining process introduces a layer into educational decision making that many, if not most, superintendents would rather not deal with, although some superintendents have shown their willingness to meet collective bargaining head-on rather than contend with the ongoing process and the mountains of paperwork incidental to "meet and confer" alternatives operating in some states with no collective bargaining laws for public education.[1] Thirty-three states now have collective bargaining legislation for public education (Phi Delta Kappan 1979).

Put another way, superintendents like to offer and put through their open board meetings slick, unopposed packages that have their individual imprints—without opposition from *any* source. New superintendents are especially interested in this. They seek to make their administrations appear as forward looking and innovative as possible. This means that there are times when superintendents will aggressively seek the approval of teacher organizations prior to introducing certain issues in open board meetings. Why? Because despite a unanimous board vote on the issue, the opposition by the teacher organization would taint the proposal or issue.

All observers should be aware that many superintendents are "career hustlers." Given the short tenure of many urban and suburban superintendents, it is perhaps understandable why much of their activity is oriented to glorification of their personal images as leaders. This variable, quite distinct from the ego needs mentioned earlier, is nevertheless an important one in predicting the probable behavior of school superintendents in collective bargaining.

There is no doubt about the impact of collective bargaining on the role of the superintendent, especially in the area of planning. This applies, of course, to others who function as members of the central administration team: supervisors, coordinators, curriculum specialists, fiscal officers, and others—all feel the presence of teacher organizations. Collective bargaining has also complicated the professional lives of school site administrators, principals, vice-

---

1. During a press conference on 8 September 1970, immediately after he became superintendent of the Oakland (California) School District, Marcus A. Foster was asked his opinion of California's Winton Act, the legislation that required school districts to "meet and confer" with teacher organizations on an ongoing basis. His reply was simple: "I'd rather meet, hammer out a contract that both sides can live with, and then get on with the business of educating children."

principals and others concerned with the implementation of bargained contracts.

☐ Principals

The effect of teacher mobilization under collective bargaining laws has been one of sweeping changes in both the actual roles and perceived proper roles of principals and in some instances, vice-principals (Benson 1980, 2–8; Blumberg et al. 1981). The impact has been felt in several areas in the professional lives of these individuals to such an extent that it has created considerable confusion as to the way they see their proper roles. This is particularly understandable in the case of those individuals who were principals some time before the advent of collective bargaining, when the system of rewards operating in school districts centered on a substantial amount of authoritative, autocratic behavior by principals.

Principals are currently caught in a cross-fire; that is, many of them feel strong allegiance to their staffs while being dependent on (and hence forced to be loyal to) superintendents and boards of education for authority and rewards. Their roles are doubled, both in bargaining and implementing agreements. Schofield makes vivid the ambiguity in the principal's role (Schofield 1976, 9).

> A kind of schizophrenic role emerges for the middle administrator. In dealing with teachers and their union representatives he or she assumes the role of management, charged with carrying out the employer's side of the contract and making sure that the teachers uphold their parts of the agreement. He must operate in conjunction with the central office administration (specifically, with the superintendent) to carry out district policy set by the school board. This function is managerial in nature.
>
> However, when the principal's own interests (such as salary, promotion, and termination) are at stake, he finds himself assuming the same relation to the board and the superintendent as that assumed by the teachers—the employee bargaining through a negotiator with the management.

The potential for rebellion in such a context is obvious, and it has already started (Karlitz 1979, 95–96). Principals and other middle administrators are now organizing. The situation is summed up by Flygare (1977, 19):

> They feel they have been isolated between the superintendent's central staff, which exercises all real power in the system, and an increasingly militant and unmanageable teaching faculty. They also point out that the laws in over 20 states permit Collective Bargaining by school supervisory personnel. These factors have combined to accelerate the growth of unions for school administrators.

Clearly, administrators have not let old loyalties prevent the emergence of protective organizations. Flygare reports that there are more than 1252 administrator locals, many independent and many affiliated with the American Federation of School Administrators.

Opinion varies considerably on the proper bargaining role of principals because of the nature of their jobs. For this reason, state laws differ on the bargaining status of these middle administrators. Holley, Scerba, and Rector (1976) found at least five distinct approaches to legislation on proper bargaining rights of supervisors: (1) exclusion of all supervisors from any bargaining unit; (2) exclusion of only bona fide supervisors from any bargaining unit; (3) full bargaining rights, but separated into autonomous bargaining units; (4) meet and confer rights having supervisors in autonomous units, but without an employer obligation to bargain; and (5) no provision regarding bargaining rights of supervisors in state statutes.

The perceptions of the primary parties to collective bargaining—school boards and teacher organizations—seem to compound the role ambiguities of principals. School boards and superintendents see principals as part of management while teachers, teacher organization leaders, and many principals themselves see them as more closely identified with teachers (Holley et al. 1976).

These perceptions carry powerful implications for participants in collective bargaining. For teacher-bargainers, it means that coalitions must be sought with organized administrator groups when possible. For administrator-bargainers, the existence of organized administrator groups within a school district can undermine the administration position in bargaining, especially whenever such a group takes a position contrary to the administration position or a position sympathetic to or supportive of the teacher organization position.

Organized groups often overlooked by both teacher organizations and administration bargainers are those of the noncredentialled or noncertificated employees of school districts. Although these groups are usually represented by other employee organizations, they represent important support or potential opposition for bargainers of both sides.

☐ Noncertificated Employees

The secretaries, custodians, bus drivers, lunchroom workers, skilled tradesmen, and other support personnel in school districts hold certain viewpoints on collective bargaining. Most of them belong to separate unions that may or may not bargain directly with the representatives of boards of education. Other arrangements are often made, so that the different occupations of support personnel are represented by one bargaining unit dealing with the board of education. Some local trades unions will permit deviation from union scale for their members who are regular employees of the school district as long as the total package offered compares favorably with salaries and fringe benefits of other union members elsewhere in the area.

These salaries will vary from craft to craft or job to job, but the ordinary fringe benefits will not in many instances. In many if not most cases, fringe benefits of noncertificated employees equal those of teachers.

Ordinary fringe benefits constitute much of the common ground among the labor organizations within school districts. This means that noncertificated employee organizations are likely to support teacher advocacy of improved fringe benefits. For administrator-bargainers, such reactions of noncertificated groups must be anticipated when counterproposals on fringe benefits are developed. For teacher-bargainers, some important allies are at hand; teacher organizations must avoid falling into the losing trap of attacking board of education policies granting fringe benefits that are extremely high in proportion to the salaries of some noncertificated employees. Such attacks often result in failure because: (1) the rationale for improved fringe benefits is grounded in improved efficiency; (2) revenue sources paying the costs of fringe benefits do not compete directly with revenue sources benefiting teachers; and (3) loss of future support of noncertificated employee organizations is predictable after such attacks.

It must be remembered that many noncertificated employee organizations have direct ties to both community-based labor organizations *and* the blue-collar constituency of the community. Administrator-bargainers and teacher-bargainers who fail to bear that connection in mind flirt with the possibility of failure at the bargaining table.

It was shown earlier that administrators are sometimes caught in a cross fire when they bargain on behalf of their boards, especially when those boards are divided on issues. Similarly, teacher-bargainers may be caught in traps when their teacher organizations are divided on issues. Although there has been considerable evolution of teacher attitudes and viewpoints about collective bargaining in the past decade, those attitudes are not yet unanimous.

☐ Teachers

Investigation of teacher attitudes toward collective bargaining is potentially cumbersome because of the wide range of issues involved. The aspects of teacher attitudes that follow were arbitrarily selected and may exclude others. Also, results reported are not necessarily generalizable to all parts of the nation.

A study conducted by the Field Service Center of the University of California, Berkeley, sought to analyze teachers' perceptions of the gains and losses for major interest groups under the collective bargaining laws of that state (Rodda Act of 1975, SB 160). The study asked a small group of specific questions (Stern et al. 1978, 33–37):

What are the perceived areas of common interest and perceived areas of conflict between representatives of teacher organizations and representatives of school districts?

How do representatives of each side view the interests of students and the community in relation to their own interests and those of the other side?

On issues outside the scope of Collective Bargaining itself, do the teachers and district representatives think they are working together more or less effectively since SB 160 took effect?

In what ways, if any, would representatives of the two sides want the Collective Bargaining law to be changed?

In districts where more conflict is perceived to exist since Collective Bargaining began, are negotiations expected to become easier or harder in the future?

Conclusive findings surfaced for all except the last question. Structured interviews were conducted in eight selected unified school districts, using questions that were subsumed under and related to the questions above. Among the major findings of the study were (Stern et al. 1978, 55–74):

1. Both sides (teachers and school district representatives) impute their own interests to students and the community. Of particular interest is the finding that teachers equate losses for themselves to losses for students and the community.

2. Teachers' representatives see more gains from collective bargaining than district representatives.

3. Teacher representatives and district representatives differ more in their perceptions of gains and losses for students and community and for administrators and school board than in their perception of gains and losses for teachers.

4. Both teachers and district representatives perceived grievance procedures as a gain for teachers more often than any other contract item. Salaries and hours were least often perceived as items on which teachers had gained due to collective bargaining.

Of special interest under the second part of question four is the finding about salaries and hours. Other findings on teachers' attitudes are reflected in the following reactions:

1. Pleasure with their growth in power but displeasure about the limitations on scope

2. Belief that expansion of scope of bargaining to include matters of curriculum and instruction would benefit teachers because these matters affect

their working conditions and their evaluations and (thus) should be subject to bargaining

3. Belief that everyone, including administrators, students, school boards and communities will benefit if curriculum and instructional matters are included in scope of bargaining

4. Belief that legalization of the right to strike for teachers would have positive effects

5. Belief that elimination of "layoff by seniority" rules would have negative effects on teachers

6. Belief that open negotiation sessions would have a negative effect on teachers

7. Belief that attempts to link teachers' salary increases over and above cost-of-living raises to improvements in the quality or efficiency of school programs would affect them negatively because, primarily, there were too many difficulties associated with measuring the *quality* and *efficiency* of programs

The reader should proceed cautiously when generalizing from this California study. However, several aspects of this study are very interesting and can serve as catalysts to further study. Not surprising, teachers wish to protect the concept of layoff by seniority and are opposed to merit pay approaches to pay scheduling.

One of the most important points surfaced in the study relates to teachers' interest in inclusion of curriculum and instructional matters in the scope of bargaining. Traditionally, school boards have insisted that curriculum matters are management prerogatives, but a haunting question in line with teachers' concern about curriculum and instruction is: If teacher evaluation procedures are *within* the scope of bargaining, how can such evaluation proceed without reference to curriculum and its operational manifestation, instruction?

But the sword is double-edged, with teachers and their organizations in a contradictory position on the other side. How can they continue to oppose merit pay issues—all based on curricular and instructional effectiveness—because such merit pay approaches would necessarily be tied to measurable instructional improvement? And despite measurement difficulties, it *is* possible to adjust expected outcomes statistically.

Teacher interest in widening the scope involves other areas of concern, some of them administrative. Sabghir's findings in New York offer evidence that teachers succeeded in widening the scope to include school day, class size, school procedures, teacher assignment, school calendar, teacher evaluation, and school facilities usage in at least 50 percent of the fifty-six school districts studied (Sabghir 1970, 64).

From the standpoint of administrator-bargainers, participation of teachers in planning of staff development and other in-service activities holds certain advantages, particularly when such staff development and in-service activity has been bargained. Bargaining holds the promise of leading to the all-important common ground between the institutional needs of the school system and the in-service needs of teachers.

In the eighteen years since Carlton (1967) surveyed teacher attitudes toward job actions, it appears that teachers have changed viewpoints about the strike as a desirable job action. They appear to be more favorable toward strikes, with the attitudinal trend attributable to several factors, among them the growth of the number of males in education and the reduction in numbers of teachers with long service (Tomkiewicz 1979).

Two other factors that may contribute to increased attitudinal militancy in teaching are economic conditions (Weintraub and Thornton 1976) and a desire for increased job autonomy (Alutto and Belasco 1974, 226). While the former is largely a function of factors outside the education community, the latter is likely to be associated with a growing desire by teachers to be perceived as true professionals, despite professional and lay opinions to the contrary (Ornstein 1981).

Ironically, the concept of professionalism and the mechanism of collective bargaining—two aspects once considered antithetical—may be moving toward compatibility, at least from the perspective of teachers (Ornstein 1981, 197):

> The spread of collective bargaining during the Seventies has also had an impact on the professional status of teachers. Many people consider collective bargaining and contract negotiations as nonprofessional or even unprofessional activities, and in many of the professions (e.g., law, medicine, the ministry) few practitioners work in organizations that have anything to do with collective bargaining. From another point of view, however, the spread of collective bargaining has significantly enhanced teachers' control over the conditions of their employment and their effectiveness in the classroom.

The foregoing observation addresses one aspect considered necessary to the definition of professionalism: autonomy in spheres of work. It should be pointed out that the comparison to the other professions above omits one important reality: the source of public school teachers' incomes is *public*.

There is evidence that the enactment of collective bargaining legislation may actually increase teachers' propensity to strike (Weintaub and Thornton 1976, 204):

> Moreover, the strong correlation between permissive bargaining statutes and the number of teacher strikes reflects the importance of the changing legal framework for collective bargaining among public employees. It suggests that as more and more states adopt legislation instituting collective bargaining machinery for school teachers, the number of teacher strikes will increase. . . . .
> The findings offered in this paper thus contradict the opinions of

some observers of teacher bargaining who contend that the enactment of permissive bargaining legislation will actually reduce strike activity by creating an atmosphere that allows teachers to vent their grievances and demands peacefully across the bargaining table. . . . Our evidence suggests instead that the granting of collective bargaining rights to teachers at least increases the probability that more strikes will occur, since the strike and the strike threat are historically the strongest weapons — indeed, the *sine qua non* — in any collective bargaining situation.

In the first-ever situation of its kind in California, teachers of the Modesto City School District exhibited considerable confidence in the collective bargaining mechanism of that state. They displayed a willingness to exhaust the collective bargaining laws and procedures as set forth in the Rodda Act, SB 160. Of much greater importance, however, is the teachers' adherence to and exhaustion of collective bargaining impasse resolution procedures that forced the Public Employment Relations Board (PERB) of the state to confront a new question of law: are there circumstances under which postimpasse strikes may be "protected"? (Bowen and Bogue 1980, 9; see also *Modesto Bee,* 24 Apr. 1981, a-16):

> PERB found such circumstances in this case when it determined that a strike, after exhaustion of impasse procedures and in the face of an apparent unlawful refusal of the employer to bargain, is not *"per se* illegal" and, in fact, may be a "protected response" to the employer's unlawful actions. Although PERB did have the strike enjoined, it did so not because the strike was deemed to be illegal, but principally because the continuation of the strike would arguably interfere with the progress of the renewed bargaining which PERB had commanded.

It is perhaps easy for teacher interests to interpret "not *per se* illegal" and "protected response" references to strikes as legalizing them. But the sides are divided as to the implications of the Modesto experience for legalizing public education strikes — and perhaps subsequently, public sector strikes in general. At the time of this writing, the issue is before the appellate court and may be resolved in the not-too-distant future.

There are some indications that teachers are modifying their attitudes in ways that accomodate new developments mandated by federal statutes and policy (McDonnell and Pascal 1979, 129–51). Those developments are (1) PL 94–142, the Education for All Handicapped Children Act; (2) federally endorsed, court-mandated desegregation plans; and (3) Affirmative Action policies and programs. Meeting these diverse mandates is often difficult for teachers and their organizations because of a necessary focus on group solidarity. Maintenance of group solidarity requires teacher organization policies that advocate and protect the individual rights of teachers in the areas of salary, transfer policies, promotion policies, and seniority. There are times when such categorical federal programs and mandates — Affirmative Action, for instance — are in direct conflict with aspects dear to teachers. Seniority is a good example: how can affirmative action "live with" seniority unless some concessions are made?

There is evidence that the current era of severe fiscal limits is forcing concessions from teachers during the bargaining scenario (Levin 1982, 34, 37–38). Many administrators now recognize the opportunity to bargain offensively rather than defensively because of the current necessary focus of teacher organizations on job security, specifically on lessening the impact of reduction-in-force decisions by school boards and their administrations. As a result, teachers are agreeing to wage freezes in lieu of layoffs, although that is not yet the typical situation all over the nation because senior members tend to lead and control teacher organizations. In some instances, school boards and their administrations are "taking back language" (rebuilding management-rights clauses) in exchange for concessions made to teacher organizations designed to lessen the organizational impact of reductions in force.

But cooperation between teacher organizations and school districts might be the feasible alternative. After all, there is a point of diminishing returns for teacher organizations, beyond which they may be forced to resort to job actions. Some examples of such cooperation are: early retirement plans including continued fringe benefits for retirees in lieu of reductions in force; reduced insurance and annuity benefits in lieu of reductions in force; and, perhaps more common, increased class sizes in lieu of reductions in force.

While the current economic situation seems to point to bargaining advantages for school boards, cooperation is possible in many other areas than the ones already mentioned. Some of those areas are: (1) only one health plan required for married couples; (2) more flexibility in teachers teaching at different sites; (3) more concessions in paid in-service activities; and (4) cooperation in developing incentives for early retirement.

Whether recession or postrecession bargaining will in the long run spawn cooperation or increased adversarial bargaining remains to be seen (Craft 1982, 431–39). In addition to the impact of the current economy, the necessity for public support of teacher unionism would seem to dictate an aggressive spirit of cooperation by teacher organizations for the duration of the recession, coupled with the projection of an image of child advocacy.

□ Parents and Other Citizens

The literature related to parent or citizen participation in the collective bargaining process is sparse, with the exception of a few writers who contend that concerted effort must be made in the very near future to accomodate effective parent input into the process. These warnings are based on the knowledge that parents and citizens ultimately control much of the basic substance of bargaining through the vote; they can make bargaining a hollow endeavor through their refusal to support tax increase elections or similar initiatives and referenda.

The financial power held by parents and citizens is only a part of what has to be contended with by the parties to collective bargaining. Certain pressures can be exerted by parents and citizens. A good example is the "back-to-basics" movement. The enactment of minimum competency testing legislation throughout the nation during the seventies represented, in many instances, showy responses to parent and citizen pressures by various state legislatures. This suggests that politicians will seek to please the general public when forced to a choice between collective bargaining interests and the public. This reality supports one central theme of this book, that public opinion is the ticket to successful bargaining.

Current conditions point to confrontation between education interests — management and teacher organizations alike — and the general public. This situation obtains because parents and other citizens are essentially excluded from effective participation in the bargaining process in most bargaining jurisdictions.

Cheng (1978, 11) holds that collective bargaining is a political process that influences the allocation of resources and policy, and as such it affects the public and its interests. The current collective bargaining model in public education, borrowed from the private sector model, excludes citizen participation and allows professionals to monopolize the process.

It is perhaps unfortunate that the most conspicuous aspect of collective bargaining in public education is the strike. This is true because of media power and its attendant sensationalism. While it is difficult to assess the general public attitude toward collective bargaining in public education, some writers offer what they believe is the fundamental attitude of the public toward public employee strikes (Zachary 1976, 11):

> The effect of granting a right to strike to public employees commensurate with that enjoyed by employees of private employers could result in frightful social consequences. For example, the prospect of a city at the mercy of criminals and arsonists because police and firemen withhold their services is simply not acceptable. The public will not stand for it. Nor will it stand for extended strikes by teachers which impair the education of their children.

A distinction must be made between the general public attitude toward teacher bargaining and its most conspicuous aspect, teacher strikes. Whether the viewpoint expressed above is correct is not well documented in the literature. Surely the analogy between teaching and occupations like police and firemen is a rough-hewn one because (1) the nature of the services rendered are different; (2) the "products" are different; (3) the threat to public well-being is very different; and (4) both the immediate and long-term effects of protracted strikes are different.

A distinction should be made between the viewpoints of the public in general and the parent public. It is possible that teacher strikes have more immediate effect on parents because of the necessary instant changes in their daily life-styles. Working parents are often affected to a much greater extent; after all, public schools provide a relatively safe, controlled environment for their children for about six hours per weekday.

There are indications that parents and citizens want active participation in the collective bargaining process. From the venture in Florida with sunshine bargaining laws that require open bargaining, to the milder public notice provisions of California and other states, trends are the same: parents and citizens are pushing for involvement.

The implications of this increasing parent and citizen interest in collective bargaining are directly related to an oft-stated central premise of this book: *public opinion is the ticket to successful bargaining.* For administration bargainers, the future points to ongoing, active strategies for selling the administration viewpoint (and hence the school board viewpoint) to the public at every opportune point before, during, and after the bargaining encounter. For teacher-bargainers, the trend toward parent and citizen participation in collective bargaining means (1) abandonment of much of the private sector model of bargaining; (2) translating all teacher organization proposals and counterproposals in terms of benefits that accrue to children; and (3) the use of all avenues, media, word-of-mouth, and others to get the message to all individuals and agencies: teachers who benefit at parity with other professionals are better teachers — for children.

For school board members, increased parent and citizen concern about collective bargaining means that those school board members will be forced to include positions about collective bargaining in their political platforms. Such school board members will have little choice: their positions will have to be oriented to the welfare of the children. During job actions and/or work stoppages, these school board members will have to exert every means possible to keep the schools open and safe, despite previous political support by the teacher organizations.

Parents and citizens are also members of various organizations with direct or indirect interests in collective bargaining in education. Parent members of labor unions are likely to choose to support school administrations during teacher job actions or strikes when it appears that those job actions will threaten the long-term best interests of their children. On the other hand, nonparent citizens who are themselves members of labor organizations are likely to support teacher organizations.

It is difficult to formulate a rule that predicts the direction of parent and citizen support. Andree (1972, 135) offers some generalizations:

Public logic will tend to be consistently supportive of teachers if the latter maintain a posture of professionalism. There are enough conflicts in the act of negotiation without creating new doubts in the public's collective mind concerning the antics of the teaching group. Labor-oriented districts will support teachers and their tactics if the professionals do not overreach their advantage and make their demands exceed those made by the groups they serve.

On nonparent citizens (Andree 1972, 135):

> There is an ever-present barrier between the schools and that portion of the public having no children in the schools. Yet, there are many instances, where appeals to the older generation have been successful—appeals for better instructional materials, safer school classrooms, and the care of exceptional children. Teachers seldom find the peripheral public against their programs on such issues.

Tempered with a note of cautious optimism about the attitude of the public toward collective bargaining, Andree (1972, 136) supports the central premise of this book: that public opinion is the ticket to successful bargaining and public support can be developed though the bargaining process:

> We need not discuss specific ways and means at this time, for there are few fool-proof general rules. Each community must be analyzed for the most-likely-to-succeed methods of engendering public support of the negotiative process. There are enough examples, extending back to the 1940s, to know that such support *can* be developed, and that the impact of that support on school boards and other resistant communities can be most effective.

Thus public support is not an aspect that accrues automatically to either side because of the nature of their roles in the education of children. It must be worked for on an ongoing basis, using long-range welfare of children as the weapon.

☐ Summary

There are certain basic viewpoints related to collective bargaining, all dependent on the socioeconomic orientation of the parties observing the bargaining endeavor and more or less related to the threat value carried by collective bargaining. This is, of course, a strong generalization, and the observer of the dynamics of collective bargaining must be cautious and relate to the specific actors and circumstances under observation.

There is no doubt that collective bargaining carries with it the potential for altering some of the most basic relationships in American society. Teacher organizations and their leaders must be aware of the threat value of their weapon at all times. Such awareness can help to predict the behavior of others in the bargaining endeavor. Also, it can help to temper the approach of teacher organizations and avoid single-minded reliance on the heavy-handed tactics of private sector bargaining. Such tactics are likely to generate a backlash by the general public, especially when those tactics appear to threaten the long-term best interests of children.

Viewpoints toward collective bargaining held by many, if not most, school board members are related to socioeconomic status. School board members hail from higher socioeconomic strata and are usually entrepreneurs and/or high-level executives. Their attitudes toward collective bargaining, basically in opposition, reflect their socioeconomic status. One important aspect often escaping the attention of board watchers is the reality that memberships on boards of education, often explained in terms of community service and altruistic concern for quality education, are really excellent positions to be in for purposes of "watchdogging" against increased taxes—all while building backlogs of political experience necessary for higher political offices. But there are thousands of school board members having no hidden political or economic agenda who seek quality education for children and nothing else. Many of these school board members will defy political forces who seek to control them and advocate higher taxes and higher expenditures for teacher salaries and other budgetary aspects if those expenditures promise higher quality education.

Superintendents of schools often oppose collective bargaining for several reasons, the most important of which is that bargaining forces an additional decision-making layer that many, if not most, superintendents would rather *not* have to contend with. Also, collective bargaining adds myriad complexities to the politics with which the superintendents have to cope.

Principals, vice-principals, and other middle administrators are currently in ambiguous positions concerning collective bargaining. They are torn between boards of education and superintendents on the one hand and the teachers they work with on the other. In response to this ambiguous position, they are organizing rapidly in the interest of bargaining collectively and effectively in separate relationships with their boards of education.

Noncredentialled employees represent forces that both administrators and teacher organizations must seek to form effective coalitions with whenever possible. Many of these noncredentialled employees are members of labor organizations in the community. As such, they cannot be run over in roughshod fashion because they are smaller labor organizations within the school district. Administrator-bargainers who do so can find themselves and their positions opposed by coalitions of labor organizations in the greater community. Similarly, teacher organizations can lose the support of organized labor in the community when they fail to seek compromise positions with organizations of noncredentialled employees.

Teacher organizations are interested in a wider scope of bargaining, including all aspects that impact on the quality of their work life. For all practical purposes, gone is the "one big happy family" concept that shackled teachers for so long. Another important trend in teacher attitudes toward collective bargaining is abandonment of the belief that professionalism and collective bargaining are mutually exclusive, that collective bargaining is blue-collar activity and must be avoided. There is evidence teacher attitudes are changing to acceptance of some national trends and policies that would otherwise be on a collision course with teacher seniority, one of the oldest and most durable planks in teacher organization platforms.

Parents and other citizens, too, have shown evidence of interest in participating in collective bargaining in education. In response, legislators have incorporated many types of parent-involvement provisions in collective bargaining legislation. These range from after-the-fact public information requirements to sunshine or outright open bargaining with parent/citizens as observers. The implications of this stepped-up parent interest in collective bargaining are clear: teacher organizations will have to alter their basic approaches to bargaining to embrace some form of productivity bargaining. Administrator-bargainers will be forced to develop proposals and counterproposals that insure certain commitments by teacher organizations to output in the form of better quality teaching.

PART 2

The Struggle for Bargaining Posture

□ CHAPTER 3

Some Determinants of Bargaining Climate

"BARGAINING CLIMATE" is the context in which bargaining occurs. "Good" bargaining climate implies a context conducive to effective bargaining. Conversely, "bad" bargaining climate operates against effective bargaining.

But such definitions are extremely simple, almost simplistic, because they involve several assumptions vulnerable to challenge. These assumptions are: (1) bargaining climate can be defined in handy, easy to understand terms; (2) it is possible to capture, in discussion, most of the conditions that make for good or bad bargaining climate; and (3) the determinants of bargaining are discrete and identifiable as such.

Despite the difficulties involved in discussing bargaining climate, an attempt must be made. The behavioral sciences beg for models and paradigms that lead to conceptual order. For that reason alone, the time and space used here is justified. For discussion purposes, certain limitations and assumptions are necessary. The major limitation is that any inferences drawn from the discussion in this chapter apply only to situations where there are collective bargaining laws for public education. The assumptions are that limited but adequate financial resources are available and there is prior history of collective bargaining in the school districts discussed.

This chapter is devoted to examination of these factors that determine bargaining climate:

School District Governance Factors
Power Status of Superintendents
Teacher Organization Factors
Community Factors
Situational Factors

□ School District Governance Factors

With the exception of financial aspects, the primary school district governance factors determining bargaining climate are school board dynamics and the power status of the superintendent. Both are complex aspects requiring elaboration.

☐ **SCHOOL BOARD DYNAMICS**   Although it is difficult to generalize about school boards and their modus operandi, it is possible to observe their behaviors, understand certain community linkages with board members, identify the behaviors of individual board members from issue to issue, and analyze the consistency or contradictions in economic and political positions taken. It is perhaps incorrect to call such observations "analyses" in the same sense that scientists observe phenomena in the interest of explanation and prediction. But paying close attention to certain events, human relationships, and power plays in educational bureaucracies can improve the ability of observers to predict behavior.

The following topics or broad areas are important to look at when examining school district governance factors:

Unanimity of school boards. As explained in Chapter 2, the solidity of a school board is closely related to its level of certainty or, inversely, to its level of uncertainty. Unanimous school boards are those that vote as a bloc on most issues. It is not unusual to see unanimous school boards immediately after the appointment of a new superintendent, for they tend to rely on the decisions of that superintendent. Also, unanimous school boards with adopted positions against teacher gains in collective bargaining usually operate against effective bargaining, for they tend to do as much as the law requires and no more. Moreover, their positions against bargaining often stiffen when they sense community support.

On the other hand, unanimous school boards elected on quality education platforms are likely to support effective collective bargaining when and if it can be shown that teacher gains from bargaining translate to higher quality education. School boards that are divided may be more common. Such school boards should be analyzed.

Power relationships on school boards. Social scientists and other political observers are divided about the nature of school board control by outside power influences. They also differ as to whether school boards are controlled by one, more than one, or no groups at all. (In order to put school board–community relationships into some kind of perspective, the observer needs a conceptual model for observing these relationships. For an excellent model see Hickcox 1967 and the study by McCarty and Ramsey 1967.)

However, there is a tendency on the part of some observers—administrators, particularly—to think of communities as having one strong, influential and rigid power structure to which they must relate to get support for bond issues and other school-related referenda (Boles and Davenport 1975, 32–33). This viewpoint has strong implications for those attempting to understand the behaviors of school superintendents and will be discussed later in this chapter.

The occupational groups from which many school board members come were noted in Chapter 2. If there are ongoing relationships between these board members and outside persons, it is likely that observable changes in the behavior of these board members can be noted, especially when there are basic issues that force open votes.

When such relationships exist, they are not usually easy to see. They are apt to be operational rather than titular. Persons behind the scenes pulling strings do not want to be seen. Money is usually the central issue; the pointed concern of such string pullers is control of the impact of the public schools on the tax structure of the community.

Ego-laden issues such as who determines the curriculum or whether Black history, Chicano history, or ethnic studies will be taught are secondary, even tertiary, to such power elements. Moreover, these issues are sometimes used as diversionary ones, bait for those who bring their emotions to relatively unpopular subjects like busing and desegregation. Often the effect is to protect the real culprits, those who would systematically keep school revenues at dangerously low levels. The method of diversion is quite similar to that of the thief who throws a picked bone to dogs and steals chickens while the dogs fight over the bone.

The power makeups of school boards are not always easy to identify. Doing so requires exploration of two specific aspects of school board dynamics: power relationships *among* school board members and relationships between school board members and community members.

Power relationships among school board members. These relationships are often tied to *how* certain individuals became board members. In some states it is legal for incumbent board members to fill vacated board seats by appointing community members of their own choosing. The strategy is deliberate; the outgoing board member is often asked to resign well before his or her term is over so that a replacement can be selected and permitted to serve for a period. When this is done, the appointed board member often has time to establish an incumbent identity that offers a definitive advantage during the election. The practice is a common one. The self-perpetuating aspects of the practice are obvious: persons of similar political persuasions can control school boards forever.

Of more importance to the current discussion is the political debt that is created. The new incumbent clearly owes the older board members, especially the one or two who lead the others. The impact of this debt on the behavior of the new board member will vary, depending on whether that individual has higher political ambitions and how the new board member perceives his support during reelection. If the new board member has higher political ambitions, it is likely that he or she will follow the line of least resistance, with acquiescence to the power elements on the board until time to move to another legislative body or judgeship (this often happens when the board member is also an attorney). Even when new board members make themselves visible on issues, they are not issues dear to the controlling elements on the board. Liberal utterances in support of quality education, human relations, avant-garde issues, and others are heartwarming. Indeed, even the most conservative board members will often chime in: after all, these utterances and positions *cost* nothing.

The debt between the new board member and the others is diminished if the new board member is required to rely on coalitions of several identifiable elements in the community to get re-elected. This has implications for administrator-bargainers formulating bargaining proposals and counterproposals as well as teacher-bargainers doing the same.

Another aspect related to the effect of school boards on bargaining climate within a school district is the level of uncertainty on the board. Both administration bargainers and teacher-bargainers have stronger chances of having controversial issues accepted and/or adopted by school boards when those boards are *not* controlled by identifiable individuals, unless those individuals are sympathetic to or supportive of the issue. School boards tend to resist bargained issues when they are certain or reasonably certain that they are supported by significant power elements to whom they relate.

One question should arise here: what about board members' representation of their constituents, the masses who supported them in their campaigns? There are indications that the control of public education has evolved to such an extent that board members' perceptions of their roles are almost exact opposites of what boards were originally established for. Zeigler, Tucker, and Wilson (1976) comment:

> In fact, most board members do not view their role as representing, or speaking for, "the public." Rather, they view their role as speaking *for* the administration *to* "the public." Such views are a natural consequence of reform. Lacking a constituency (as a consequence of at-large elections) and lacking a systematic recruitment mechanism (as a consequence of nonpartisanship), they are normally recruited through the civic-business elite, sometimes by the existing board.

It should be pointed out that this statement might be a bit extreme with its indication that the public simply does not matter in educational decision making. There are, to be sure, communities where this is true. But there are many communities where public opinion prevails. Also, there are several types of community power structures.

Figure 3.1 is a simplified scheme that illustrates the relationship of the makeup of school boards to the operational style of superintendents. This scheme is an adaptation of the conceptual model devised by McCarty and Ramsey (1971). This model uses four descriptors for school board makeup: dominated (Type I), factional (Type II), status congruent (Type III), and

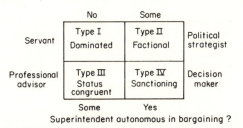

	No	Some	
Servant	Type I Dominated	Type II Factional	Political strategist
Professional advisor	Type III Status congruent	Type IV Sanctioning	Decision maker
	Some	Yes	

Superintendent autonomous in bargaining ?

3.1. Superintendent style and bargaining autonomy as a function of school board makeup.

sanctioning (Type IV). *Dominated* structures mean there is evidence decisions are handed down, that the values of power figures in the community prevail in decisions. Such boards show many unanimous votes, long terms for board members, actual instances of top power figures being sought by board members, and definite leader-follower relationships on the board with each board member knowing which board member to follow. *Factional* boards are obviously polarized, with visible alignments, two sets of leader-follower relationships, and obvious awareness and suspiciousness of the other side. *Status congruent* boards exhibit verbal expressions of support for other board members, changes of opinion in board meetings during discussion, many unanimous votes and no consistent sides in voting, and many questions on theory and research asked of the superintendent. *Sanctioning* boards show high respect for the superintendent, voting on his or her recommendations with little or no discussion.

It is difficult to consider relationships among board members separately from the relationships of board members to community members. This is true because certain powerful community members are often instrumental in putting many—if not most—board members on boards, mainly through the procedure detailed earlier, that of replacing incumbents by appointment.

Certain special relationships may exist between board members and powerful community members. These are possible, not necessarily actual, relationships, and they are offered to stimulate the awareness of interested board watchers.

Relationships between school board members and community members. Occupational and social connections of school board members are the key to understanding their relationships to community persons. As mentioned earlier, the central issue is often the tax impact of the schools, especially the extent to which school taxes reduce the profits made by local industry.

This impact can be so strong that leaders of local industry can be prompted to support candidates for the school board. The motivation for this can be understood when one applies the school portion of the tax bill to the total real property valuation of one of the local industries in any American city. While a residence worth $40,000 taxed at $15 per $100 assessed valuation costs $1500 in taxes, an industrial operation worth $4,000,000 costs $150,000—a proportionate figure. The school's portion of such a rate ($6.50, for example) would cost $650 or $65,000 respectively.

Industrial leaders argue that the rates for industry should be lower, that individual homeowners should bear the heavy burden of taxes; after all, the invested capital of industry generates the jobs of the homeowners. The opposing argument, of course, is that tax rates on industrial property should be higher; after all, they have a higher impact on tax-supported services like police and fire protection, highways, roads, and others.

Because of this tax impact, the school board is often a target for participation by representatives of industry. Some corporations reward their executives and aspirants to higher status within the corporation for participation in what is sometimes referred to as "public service" activity—especially when they gain seats on school boards, city councils, county boards of supervisors, and other agencies making decisions that result in tax impact.

Dahl (1961) and his researchers found that "social notables" and "economic notables" were influential in decisions that directly involved business prosperity. Other researchers conclude that there are various degrees of political power wielded by these "notables."

The mechanics of such power exercises are usually subtle and vary from context to context. Participation on a school board and being responsive to the wishes of powerful people can be rewarded in many ways. Several ample legal retainers can come to the law firm of a school board member every year; fleet-lease transactions can come to the firm of a school board member who is a car salesman; the husband of a school board member is suddenly made a vice-president of a manufacturing firm; an accountant-school board member's firm receives the audit contract for several firms controlled by the economic notables in the community.

School administrators, especially superintendents, are often caught in cross fires between their own relationships with community persons and the relationships of board members with those same persons (or others with whom those persons have business or social relationships). Whenever that happens, those administrators are sometimes forced to change the nature of their relationships with those persons.

It is often said in school administration circles that "a school board has one task, and that is to hire a superintendent." Implied in the statement, of course, is that school boards should hire a superintendent, then stick to voting on the policy recommendations the superintendent brings to them. Also implied is that once school boards are dissatisfied with their superintendents, they should fire them and hire others.

There is merit in the quotation above. Much of what has been said in the foregoing section on the makeup of school boards and the dynamics of school boards can be confounded simply by the hiring of highly capable, charismatic, and impressive superintendents. For this reason one should explore the power status of superintendents as that power status influences school boards, communities, and other administrators — all of which influence the bargaining climate in a given context.

☐ Power Status of Superintendents

Power status of superintendents as referred to here is important to the extent that it affects the degree of autonomy and independence enjoyed by superintendents in decision making in bargaining. School boards tend to clamp down on and challenge superintendents in whom they have lost confidence. Conversely, school boards tend to give ample decision-making latitude to superintendents they believe in, as long as those superintendents adhere to the political positions of their boards. Figure 3.2 is a very generalized illustration of the relationship between the tenure of superintendents and the decision-making latitude they enjoy in bargaining.

New superintendents with strong board support are likely to make most, if not all, decisions related to bargaining with a minimum of consultation with board members. This is especially true if those superintendents were promoted from within, because they probably would be familiar with the board members' attitudes and values about collective bargaining. But whether promoted from inside or outside, new superintendents usually enjoy honeymoon periods during which it is difficult for their boards to challenge their decisions without looking indecisive. The effect of such new superintendents on the bargaining climate is simple: if they are predisposed against collective bargaining, the bargaining climate can suffer; if they are positive about it, the bargaining climate is enhanced.

Superintendents long in office who have strong board support are perhaps the most autonomous decision makers simply because they have run credibil-

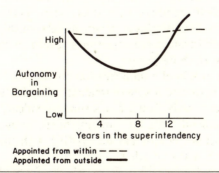

3.2. The relationship of superintendent tenure to bargaining autonomy.

ity gauntlets over a long time and still managed to retain board support. Their attitudes toward bargaining are perhaps the strongest single influences on bargaining climate within districts, all other things being equal.

Midterm or superintendents long in office but with poor board support are the most indecisive of all with respect to bargaining issues. The effect of such leaders on bargaining climate is difficult to generalize about. One consistent effect is time delay. This happens because these superintendents often need to consult their boards on each issue. When superintendents have poor support, observers would do well to base their predictions about the bargaining climate directly on the makeup and dynamics of the school board, totally discounting the impact of the superintendent. It is not likely that such superintendents will advocate any particular position in the bargaining context because they are interested in maintaining the little credibility and "idiosyncrasy credit" they have remaining. (This term is related to the expectations by others for certain positions. See Hollander 1958, 117–27.) After all, they have to be able to move to new superintendencies.

One note of caution to the observer attempting to predict bargaining climate: of key importance is the *reason* such superintendents have poor board support. Sometimes these superintendents enjoy the respect of their school boards even though they do not get the support they need. This confusing state of affairs happens when school boards find it necessary to "throw away" a superintendent in order to salvage their own collective public credibility. This usually results in a well-publicized dismissal of the superintendent followed by press releases and public statements saying outright or implying that the negative aspects of the school district are the superintendent's fault.

The relationships of administrators with one another also bear watching when calculating bargaining climate.

☐ **POWER RELATIONSHIPS AMONG ADMINISTRATORS**   These relationships are most evident during times of transition, turnover, or reorganization. Behavior of administrators during such times is often quite vicious and ruthless — even embarrassing. Of course, administrator-bargainers are likely to be tuned-in to such relationships. Unfortunately, teacher-bargainers are not.

Much of what transpires in relationships between administrators depends on the reason the superintendent was hired. If the superintendent was hired from the outside, it is likely that the board of education perceived the need for some kind of change. If the superintendent was promoted from within, it is likely that the board of education did not want much change or the *appearance* of change. In the first case, administrators react by conspicuous changes in both their administrative and personal behaviors. In the second case, there are often no observable changes in behavior on the part of administrators.

These changes in observable behavior are oriented to survival in certain positions or to vertical mobility in the administrative hierarchy. If the superintendent is basically positive toward collective bargaining, for example, administrators are likely to reflect that attitude. Conversely, if the superintendent is a hard-line type against collective bargaining, the bargaining climate might worsen.

Incoming superintendents often try to maintain a balance between the status quo and change; too much change early in an administration can be threatening to established persons in the administrative bureaucracy—so much so that ad hoc groups form in opposition to a superintendent's policies. Some new superintendents attempt to minimize the appearance of change (and hence threat to persons and positions in the bureaucracy) until they are familiar with the details of bureaucratic operation. This requires that reorganization plans and strategies be kept top secret until time for implementation.

Line and staff relationships are important targets for observation by students of bargaining. Superintendents tend to put persons they trust in line positions and others in staff positions, although all positions may be at the cabinet level. So lonely is the life of superintendents that they often promote persons of lower competency levels—or even minimally competent persons—simply because of their loyalty.

Promotions are prime indicators of power relationships among administrators. Line and staff relationships often display the true relations of the superintendent with his or her senior level administrators. Changes in job descriptions from line positions to staff positions, although there are no changes or reductions in status, can sometimes be interpreted as demotions.

Times of administrative transition are particularly important in attempting to assess current or future bargaining climates. In such times, certain issues are likely to meet with positive reception, depending on the extent to which they agree with superintendents' desires to project forward-thinking images. Curriculum-related proposals that require minimal expenditures can often be sold with ease. Conversely, money issues are extremely hard to sell because many superintendents tend to be fiscally conservative during transitional periods.

The model put forth by McCarty and Ramsey (see Fig. 3.1) offers a good starting point for observers interested in the dynamics of school boards and their administrations. However, much of the behavior of school boards depends on how those boards perceive their political survival needs. This means that even though the power status of superintendents is offered here as an important determinant of bargaining climate, it should be remembered that superintendents serve at the discretion of their boards. Thus the overall goal-setting and power-retention needs of school boards dominate; in the absence of such needs, the power status of the superintendent dominates, even to the extent of *controlling* the school board.

Another prime determinant of bargaining climate is the teacher organization itself. Its effectiveness in influencing bargaining climate depends on how it handles certain strengths, weaknesses, and problems.

☐ Teacher Organization Factors

Teacher organizations must assess the bargaining climate before selecting issues for bargaining. Such assessment requires consideration of many separate but interrelated factors. The obvious ones are not teacher organization factors. For example, issue admissibility depends on the bargaining laws of the state; comparability factors depend on the demographics of neighboring districts and are situational factors. The same is true of previous bargaining history. Teacher organization factors may be described as those that influence the ability of the organization to project an appearance of organized support for the issues, whether such support comes from organizational unanimity, support groups, or the general public.

The nature of the issue or issues is important. Some issues are recurrent; others are episodic. Annual bargaining for pro rata pay for teachers doing in-service work after school hours can be a totally different matter from bargaining for policy wherein teacher organizations receive monthly printouts of account balances for each school site. In the former case, the precedent for bargaining the pay issue is already established; that is, it is not likely that administrator-bargainers will argue against the issue itself. Resistance will focus on rates of pay. On the other hand, the printouts issue might meet with strong resistance simply because it is a new idea.

Some teacher organization factors that impact on the bargaining climate are: (1) unanimity of members' opinions; (2) positions of other large, competing teacher organizations; and (3) support of other labor organizations within the same district.

☐ **UNANIMITY OF MEMBERS' OPINIONS**   Of major significance in assessing bargaining climate is the collective opinion of district teachers. By definition of its role, the exclusive representative speaks for the majority of district teachers. However, of concern to teacher-bargainers is unanimity of opinion of all district teachers; that is, the existence of a large, competing teacher organization within the same district can detract from the appearance of unanimity so essential to effective bargaining.

Thus appearances of teacher solidarity must be sought at all times, and one prime method of doing so is the selection of issues likely to be supported by all district teachers, whether they are members of the exclusive bargaining agent or not. One effective tactic in this regard is selection of issues that may be advocated and/or defended on the basis of comparable practices in other school districts.

Properly used, the comparability strategy can result in enhanced teacher solidarity as well as contracts acceptable to all teachers, whether they are members of the exclusive bargaining organization or not. Because comparability is often an effective strategy, comparability assessments of other districts can be used to develop issues that unify teachers and estimate the bargaining climate for those issues. As a tactic, it capitalizes on the following realities: (1) school boards tend to base their long- and short-range activities on certain policies as guidelines for maintaining consistency, often using the criterion of practice in other school districts; (2) school boards are political entities that sometimes view excellent salaries and fringe benefits of employees as political assets, indicative of school board leadership; and (3) administrators are less likely to resist salaries and fringe benefits based on established schedules if and when revenues permit. (The comparison strategy of collective bargaining is discussed in Chap. 8.)

□ POSITIONS OF OTHER COMPETING TEACHER ORGANIZATIONS

While collective bargaining laws force school boards to bargain in good faith with the teacher organization that can document the membership of the majority of teachers through elections, they do not preclude the existence of other teacher organizations. This means large, competing teacher organizations possess a latent power whenever their positions on certain issues are contrary to the positions of the certified organization. Thus the larger such competing organizations are, the greater the teacher divisiveness on the issues. The implications for bargaining climate from the standpoints of both teacher organizations and school boards is obvious.

Such a situation argues for careful selection of issues by the certified organization. Issue selection should be based in large part on criteria of interest to *all* teachers within the district. Other issues should be based on the mutuality of interest of the teacher organizations.

For this reason as well as the ongoing battle for power of representation, teacher organizations should maintain liaison with other teacher organizations within the school district. Another aspect which influences bargaining climate is the relationship of the majority teacher organization with other labor organizations within the school district.

□ SUPPORT OF OTHER LABOR ORGANIZATIONS The viewpoints of nonteaching labor organizations within school districts were discussed in Chapter 2. These viewpoints must be taken into account when teacher organizations assess bargaining climate.

An example will illustrate this point. Before and during job actions (sickouts, work stoppages, or general strikes), teacher organizations must have the support of organized labor in the community. Suppose a teacher organization has openly opposed fringe benefits for nonteaching employees because they are equal to those of the teachers, despite lower salaries. How could such a teacher organization expect the support of other labor organizations in the school district, despite the rightness of its position related to the cause of the job action?

The relationship(s) of teacher organizations with other labor organizations, both inside and external to the school district, is of vital importance when assessing bargaining climate. Failure to include this important variable can result in stiff opposition at the bargaining table.

☐ Community Factors

Public opinion in support of teachers' rights to bargain collectively is without question the strongest single community factor influencing the bargaining climate in school districts (Andree 1971, 134–36). But certain findings (Gallup 1976, 195) point to a relationship between the size of a community and the attitudes of community members toward teacher unionization. Although the majority of respondents polled thought that teacher unionization had hurt the quality of education, more respondents in cities of 50,000 population or more believed that unionization had helped the quality of education. In the same study, larger communities—including those larger than 1,000,000 population—supported extension of the scope of bargaining for teachers to include class size, the curriculum, and teaching methods.

The connection between the size of cities and attitudes toward collective bargaining in education reflects the parallel growth of teacher unionism and private sector unionism. One of the most visible examples of this parallel growth is the American Federation of Teachers of New York City, which developed right along with other unions there (Braun 1972).

A newer poll revealed public support for the requirement that nonunion teachers pay union dues (Gallup 1980, 43). In this poll, about half of the respondents felt positive about the requirement.

There is evidence that the mean age of the population affects its attitudes toward unionization of teachers and collective bargaining. Persons between the ages of 18 and 49 tend to be more receptive to the notion of teacher unionization (Gallup 1976, 195). There is a possibility that this finding is related to the attitudes of parents of school-age children, who are also in this age group.

Level of education attained appears to influence attitudes toward unionization of teachers (Gallup 1976, 195). Twenty-nine percent of persons with college educations supported teacher unionization, while only 20 percent of persons with high school educations and 18 percent of persons with grade school educations had the same attitude. This statistic might be closely related to the reasons certain education-oriented referenda pass in some college towns.

There are certainly other factors that affect bargaining climate within communities. Some are spin-offs from the factors cited above. An example of one such factor is the revenue flexibility of the local board of education (Thomas et al. 1966, 61). The revenue flexibility of boards of education refers to the latitude that those boards have for meeting teacher demands while being responsive to other constituencies.

Community factors are fixed for any time and any given community; that is, they are demographic, dependent on the overall makeup of the community. Situational factors are not. They fluctuate from moment to moment, depending on what has occurred previously.

☐ Situational Factors

Situational factors may be thought of as factors resulting from combinations of school governance, community, and teacher organization factors. Factors related to the power status of superintendents are subsets of school governance factors. Of importance is the manner in which these factors mix to produce a good or poor bargaining climate in a given situation. For example, the superior revenue flexibility that a school board enjoys in a rich community might not translate into improved bargaining climate for teacher organizations because of the presence of a new superintendent with a reputation for fiscal austerity. The combination of factors results in a situational factor.

In Chapter 2 it was proposed that collective bargaining is a dynamic activity, and the relative bargaining power of either party must be thought of as an instantaneous quantity or magnitude due to the impact of positive or negative events. Those negative or positive events are the school governance, teacher organization, community, and power status of superintendents – factors discussed earlier – as well as factors resulting from combinations of these. Some situational factors are the results of such combinations and others are not. Figure 3.3 is a simple illustration of the interrelationship of the determinants of bargaining climate.

Previous bargaining history is an example of a situational factor resulting from combinations of other factors. Assessment of the bargaining climate depends heavily on what has been bargained previously. Also, the relative ease or difficulty encountered while bargaining will affect the future bargaining climate.

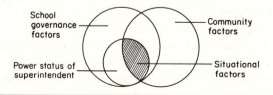

3.3. The interrelationship of the determinants of bargaining climate.

Some specific aspects of previous bargaining history must be considered in detail. Among these are: (1) the history of an issue within the school district, (2) reactions of board members to the issue and similar issues, (3) competing money issues, (4) support or resistance by business groups, (5) positions taken by media in editorials and other articles, and (6) support or resistance by special interest groups.

Some situational factors are generated by grievance history. If a matter has gone to arbitration and resulted in an award to a teacher organization, the relative bargaining power of that teacher organization is likely to be enhanced when bargaining issues similar to the one central to the award. For example, an arbitrator award using the criterion of comparability with neighboring districts for resolving a contractual conflict about extra-duty pay will probably encourage the use of that criterion by teacher-bargainers in the future and make it difficult for administrator-bargainers to refuse to bargain related issues, assuming, of course, that all other aspects are equal.

The support of organized labor can be an ongoing teacher organization factor or a situational factor; that is, such support can occur after the interaction of the three major determinants. The extent to which it enhances the relative bargaining power of teacher organizations depends largely on the impact of the labor bloc on the election of public officials in the area of jurisdiction in question.

Specific situational factors vary with context because they depend in large part on the interactions of school governance factors, teacher organization factors, and community factors. Moreover, they depend on *the perceptions held by each side with respect to the political effects of the interactions.* It will be shown in Chapter 7 that much of the closure in bargaining depends on proper calculation of the costs of proposals or counterproposals, and that such costs are based largely on an estimation of the political effects of those proposals or counterproposals.

The interrelationship of determinants of bargaining climate can be clarified by returning to the example of newly appointed superintendents discussed earlier. In many cases, school boards attempt to cleanse themselves politically by hiring well-known, bright superintendents with excellent images. Clearly, the perceptions of such school boards are that their own political images and futures are enhanced by the hiring. From the perspective of teacher organizations in such situations, bargaining climate might be worsened by the hirings because of the power status of these superintendents, especially if the superintendents are basically against collective bargaining.

While quantification of the inputs to the determinants of bargaining climate is virtually impossible, it is fairly easy to conceptualize those inputs as they enhance, detract from, or otherwise modify bargaining climate. Figure 3.4 illustrates the impact of selected factors on bargaining climate. In addition to the usual limitations of conceptual models, the reader should be aware that:

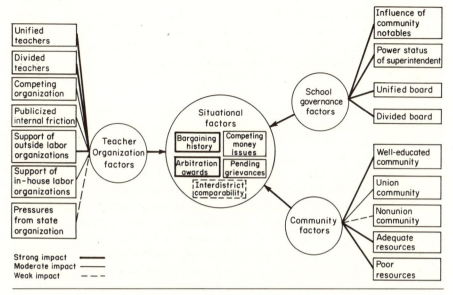

3.4. Interaction of the determinants of bargaining climate.

(1) strength of impact can be positive or negative, depending on actual situations; (2) many other factors not included in Figure 3.4 are actually in operation in the determination of bargaining climate; (3) factors are not necessarily discrete; (4) no hierarchy or order of determinants is suggested in the illustration; (5) strength of impact is a relative concept; and (6) good and poor bargaining climates are subjective concepts, depending on the perception of the observer.

☐ Summary

Bargaining climate refers to the context in which bargaining occurs. Various factors influence bargaining climate; their interactions enhance or detract from it. Those factors are school district governance, teacher organization, and community. The power status of superintendents is a factor that subsumes under district governance factors.

Many of the tactics and strategies of collective bargaining, from both administrator and teacher organization viewpoints, depend on the ability to capitalize on existent bargaining climate or to manipulate certain variables that impact on it. However, in the final analysis the estimation of the relative strength of each factor, as well as the combined strength of several factors, is subjective. The actual estimation of bargaining climate depends, of course, on the specifics of the context.

CHAPTER 4

Nine Vital Principles

IT CAN BE STATED SAFELY that the preparation of bargaining teams of both sides should cover every aspect of school district operation, salaries, fringe benefits, conditions of employment, curriculum, personnel policies, and overall budgetary matters — to name a few. This content is the meat of the homework that bargaining teams must accomplish in order to be effective.

Equally important for effective bargaining is the behavior shown during the bargaining encounter. Even when they are well armed with background information, it does not necessarily follow that bargaining team members will always behave in ways that enhance the effectiveness of their teams.

This chapter is intended to acquaint bargainers and other readers with the "best" behaviors they can take to the bargaining table. It includes the following topics:

Encouraging Viewpoint Expression
Equality of Status among Individuals
Developing Agreement Momentum
Blaming the Absent Third Party
Clarifying Legal and Institutional Limits
Stressing Common Ground between Parties
Providing Necessary Emotional Outlets
Pinning Down Agreements as Soon as Possible
Leaving the Table as a Winner

☐ Encouraging Viewpoint Expression

This principle is based on the notion that in successful bargaining, both sides win. While bargaining involves a potential alteration of power relationships, it should not devastate the opponent. Mutual respect, then, is of vital importance at all times in collective bargaining.

A point of disagreement at the table can be met with one of three responses: outright disagreement, neutral reaction, or displaying interest in a point of view expressed. The first reaction usually closes discussion, but the second and third ones are usually better because they help to reduce tensions and leave things open for exploration of ideas that can be possible bases for compromises later.

The broad area of communications is important for study by team members because it can help them with techniques of encouraging expression of viewpoint in others. (See Berlo 1970; Thayer 1968.) However, it is a sophisticated area of study that takes considerable time. One helpful training approach is that of bringing in consultants steeped in communications theory and conducting training sessions for team members. It is also advantageous for team members to attend counseling seminars when possible.

☐ Equality of Status among Individuals

The bargaining situation is one that often tempts both teacher-bargainers and administrator-bargainers to open up and (verbally) abuse one or more members of the opposing team. This temptation must be resisted. Just as administrator-bargainers must refrain from condescending remarks that draw attention to their socioeconomic advantages, teacher-bargainers must strive to do the same. Members of both teams should treat their opponents as individuals of equal human status, irrespective of the positions and titles held by persons at the table.

Bargaining team members must be selected very carefully. After screening, training through simulation can do much to prepare team members for sensitivity to equivalence of status during bargaining sessions. Maintenance of an atmosphere of equivalent status can foster and maintain agreement momentum.

☐ Developing Agreement Momentum

This principle of bargaining is simple, based on the notion that once a pattern of agreement is started, it is easier to continue. When both parties prepare for bargaining, they should attempt to predict the amount of difficulty they are likely to encounter with each item or proposal, then rank-order all proposals from easy agreement to difficult.

In many instances both sides will be more or less in tune on the easier items. Once agreement is reached on some bargaining items, it will be easier to deal with difficult or controversial items. This happens because both parties will seek to maintain the momentum of agreement. On difficult items, the parties can agree to table certain aspects and keep the bargaining going. Often, other intervening issues will suggest solutions to the difficult (tabled) ones.

Effective bargaining means that both parties should actively seek to overcome obstacles to progress in bargaining. One prime technique for doing so is to blame the absent third party.

☐ Blaming the Absent Third Party

Hostility at the education bargaining table often results from the day-to-day involvement of teachers and administrators with each other. This likelihood is great in small school districts. In such districts both teams are often forced to bargain on one day and work cooperatively at schools the next day. In such contexts, changing hats can be difficult, leading to increased tension at the bargaining table *and* on the job.

Such hostility must be avoided. Administrators can (and do quite often) blame their school boards for a hard-line stance on a certain issue. Teacher organization representatives can blame their memberships for inflexibility in certain instances. While the blaming device seems overly simple, it often works because it avoids or delays confrontation on certain issues. In many cases, the agreement momentum maintained leads to alternate solutions later.

Much of collective bargaining is determined and controlled by forces external to school districts and these forces should be recognized by both sides.

☐ Clarifying Legal and Institutional Limits

Besides collective bargaining laws, per se, other legalities impact on various aspects of the bargaining process. An example is the legal requirement related to school finance in a given year. The time lines and procedures for budget submission, approval by external agencies, and other factors can change the entire bargaining context.

This means that open communication involving interpretations of the legal and institutional boundaries is absolutely necessary. Both sides must express viewpoints freely because legalities often lend themselves to various interpretations. So do school district policies. Clarification clears up many points of confusion, resulting in savings of time and money and maintenance of agreement momentum. One prime device for maintaining agreement momentum is personal and human.

☐ Stressing Common Ground between Parties

Often, in the heat of bargaining, members of each side are likely to feel alienated by the other side. In such situations, both sides should work quickly to build bases for trust that will maintain agreement momentum.

One way of building trust and keeping communication open is stressing the one aim both sides have in common: quality education for children. Other seemingly minor things help: one or more golfers or fishermen on each side of the table can find common ground in their hobbies. Once communication is open and flowing easily, the discussions can be steered back to the professional point in common — quality education and the relationship of effective bargaining to it.

☐ Providing Necessary Emotional Outlets

The potential for emotional flareups at the bargaining table has been discussed elsewhere. Such flareups should be avoided if possible.

Sometimes flareups are impossible to avoid. Bargaining superintendents are occasionally capable of heated expressions directed at teachers they supervised before the advent of collective bargaining. Bargaining teachers sometimes see red when facing principals they once thought supportive of teacher rights in collective bargaining.

When such outbursts occur, it is extremely important to call for a recess, caucus, or any other interruption that will buy time and permit heads to cool off. When in recess, a decision must be made as to whether that team member should continue to participate in the bargaining sessions for the remainder of the day. When sessions resume, apologies are in order.

☐ Pinning Down Agreements as Soon as Possible

This means that each team should try to lock in the verbal agreements and commitments made by the other side. Doing so is essential because it is also related to developing and maintaining agreement momentum: signatures of members of both sides attesting to agreement on a proposal or counterproposal means easier subsequent agreement on other related proposals or parts of those proposals. If and when there is agreement in writing on a proposal, those proposals can always be referred to when debating other proposals or counterproposals.

Both teams should agree as soon as possible on the method of securing agreements. This should be done during the first meeting when ground rules are being determined.

☐ Leaving the Table as a Winner

This aspect is closely related to the third point, developing agreement momentum. In a certain sense it is the same because it is oriented to keeping momentum going until the next session. It is important to keep positive attitudes and good faith bargaining going over a weekend or until the next regularly scheduled bargaining session.

Each team spokesperson can project a feeling of accomplishment with a brief statement detailing the progress that has been made, together with an expression of belief that remaining problems will eventually be ironed out,

even when very little has been accomplished. Such statements project a positive attitude to the opposing team.

□ Summary

Although these nine principles do not guarantee effective bargaining, they
can overcome many barriers to it. Training bargaining teams in these basic
principles can be achieved through simulation as well as sessions conducted by
experts in communications theory and dynamics.

These nine principles are related. Most are based on principles of respect
for human dignity, equivalence of status, and the belief that both sides want
and believe in effective bargaining. One additional principle capitalizes on the
old notion that success builds on itself, that once a pattern of agreement is
started it is fairly easy to maintain.

□ CHAPTER 5

The Struggle for Positive Images

RAPID ENACTMENT of collective bargaining laws in various states in the last ten years gave rise to teacher organization attacks on most issues within the scope of bargaining. In many instances these organizations also attempted to expand the defined scope of bargaining.

Such efforts are understandable when overall teacher power is considered. But despite the awesome nature of teacher power, much of the substance of collective bargaining in education is controlled by a larger and more powerful group—the general public. This public power derives from the ability to withhold desperately needed financial support for education.

Observation of school boards will reveal their awareness of the power of the general public. Quite often the stances taken by school board members are adopted only after they know what prevailing public thought is on the issues involved.

This means that school boards, when forced to make a choice, are likely to be more responsive to the general public than to teacher organizations. Collective bargaining laws require good faith bargaining, not agreement. Thus much of the motivation of school boards to cooperate with teacher organizations comes from the climate in which collective bargaining takes place rather than the sheer political power of those teacher organizations. The adoption of and adherence to a certain position by a teacher organization *or* a school board can only be done with adequate public support.

But adequate public support is hard to generate after collective bargaining is underway. It must be sought and maintained at all times. It is the prime weapon held by either side during bargaining. Therefore this chapter is dedicated to a discussion of tactics usable by bargainers of both sides when developing public support. Topics discussed are:

Image of Child Advocacy
Image of Professionalism
Image of Moderation
Image of Forward-thinking Leadership

☐ Image of Child Advocacy

Public or private, irrespective of level, schools exist for children. Consequently, all collective bargaining activity is, in theory at least, for the benefit of children. Both administration bargainers and teacher-bargainers must avoid conveying the notion to the general public that collective bargaining activity has made the education of children a secondary consideration.

Unfortunately, this sometimes happens. Often, during press interviews concerning publicized job actions or strikes, both teacher organization leaders and administration officials focus most if not all conversation on causes of job actions or upcoming contracts, without statements of concern or regret about the negative impact of the job actions on the education of children. Even more conspicuously absent in such situations are statements about how the outcomes of the job action could *help* children in the future.

Needed is the development of an image of child advocacy by both teacher organizations and administrations. Educators, perhaps, are the most unique group involved in collective bargaining, public or private, because of the nature of the public service they render and the enormity and variety of the public expectations held for public education. Neither teacher organizations nor administrators can afford to approach collective bargaining with the same single-minded focus on salaries, benefits, and working conditions that, say, longshoremen can. Longshoremen move goods and nothing more, while educators deal with the delicate, complex task of preparing children for survival in a changing technocracy. It is not necessary for longshoremen to project images of concern for the wares they move or the general welfare. But educators must *always* sell themselves as advocates of and for children.

As is the case in many behavioral sciences, there are no pat rules that can be offered for generating an image of child advocacy. Situations will vary with contexts, but the following points are applicable to most situations.

Teacher organizations should always strive to translate all publications and communications into descriptions of the short-term or long-term benefits to children that will result from teacher gains from collective bargaining. Organization platforms should be changed to incorporate the notion of child advocacy. Similarly, all press releases should be carefully monitored so that statements are always made about the child benefits involved. Teacher organizations should also conduct training sessions for teacher spokespersons, so that all organization members are adept at articulating organization goals as benefits that accrue to children.

Woven throughout the literature of bargaining is evidence that administration bargainers are aware of the image of child advocacy. Simple casual observations of press releases of school administrations reveal this awareness.

Closely tied to the image of child advocacy is the image of professionalism. As in the former case, there are indications that school administrations are aware of the significance of this image.

☐ Image of Professionalism

Unfortunately, educators are still struggling to achieve true professional status in America. There are many reasons for this persistent problem, some caused by administrators and some caused by teachers and their organizations. Still others are caused by the public character of education as a profession.

It can be argued that educators as a group have failed to sell themselves as professionals because they have opted to lower their political profiles to project apolitical public images. There may be other reasons for this image shortcoming, but the task of projecting professional images remains for administrators and teacher organizations. Listed below are some ways that both can enhance their professional images:

1. Seize every opportunity to publicize the education levels of their respective members. Administrators should couch salary counterproposals in terms of how such salary schedules could improve the levels of professionalism in their school districts. Similarly, teacher organizations should portray their organizations as highly supportive of higher education and advanced degrees for their members.

2. Develop for teacher organizations a separate occupational code of ethics, quite apart from similar documents and position papers offered by school boards for teachers. Such codes of ethics, based largely on moral principles, should convey the idea that violation of this code results in expulsion from the teacher organization.

3. Stress service to children. This aspect is of equal significance to administrators and teachers; however, teacher organizations probably have more to do in this regard. All of their professional documents should be edited to reflect this concern.

4. Emphasize the complex interrelationship of disciplines necessary for effective teaching. This means teacher organizations can assert that teachers deserve certain gains because they have waded through course preparations that include subject matter content as well as pedagogy. Similarly, administrators should attempt to defend their salary counterproposals (or proposals) in terms of the relationship(s) of the increments to acquired teacher skills, whether acquired through course work or experience.

There is evidence that some teacher organizations have not been aware of the necessity to bargain within the framework of the public will to support quality education. This awareness is essential.

☐ Image of Moderation

Moderation as referred to here means balance between what educators desire and the public will to support education. This does not mean that teacher demands, for example, should be abandoned. Rather, it means the teacher organization images projected should convey the idea that teachers are not unreasonable, that collective bargaining is a fact of life in America and teachers are no exception, that teachers are only interested in using the power derived from collective actions to keep themselves in step with cost-of-living indices and the advantages generally enjoyed by other professionals.

Unfortunately, because educators — especially teachers — deal with children, they are very conspicuous to the public. They are often subject to the accusation that they are overreaching the public will to support their demands. Remember that the public has no criteria by which to evaluate the demands of striking longshoremen; and even if they did, the product or service withheld by the striking longshoremen impacts on the public in the form of commodities not available. By law, these cannot be commodities essential to the survival of the nation. To the contrary, the public has a strong feeling for the tax impact of the public schools in recent times. Hence the act of withholding teacher services for protracted periods results in extremely visible events: children out of school, a lengthened school year, children on the streets, public facilities not used to their maximums, and others — all events that are perceived negatively by the public.

The image of moderation is perhaps more immediately applicable to administrators. The logic is simple: school boards are elected to determine education policy and implementation by and on behalf of the general public, administrators are hired by school boards for the same basic reasons, and (hence) administrators must consider the public will to support education.

All of the foregoing point to the unique nature of the education profession. A need exists to let the general public know at all times that educators, both teachers and administrators, are not out of line with their demands.

Some tactics to keep the public informed, usable by both teachers and administrators, are:

1. Press releases that offer simplified illustrations showing comparability with other districts. Teachers can use this tactic to support their proposals when relevant, and administrators can defend their counterproposals or other public positions with the same tactic. The comparison strategy is discussed in detail in Chapter 8 of this book.

2. Student achievement data (test scores and others) can be cited whenever it can be tied to positions taken by administrators or teacher organizations. Administrators can defend school board refusals to agree to certain issues dear to teachers, arguing that previous gains by teachers were not translated into gains for the district students. Likewise, teacher organizations can argue for higher salaries, benefits, and other perquisites when those can be

tied to greater student achievement, especially in a school year prior to the one for which they are bargaining. While causality is hard to infer, such arguments can still be mounted effectively in the popular media.

3. Teacher proposals or administration counterproposals should be interpreted by teacher organization leaders or administrators, respectively, to the public whenever those proposals or counterproposals are not moderate; that is, when they appear to overreach the public will to support education.

While the public appears to expect moderation in expenditures and other aspects, that same public expects to see educators keeping abreast of newer developments in education.

☐ Image of Forward-thinking Leadership

The era of public education since 1958 and the Sputnik scare has seen momentous changes in the character and overall goals of public education. Events like the Elementary and Secondary Education Act of 1965 (ESEA), the civil rights movement, Affirmative Action programs, and PL 94-142 have redefined the role of the public schools. Some traditional approaches to education are now dated; self-contained classrooms operating on a lock-step basis no longer meet the diversified needs of youth; minorities are assertive about their rights to quality education; and desegregation is the law of the land, often forcing the involuntary transfer of teachers themselves.

Most professional groups—administrators and teachers alike—maintain mechanisms for anticipating developments such as these so that they can assure input into the appropriate movements or legislation and be ready for changes required by the legislation or movement.

In addition to anticipation of trends, both teacher organizations and school administrations must convince the public that they are receptive to American ideals supporting quality education for all children. Put another way, both parties to collective bargaining must let the general public know they possess futuristic attitudes about the education of children and about issues ranging from legal aspects (an example is PL 94-142) to innovations.

Like most other aspects of the behavioral sciences, there are no hard, fast rules for projecting images of forward-thinking leadership. Doing so involves:

1. Staying abreast of pending legislation and other developments at the national and state levels and translating them into local concerns long before they become law
2. Developing and maintaining regular publications that address the realities of upcoming legislation and other developments and explaining their local implications

3. Issuing position papers or other prepared statements against certain upcoming changes or developments *before* the development is enacted or finalized

☐ Summary

The images of the two parties to collective bargaining in public education can make or break either or both parties in their communities. Certain images must be shaped and reshaped constantly. This can be achieved, in large measure, through teacher and/or administrator strategies oriented to developing and maintaining images of (1) child advocacy, (2) professionalism, (3) moderation, and (4) forward-thinking leadership. Such images are best achieved through media campaigns based on proactive rather than reactionary strategies.

CHAPTER 6

The Battle for Public Support

BOTH TEACHER ORGANIZATION leaders and administrators preparing for bargaining for the first time often learn—much too late, unfortunately—that they are bargaining in a climate hostile to their best interests. They learn they are opposed in principle by civic, business, and parent group leaders because their true ideals, beliefs, attitudes, and zeal about children and doing what is best for children has not been communicated to those groups.

Communicating with various public quarters is related to, but quite separate from, "The Struggle for Positive Images" in bargaining, which was the focus of Chapter 5. Proper communication can offset the negative perceptions of those groups focusing on one glaring item—the soaring costs of education in an already overburdened tax structure. In almost every American city or town, the greatest single rate on the tax bill will be the one generated by the public schools. In some large urban centers, the schools appear even more expensive because of relatively higher costs in those areas.

The first aspect of the message to be communicated is simple: a well-educated public is one of the heavy costs of democracy. It is the responsibility of teacher organizations *and* administrators to sell that point to the public. The promotion of this idea should be part of the policies of both administrations and teacher organizations, and it should be done continually—certainly long before bargaining time for items that increase the tax rate. Moreover, the sell job should be done through all possible media with one recurrent theme: that educator welfare translates into increased benefits for children.

To sell their roles as transmitters of educational benefits to children, teachers and administrators must seize every opportunity. This role should be as ever present in the minds of parents and community leaders as are television commercials. Opportunities for selling the significance of their roles exist at all times—at community gatherings, during election campaigns, during the school year, over the holidays, and in connection with other related political issues as they surface.

This chapter explores methods of getting public support for the positions involved in collective bargaining. It covers the following topics:

☐ The Message That Must Be Sold

The logical sequence of the message to be sold is simple: children are the hope of the future; educators (both administrators and teachers) are the custodians of children and as such are the main shapers of many of the values, skills, and (hence) life chances of those children; better educated and adjusted educators will transmit better educations to children. While the adversarial aspects of collective bargaining will force teacher organizations and school administrators to adopt competitive variations on this message, the basic message is the same.

While this message appears simple, it is difficult to transmit to the public for many reasons. Several of these reasons are: (1) other more verbal public servants have sold themselves as more important from the standpoint of overall public safety and as such have become more competitive for the tax dollar in an era of fiscal restraint; (2) educators—teachers and administrators alike—have failed to establish measurable causal relationships between effective teaching and student achievement; (3) educators have taken defensive postures when reacting to public outcries against the costs of education, resulting in cuts in educational services that in turn led the public to believe those services were not important to begin with; and (4) perhaps most important, educators have failed to establish a firm meaning of quality education, a failure that resulted in no true definition of the basic costs of quality education.

Points (3) and (4) deserve further elaboration. Educators often cite mean expenditures per pupil as the criterion for costs within a given state. This is simply an average, but the quality of education purchased by that figure is never established through detailed description. It is quite possible that *true quality education* costs two or three times as much per pupil. Until the fundamental concept of quality education is defined and priced in ways understandable to the public, it is likely that education will get "seconds" at the salary marketplace. Furthermore, as long as educators continue to make cuts in reaction to public pressure and still manage to keep schools reasonably effective, establishing the baseline costs of true quality education is difficult if not impossible.

The brunt of leadership in countering these negatives in public perception falls on both bargaining parties, teacher organizations and administrators. While the overall message is the same, slight variants may be used by each to gain an edge in public support. The fundamental teacher organization message should be:

1. Teachers are daily custodians of the most precious thing of all, children
2. Better teachers develop better students
3. Better teachers have an American right to better salaries and other perquisites because they have worked harder to attain better educations
4. While some school districts have moderate-to-admirable educational programs, they are far below what must be considered ideal
5. Teachers deserve to participate in the formulation of policies related to curriculum and instruction because they are intimately involved with these areas on a daily basis
6. Teacher organizations are quite willing to assume responsibility for student achievement, provided:
   a) Teachers participate equally in the formulation of criteria for evaluating that achievement
   b) Other groups (administrators, parents, and others) have parallel and supporting responsibilities

The message to be delivered by administrators on behalf of their school boards is slighty different:

1. The school board has the legal responsibility for the quality of education, including:
   a) Determination of the policies of the school district
   b) Determination of the goals and objectives of the school district
2. The collective will of the public, represented by the members of the school board, is best for the long-term interests of the children of the district
3. The school board is aware of its responsibility to protect the tax-supported interests of citizens
4. The school board is interested in quality education and quality teachers and strives to achieve that quality within the framework of the public will to support it

☐ Getting the Message Out
Perhaps the most important aspect to remember about the message(s) is that they must be delivered constantly—not just *during* bargaining sessions.

Teachers or administrators who wait until bargaining sessions begin are inviting failure. Listed below are some excellent avenues to public opinion, together with some "do's" and "don'ts."

☐ **OTHER LABOR ORGANIZATIONS**   While this appears to be a natural avenue for teacher organizations, the administration message can be effective at times. Centralized labor councils in certain areas, organized for coordinating labor activities, afford a natural arena for delivery of the message.

For teachers, it means that ongoing communications with these labor councils must be maintained to merit their support when needed. Ongoing communications will insure that teacher organizations stay knowledgeable about: (1) the extent of general labor support for the teacher organization and its position(s), (2) the location of pockets of resistance to teacher organizations in the labor community, and (3) the opinion of the parent portion of these labor organizations, and (4) the limits of support. Some practical don'ts apply here:

1. Don't assume the support of other labor organizations, especially other teacher organizations
2. Don't communicate in educational jargon
3. Don't forget that it's all in the name of children
4. Don't forget that other labor organizations are interested in their own survival and that presentations must address that concern

Administrators who represent their school boards must translate the school board message to the same labor councils. In addition to the general school board message described earlier, administrators can take the basic position that collective bargaining alone does not guarantee protection of the interests of children. While collective bargaining is a fair mechanism in a general sense, the mission of the school board is oriented to the best interests of child equity and taxpayer equity in the community and is only opposed to teacher interests when those interests threaten what is best for the children and the taxpaying public.

Some of the most important organizations in the community are church organizations, and they are often influential in determining the collective bargaining climate.

☐ **CHURCH ORGANIZATIONS**   Either bargaining party can generate strong advocacy when they are able to get the endorsement and support of church organizations on issues. The basic strength of such support derives from the following:

1. Churches have public images that include the education function
2. Many factions otherwise hostile to the interests of educators can some-

times be neutralized

3. Church organizations have clear access to audiences (ethnic and racial groups, for example) that educators might otherwise have trouble reaching

Access to church organizations can be gained through the leadership of those organizations. That leadership is usually positive about the public schools of a given locale. It is important to mount an aggressive program for support from the leadership of various churches, irrespective of denomination or faith.

Be aware that these church organizations have in-house politics that must be respected. This means that proper channels of communication should be observed. It is usually best to direct communications to the minister, pastor, or other top official of the church.

It is best to *go* to the church organization. Brochures, advertisements, documents, or other publications lose their effectiveness unless they are accompanied by representatives who explain them. Also, the language used must fit the cultural or ethnic backgrounds of the audience. For this reason it is sometimes best to send a representative from those backgrounds or one thoroughly familiar with them.

One more caution: many church groups are conservative, which means that certain avant garde or controversial issues must be approached with extreme care or be avoided altogether. Sex education, for example, can be a very adventuresome topic for such organizations.

Now for some don'ts:

1. Don't focus arguments on money unless children are the obvious beneficiaries

2. Don't ignore the status of the religious leader. Give him or her credit whenever appropriate

Another type of organization present in most, if not all, communities is the business organization. Ways of getting messages to these organizations should be explored.

□ **BUSINESS ORGANIZATIONS**   Administrators and teacher organization representatives should inform members of the business sector about the rationale of particular issues, proposals, counterproposals, and other well-known positions. Often, the simple act of communication neutralizes would-be opponents.

Despite traditional opposition to increased taxes, many business groups realize they have vested interests in quality education in their communities. Many giant corporations would like to see high schools training students to become productive employees at the time of *entry* into corporate activity. Given such interest, school board representatives and teacher organization representatives benefit by presenting themselves as supporting such training when the resources are available.

Small business operators should be remembered too. These persons often belong to associations of small business operators and these associations must be sought by both bargaining parties.

The following don'ts apply to both administrators and teachers:

1. Don't be uninformed about budget and tax impact
2. Don't forget to do your homework about the various special interests that might be present at the meeting
3. Don't forget the parent faction in the audience — their interests are likely to be similar to those of parents anywhere

☐ **PARENT GROUPS**   The message that sells collective bargaining as ultimately benefiting children is the most effective message when dealing with parents. However, some additional aspects deserve mention because of the unique nature of the parent perspective. In communicating with parent groups, both teacher organization representatives and administrators should stress:

1. The nurturing role of the schools
2. The importance of achievement at parity with national standards
3. The rights of parents to participate in the definition of goals for their children
4. The complexities related to proper evaluation in education
5. The importance of the affective domain in the development of the total child
6. The necessity for parent-educator teamwork

Meetings with parent groups can and often do lapse into verbal attacks on educators — administrators and teacher organization representatives alike. Such attacks are often based on minor incidents that have displeased the parents. Teacher organization representatives and administrators should avoid getting caught in such confrontations, especially when newsmen are present.

The best format for educator meetings with parent groups is panel discussions chaired by knowledgeable parents and made up of both parents and educators. The agenda should be carefully drawn up and should involve a carefully sequenced group of topics of primary interest to parents. The panel discussion should be followed by questions and answers.

Without a doubt the most difficult message to convey to parents is the position that while standardized test achievement is a worthwhile goal, it is not an adequate one. Other aspects of the child's education must be focused on at the same time. Put another way, aspiring to and working toward achievement at parity with national norms on standardized tests tends to limit the thrust of the schools at the expense of other subjects that are equally vital to the total development of children. This message is doubly difficult to sell because of current parent interest in "basics," but it must be conveyed.

The specialized interests of minority parents must be addressed, too. Although these interests are essentially the same as those of other parents, educators would do well to familiarize themselves with some special approaches to communication with minority parents.

□ ORGANIZATIONS REPRESENTING MINORITIES: A SPECIAL NOTE

Minority parents and minority organizations are often overlooked as sources of support for educators, administrators, or teachers. This support can be a dominant force, especially in urban education. The net effect of overlooking such support is that educators—especially teacher organizations—can run into unanticipated opposition, often at times when such support would be crucial. In recent years teacher organizations have gained considerable momentum from positions taken in advocacy of minority children, particularly those from low-income households. Such momentum has put school boards on the defensive about their policies involving these children. But school boards are often revitalized when teacher organizations are contradicted by the parents of the very children for whom those teacher organizations are advocates, especially when these attacks occur during open board meetings.

School boards and their administrators, too, can gain considerable support from minority quarters with aggressive, forward-thinking programs and publicity. Their key to success is consistency in outreach, long before the bargaining process occurs.

Access to minority organizations and interests can be gained through churches, community improvement and/or community action organizations, many of which are affiliated with mayors' offices in various cities and towns. Representatives of minority organizations are usually willing to exchange opinions with school-related organizations, especially school boards.

The message to these organizations should be no different from those delivered to other organizations. However, remember to express that message in lay language.

Some don'ts are in order:

1. Don't forget to follow channels of communication that respect the leaders of minority organizations.

2. Don't forget that special categorical programs (Chapter I, Bilingual Education, and others) have special importance to minority communities.

3. Don't overreact and defend particular administrators or teachers whose names surface during discussions; it is best to promise to return to the group with more information about an incident (not a person). A good way to avoid being put on the spot in such situations is saying, simply, that it is unfair to discuss the person unless the person is there.

☐ Dealing with the Media

Distortion of fact in popular news media frequently occurs because of the ever-present commercial appeal of sensationalism. Most news editors and their assistants are not qualified to decide the relative merits of positions of parties to a collective bargaining confrontation or a dispute arising out of collective teacher actions. Also, these newsmen are not qualified to select or ferret out the newsworthy information in such a confrontation. They tend to select sensational news for presentation to the public.

For these reasons, news releases to media must be developed with extreme care. Additionally, copies must be kept of all articles submitted to the newspapers so that educators are protected against publication of false or misleading information.

Most school districts of considerable size will have reasonably well-organized news programs aimed at control of their relations with media, but specifically at development and maintenance of their images. The mere existence of an organized news program leads newspeople to seek it out and look to it as representative of the school district posture on an issue or array of issues.

There is a lesson here for teacher organizations. They should develop ongoing news programs structuring their public images. Whether for teacher organizations or school boards, such news programs should:

1. Stress positive reportage, with emphasis on leadership roles on issues that translate to benefits for children. This sometimes means news coverage of seemingly unimportant issues long before bargaining begins.

2. Rely *only* on controlled, well-written releases.

3. Avoid candid interviews unless with persons experienced in dealing with the media.

4. Stress facts.

5. Avoid accusatory, finger-pointing statements whenever possible.

6. Include documentation of facts, listing sources whenever time and space permit.

☐ Summary

All public factions should hear the viewpoints of the parties to collective bargaining on an ongoing basis. Bargaining is much more effective with public understanding of and support on issues. Merely getting the message out during or just before bargaining is poor practice. And the message should be simple. It should be couched in terms of the overall welfare of children and tailored to the understanding levels of the groups which it wishes to influence.

PART 3

Preparation for Bargaining

CHAPTER 7

Toward Practical Bargaining Philosophy, Strategy, and Tactics

A PHILOSOPHY OF COLLECTIVE BARGAINING in public education implies a basic mind-set about the nature of the bargaining process and what it should yield for the participants and those they represent. Such a fundamental outlook is the necessary first step in the triad in the title; that is, philosophy should lead to bargaining strategy that in turn should lead to bargaining tactics appropriate to accomplish desired ends.

Strategies and tactics of collective bargaining in public education center on aggressive attempts by both parties to orchestrate as many positive events as possible while reducing or neutralizing as many negative events as possible for one's side. A positive event for a school board might be landslide re-election victories for two or three incumbents; similarly, a positive event for a teacher organization could be a merger with another smaller teacher organization. An example of a negative event is a proven conflict-of-interest action by a board member or an exposed illegal handling of funds by a teacher organization. One teacher organization tactic might be publicity and exposure aimed at focusing pressure on the school board. Similarly, a school board tactic might be publicity aimed at exerting pressure on teacher organization leaders.

The strategies and tactics of bargaining depend on the philosophy of the bargainer or bargainers. This chapter will explore the ways of developing bargaining philosophies, strategies, and tactics and the basic dynamics of collective bargaining in public education. It covers the following topics:

Toward a Philosophy of Collective Bargaining in Public Education
Strategies and Tactics: An Important Distinction
Common Bargaining Tactics
Selection of Bargaining Issues
Bargaining Range, Permissible Range, and Settlement Range
Basic Dynamics of Collective Bargaining

☐ Toward a Philosophy of Collective Bargaining in Public Education

There is no need for a definition of philosophy here. In this context, the term refers to a fundamental outlook about collective bargaining in public education. Achieving such a fundamental outlook requires an exploration of several propositions.

Proposition 1. Collective bargaining as a process in employer-employee relations exists because of a conflict of interest. Examination of this first proposition forces the question: Is collective bargaining an adversary relationship? The answer requires a look at what is at stake in education bargaining. Certainly there are many topics under consideration in education bargaining and many are basic to the living standards of education professionals; salaries, benefits, and other perquisites, for example. But what of other rights demanded by teachers and education professionals? An example is a teacher organization demand for participation on a panel interviewing candidates for a principalship.

The key here is power. The answer to whether bargaining is an adversary relationship may be found in the unending quests of teacher organizations for ways of widening their scope of bargaining. Another answer may be found in the staunch resistance of school boards to binding arbitration. The decision about the adversarial or nonadversarial nature of collective bargaining in public education is left to the reader.

Proposition 2. Success in collective bargaining in public education depends on public perception of the basic justice of the matter, the roles of the constituents of each bargaining group, and the effect that the issues of bargaining may have on the public. This second proposition is one of the fundamental premises of this book. However, it is not offered here as fact; rather, it is left to the reader to ponder in the interest of a broadened philosophical outlook about collective bargaining in public education.

Proposition 3. Bargaining demands must be perceived as good by the bargaining team's constituency. The third proposition requires that a set of demands reflects the current bargaining philosophy of an entire group of education professionals. Such a philosophy is put into action in the form of goals, catalyzed by teacher organization leadership, school administrators, state and national organizations to which the education professionals belong, legal counsels and outside advisers to bargaining teams, and difficulties experienced in the implementation of the present contract.

Proposition 4. Financial terms of collective bargaining contracts represent compromises based on the priorities of each side. This implies that school finances represent a fixed resource, limited by the willingness of the public to pay. The collective bargaining process is a method of finding the middle ground between priorities determined by education professionals and priorities determined by school boards.

Proposition 5. Collective bargaining in education deviates significantly from private and other public sector bargaining because of the nature of the product of public education. Unlike the private sector, education professionals are involved with the futures of their products, the children. When teacher organizations bargain with their school boards, the across-the-table relationship is not totally polarized as it often is in the private sector. Because of public perception, teacher organizations must display concern for the rights of children at all times. This same bargaining "burden" is present for school boards and the administrators who represent them. The result is that both parties must modify their goals for the sake of a third party; and both parties must decide at each point in bargaining whether the decisions they make will be determined by their own needs or the needs of their clients.

Proposition 6. Effective collective bargaining in public education involves exchanges of concessions between two parties, none of which are beyond the long-term capabilities of either side. This proposition advances the notion that in effective bargaining, each side must gain something. Equally important, neither side must be forced to concede something that will be damaging to its long-range survival. This means that teacher organization proposals and administration counterproposals must take into account the total capabilities of the parties who must respond.

Proposition 7. The total cost of a proposal or counterproposal is related to the recipient's *perceived* total implementation cost. Proposals mean different things to the parties to bargaining. Rarely are proposals evaluated strictly in terms of dollar costs. Perceived implementation costs are other "prices" that may include teacher strikes, board recall movements, divided teacher memberships, lost elections, and many others.

These simple propositions are offered as part of a framework for the development of a bargaining philosophy. Needed also is a firm grasp of the basic strategies and tactics of bargaining.

☐ Strategies and Tactics: An Important Distinction

Bargaining *strategies* are the sustained, long-range actions undertaken by either party for the accomplishment of desired goals. On the other hand, bargaining *tactics* are the moves made by administrations or teacher organizations prior to, during, and immediately after at-the-table interchanges with the other party. Perhaps the best way to understand the distinction between strategies and tactics is to consider the analogy found in aerial warfare: strategic actions like regular bombings are calculated to destroy the will of an enemy to wage warfare by reducing or destroying resources that support military actions, while tactical actions like attacking enemy fighter planes, strafing, and destroying troop trains, ships, and air bases are more or less localized, immediate, and centered on a specific theater of operations — although they are also aimed at achieving the overall strategic end.

It may be said that tactics are subsets of strategies. But both are important to the accomplishment of the desired goals and objectives of each party to bargaining. Strategies and tactics are closely related to long-range and short-range goals, respectively.

However, strategies and tactics are interdependent. Strategies may lead to achievement of short-range goals, and—conversely—tactics may lead to achievement of long-range goals. The interdependence of strategies and tactics may be further illustrated with a simple example: when a teacher organization decides that its long-range salary goal should be maintenance of a position in the top-paid fifty school districts in the state and finds itself below that goal, it may be forced to adopt a series of tactics related to accomplishment of the goal. Such tactics could be: (1) pressure during open board meetings, aimed at forcing the school board to place a tax-increase measure on an upcoming ballot; (2) coalescing with other groups; and (3) a series of public presentations against certain competing money issues that are likely to be on the same upcoming ballot.

A similar example applies to administrators. Under parental and other pressure for increased measurable achievement (in reading and mathematics) on standardized tests, a superintendent and team of administrators might decide they must extract a firm commitment from teacher organization leaders to support, say, achievement at parity with national norms in these two subject areas. The goal of parity with national norms is, in this instance, a strategic one. Tactics that might be employed could be (1) widespread publication of the administration intention to extract the commitment from the teacher organization; (2) well-written press releases by each school board member demanding such teacher organization commitment as a condition of collective bargaining; and (3) well-publicized progress reports after bargaining sessions, all calculated to show that the administration is holding out for the teacher organization commitment as a requirement for teacher organization gains in collective bargaining.

The determinants of bargaining strategy are related to the determinants of bargaining climate, discussed in Chapter 3, which therefore will not be discussed here. More central to the purposes of this chapter are the tactics of bargaining that are determined in part by the strategies adopted.

□ Common Bargaining Tactics

There are certain tactics commonly used by the parties to collective bargaining in public education. Tactics adopted vary according to the desired ends of the bargainers. Descriptions of some of these commonly used tactics follow.

□ **REACHING FOR THE MOON**   This tactic is commonly used in real estate sales. The approach is based on ambitious proposals that form a backdrop for the gradual reduction and haggling that follows. The more common examples in collective bargaining in public education are: (1) introduction of higher salaries and fringe benefits than expected; (2) introduction of proposals focused on teacher organization participation in decision making in certain areas (purchasing, interviews of new administrators, certain curriculum concerns, etc.) that are logical and plausible; and (3) introduction of nonessential demands, some of which are plausible and potentially enhancing to the educational program.

In all three instances, the basic tactic centers on dropping the demands as a compromise gesture in return for agreement on other more essential items. Tied to this, but another tactic altogether, is introduction of futuristic issues.

□ **LOOKING TO THE FUTURE**   New items are introduced, even though there is little chance for their acceptance. These items are introduced primarily to educate the opponent about their basic concepts, costs, and educational benefits so that bargaining on them is easier in the future. These items often serve the same purpose as those in the preceding section. This tactic is part of "Bargaining as Attitude Restructuring," discussed in Chapter 1.

□ **THIRD-PARTY THREAT**   This is a basic teacher organization tactic that can also be used by administration bargainers under certain circumstances. If and when one team learns that the other team has strong feelings against the use of fact-finders, mediators, and arbitrators, it is sometimes possible to use the threat of calling in such outsiders to advantage. Doing so helps with movement toward agreement sometimes. Such threats are effective when used subtly, but the team making them must be prepared to carry through on them if called to do so by the opposing team.

□ **USE OF PUBLIC SENTIMENT**   Publicizing the issues being bargained sometimes forces meaningful cooperation by the opponent. However, the party attempting to capitalize on public sentiment must be sure of the public opinion on the issue.

The strongest case that can be made to the public is one made on emotional grounds. There is only one basis for such a case: children. Put another way, the opposing side must be made to appear as though it is obstructing or opposed to what is best for children. There are some serious limitations to this tactic, especially during mediation, fact-finding, or arbitration, processes that are often considered confidential. Also, there are times when previously agreed-upon ground rules preclude this tactic.

□ **HOT ISSUE TECHNIQUE**   Certain issues are "hot" in the sense that they elicit strong reactions from the opposing team. One example is an administration team insisting on consultation rights with a smaller teacher organization that is a vigorous competitor with the exclusive representative. Another example is a nationally popular issue that might be locally unpopular, like Cinco de Maya observances for the schools. Teacher organizations advocating such issues can sometimes put administrations and their school boards in awkward political straits with such issues. In any case, the central idea in the hot issue technique is forcing the opponent to be willing to bargain on another difficult issue.

□ **TIME AS A TACTIC**   Time is as important in collective bargaining as it is in the National Football League, where league championships often depend on the use of the clock and knowing when to move and when not to move. In collective bargaining, three aspects of the use of time are significant:

1. When starting bargaining sessions, two uses of timing are common. Some bargainers like to start months ahead of the expiration date of contracts. The idea is that the extra time permits airing of issues and differences. Other bargaining teams take on the opposite attitude, postponing bargaining until just before the expiration date of the contract in hopes that the limited time frame for bargaining will limit or decrease the obstacles to bargaining. The approach selected is strictly a matter of judgment, related to the specific conditions faced.

2. Money matters are also related to timing. Typically, money items are the last ones agreed upon in collective bargaining in public education. School administrators attempt to leave money issues to the end of the bargaining period because slow movement on money issues induces more trade-offs from teacher organizations, there is increased likelihood that the teacher-bargainers will settle for less than the board's best offer, and teacher-bargainers gain more satisfaction because the slow process offers them the opportunity to illustrate their importance to their organizations. Generally, the slow, incremental movement toward agreement on money matters by administrator-bargainers tends to enhance the perceived worth of gains from the perspective of teacher organizations.

3. Experienced bargainers know there is a certain time in the negotiations when both parties are ready to begin compromising. This moment is usually after the demands of both sides have been examined, discussed, and "costed."

It is difficult to quantify such a time; that is, it is strictly a human phenomenon that occurs in bargaining. Timing such an occurrence is a matter of judgment, depending on the personalities, the issues, the external pressures, and other variables.

□ **REDUCING THE OTHER SIDE'S EXPECTATIONS**   This is a tactic used primarily by school administration bargainers wherein their counterproposals are intentionally unreasonable and far below the expectations reflected in teacher organization proposals. The intention of the tactic is centered on lowering the minimum floors sought by teacher organizations.

☐ **PACKAGING TACTICS**   Used by administrator-bargainers and teacher-bargainers alike, this tactic involves the inclusion of desirable and undesirable (or less desirable) aspects within the same proposal or counterproposal. The idea is to force the other side into acceptance of the less desirable aspect to achieve the desirable one. A typical example may be found in current administrator bargaining: tie money gains to regaining lost management rights.

Generally, teacher organizations attempt to deal with money issues one at a time. This tactic is intended to increase the possibility that administrator-bargainers will not connect the costs of money items or will somehow overlook the total cost of money items. Conversely, administrator-bargainers usually offer packages, which retain focus on the total economic impact. Such total packages typically include salaries, fringe benefits, leave costs, sabbatical costs, and all other economic items. By packaging, administrator-bargainers ensure that trade-offs remain within budget capability and force teacher-bargainers to accept some undesirable economic features along with desirable ones.

☐ **CONVERTING OPPONENTS' LANGUAGE TO ONE'S OWN**   Generally, teacher organizations favor broad, philosophical language that permits equally broad interpretations in contract areas in which they are interested in gaining concessions. Conversely, administrators attempt to tighten contract language in most areas, primarily because contracts written in precise terms are easier to maintain or adhere to. Also, tight language, from the standpoint of administrators, is a prime defense against being forced to make unnecessary concessions to teacher organizations.

As a result of these opposing interests, much of the activity during the trading of proposals, counterproposals, and new proposals is focused on the conversion of the specific language of opponents' documents. Although this tactic is used by both sides, it is a primary device for administrator-bargainers because it:

1. Helps to create the appearance that the language writer is basically in control of the bargaining encounter

2. Helps to retain present contract language, forcing the opponent to introduce – and defend – any new language in terms of the need for change

3. Helps to project an image of compromise while actually protecting the status quo

☐ **LOADING THE OPPONENT WITH THE BURDEN OF PROOF**   This is a tactic that can be used by both sides. However, it is more commonly used by administrator-bargainers. It is similar to the legal principle wherein the accuser must bear the burden of proof. In the collective bargaining scenario, teacher organizations are in positions roughly analogous to those of "accusers," simply because they are trying to change or upset aspects of the establishment — the school board and its administration. One prime device at the disposal of administrators, then, is forcing teacher bargainers to prove the need for a proposed change *and* that the specifics of their proposal satisfies that need. A special category of this tactic is discussed in the next section.

□ **FORCING JUSTIFICATION OF PROPOSALS IN TERMS OF CHILDREN'S NEEDS**   This tactic is a clever one that can be used by each side. It is related somewhat to the tactic of reducing the expectations of the other side, discussed above, and it is particularly effective in contexts where the public must be informed on an ongoing basis. The net effect of the tactic is to slow down the bargaining and sometimes reduce the number of proposals and counterproposals.

□ **TYPICAL ADMINISTRATOR BARGAINING TACTICS**   While the specific tactics used will vary depending on the context, certain tactics are regularly used by most administration bargainers. They are:

1. Pushing for early written agreement — actual or implied — on the basic financial structure on which the bargaining is to be negotiated.

2. Attempting to limit the breadth of the definition of grievances by seeking language that limits grievances to specific contract matters only.

3. Resisting teacher organization proposals that use exact language borrowed from board and/or administration policy documents. The effect is to narrow the language and hence the scope of teacher organization proposals.

4. Attempting to include the statement that school board authority prevails over all issues not covered in the contract; and a no-strike clause, whether provided in state collective bargaining laws or not.

5. Pushing for exclusion of teacher evaluations (as distinguished from teacher evaluation *procedures*) from arbitrability whenever arbitration, advisory or binding, is a feature of the contract.

6. Bargaining for reduction-in-force procedures that are based on grade levels at the elementary school level and on certified fields of competence at the secondary level. This tactic is oriented to protecting the quality of instruction in school districts.

□ **TYPICAL TEACHER ORGANIZATION BARGAINING TACTICS**   Teacher organization bargaining tactics are a "mixed bag," so to speak; that is, some are direct opposites of those used by administrator-bargainers while others are exactly the same. However, there are certain tactics common only to teacher organizations. Some of these are:

1. Introduction of proposals based on grievance arbitration awards favorable to teacher organizations, or more common, proposals based on problems that have arisen during implementation of the current contract. Certain of these proposals present a threat to administration bargainers, and the threat aspect can sometimes force concessions in other areas.

2. Framing as many teacher organization proposals as possible in terms of benefits that accrue to children. The tactic is a powerful one, especially when and where media releases are involved.

3. Basing salary and fringe benefits proposals on comparisons with those of other school districts whenever they are higher. This tactic introduces criteria that are difficult for administrator-bargainers to counter, especially if the comparison districts are perceived positively.

4. Attempting to use the consumer price index — as distinguished from localized cost-of-living indices — as a credible basis for salary negotiations (Greenfield 1982, 25–26). The tactic can sometimes extract commitment of higher salaries than otherwise, together with greater acceptance by the constituency of the teacher organization.

5. Introduction of certain aspects to be included in reduction-in-force portions of bargained contracts, whenever there are no specific provisions in state collective bargaining laws. These are adherence to strict seniority criteria, with categorical provisions that meet affirmative action mandates; avoidance of teacher evaluation criteria; and special provisions that exempt teacher organization officers and negotiators from reduction-in-force criteria (and lay-offs) under the rationale that they are essential to the maintenance of teacher organization continuity.

☐ **GENERAL**   There are many other tactics available to and used by the bargaining parties, depending on the context — specifically, past bargaining history. For example, in the lengthy bargaining dispute between the Modesto School Board and the Modesto Teachers Association cited earlier, as soon as negotiations reached a stalemate over the annual calendar, the board adopted a strike manual detailing procedures to be followed in the event of a strike. Additionally, the board voted to increase the pay of substitute teachers from $38 to $80 per day. The overall tactic was aimed at (1) establishing public confidence — specifically, that the Board had provided for the strike possibility, and (2) destroying or reducing the collective will of the teachers to strike. Although teachers eventually struck on 4 March 1980, the initial strike vote taken on 4 September 1979 failed (*Modesto Bee* 1981).

Impasse is also a tactic in collective bargaining, usable under certain conditions. However, because impasse and its resolution is such an important topic, it is discussed separately in Chapter 11.

☐ Selection of Bargaining Issues

As discussed previously, teacher organizations receive bargaining goals from many sources. Selection of issues for bargaining requires ranking them in priority order, which in turn requires consideration of teacher organization interests, probable support of the constituent group of teachers, the ability of the school district to meet the demands, and probable public attitudes about the demands as presented.

Mind-sets of school boards and their bargainers may be somewhat different. It is important to understand, for example, why school boards frequently fail to demand something in return for bargained contracts, similar to the "in workmanlike fashion" clauses found in private industry contracts.

Before the advent of collective bargaining in public education, many school boards were more or less confident that the bulk of policymaking and decision making in public education was vested in them. But collective bargaining laws, combined with the political power of teachers, has stripped away much of the unilateral power of school boards. Consequently, a feeling of resentment remains in the hearts of many board members toward collective bargaining. The result has been a tendency to resist most bargaining demands, irrespective of worth; and perhaps more important, a failure to demand concessions of equal magnitude from the teacher organizations. Effective bargaining requires something of equal worth for a concession yielded. It is imperative that teacher organizations be forced to accomodate to the changing needs of their boards of education.

Because of this passive tendency of school boards, many of the powers and prerogatives of middle management personnel (principals, curriculum supervisors (and others) are eroded or conceded away. Another example of the negative effect of such board attitudes toward collective bargaining is seen in the reality that despite teacher gains through bargaining, true quantifiable teacher accountability (as a quid pro quo) is not yet the case in most school districts.

Administrator-bargainers who represent their school boards in bargaining must consider:

1. The educational philosophy of the school district
2. The legal responsibilities of the school board
3. The probable support of the total board for the counterproposals as presented to teacher organizations
4. The ability of teacher organizations (teachers) to comply with the counterproposals

5. The long-term effect on student and teacher morale
6. The effect on the day-to-day operations of the schools
7. Probable public attitudes about the counterproposals

It is possible to offer simple issue selection schemes for both teacher-bargainers and administrators. Such models should incorporate certain political realities faced by each side as well as some very plausible steps necessary for effective bargaining. Figure 7.1 depicts an issue selection sequence for a typical teacher organization.

Although teacher organizations will vary considerably regarding their in-house political relationships and general organization, common sense dictates adherence to a certain basic sequence in issue selection. For example, the feasibility review in Figure 7.1 should be performed *before* the membership is surveyed because the long-range credibility of the teacher organization leadership is at risk when teacher expectations are heightened by issues that are neither realistic nor consistent with teacher organization strategy or state teacher organization strategy.

Issue selection by administrator-bargainers is slightly more complex because of two aspects: (1) administrator-bargainers typically wait and react to teacher organization proposals submitted; and (2) final decisions depend on the wishes of school boards, politically visible bodies that are sensitive to

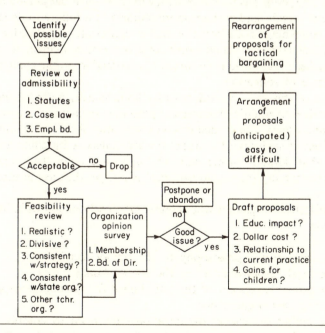

7.1. A simple scheme for issue selection by teacher organizations.

media, public opinion, and school district staff opinion as well as the overall teacher membership. Consequently, administrator-bargainers must react to teacher organization proposals *and* generate new proposals when appropriate. Figure 7.2 offers a hypothetical issue selection scheme for administrator-bargainers.

During the feasibility review phase, administrator-bargainers evaluate teacher organization proposals in terms of their relationships to arbitrator awards. Teacher organization proposals similar to or closely related to arbitration awards favorable to teachers will have a certain momentum for that reason. In such instances, it is likely that administrator-bargainers might feel compelled to change many aspects of such proposals by submitting related counterproposals.

Once teacher-bargainers receive a set of counterproposals from the administrator-bargainers, they will have to review those counterproposals by

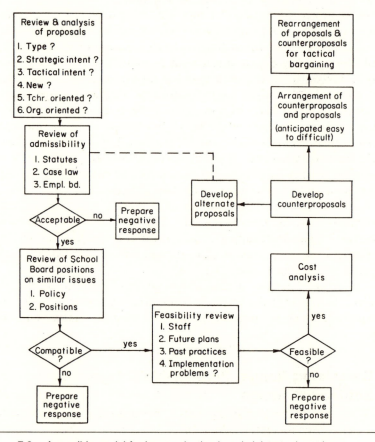

7.2. A possible model for issue selection by administrator-bargainers.

considering essentially the same questions that administrator-bargainers were forced to consider. These questions cover the type of counterproposal, strategic intent, and tactical intent.

When proposals are introduced during the "reopener" period of an existent contract, they should be evaluated as to whether they are consistent with the conditions of the reopener clause or clauses. This aspect applies to both teacher proposals and administrator counterproposals.

Time is an important determinant of feasibility because many proposals require considerable time prior to implementation. An example of this is a teacher organization proposal for parent education classes in schools in low-income neighborhoods, wherein parents are kept aware of what various teachers are teaching, all in the interest of increased parent support of the educational objectives of the teachers. Obviously, such a proposal requires logistical planning, secretarial support, community liaison, and equally important, concerted in-service activity for the teachers involved.

As indicated in Figures 7.1 and 7.2, proposals and counterproposals should be organized for bargaining. Generally, it is best to arrange them in order from easy agreement to difficult. Such organization observes the principle of developing agreement momentum discussed in Chapter 4. However, in many instances the tactics of bargaining dictate otherwise. For example, a teacher organization might want to introduce a difficult proposal involving teacher organization rights of rejection of college or university supervisors of student teachers—opposed by the school board in the past—in the interest of getting administrators used to the idea before introducing this concept in altered form two years later. Similarly, administrator-bargainers might want to surprise the teacher-bargainers with an unexpected concession designed to get teacher organization agreement on another difficult item.

Issue selection can be a complex undertaking. Many factors, including the publicity surrounding certain issues, the unanimity of both sides for such issues, feasibility, parent support, and many other considerations go into issue selection criteria. The schemes shown above should be used cautiously and tempered by the realities they face.

The actual dynamics of bargaining are discussed later in this chapter. However, before such discussion it is important to explore three important concepts in bargaining: bargaining range, permissible range, and settlement range.

☐ Bargaining Range, Permissible Range, and Settlement Range

While the terms bargaining range, permissible range, and settlement range can be used to apply to almost all items or issues of bargaining, they are perhaps best illustrated with salary items. Typically, teacher organizations submit salary proposals that are much higher than they expect to get. Using the lowest point on the salary schedule as a reference, these bargainers submit a proposed figure — $17,000 for example. Using the same reference point, administrator-bargainers answer with a counterproposal aimed at a starting salary of $12,500. The difference between the teachers' initial demand of $17,000 and the administration counter of $12,500 is the *bargaining range.*

Permissible ranges and settlement ranges are not as simple to understand. After the opening rounds and the establishment of bargaining ranges, both parties are aware that the figures they have presented are unrealistic; that is, administrator-bargainers in the example above know that the figure of $12,500 is too low to satisfy the teacher organization. Also, teacher-bargainers know that the $17,000 figure is unrealistically high and that administrators will resist it.

There exists a point below which teacher-bargainers will not go and there exists a point above which administrator-bargainers will not go. These may be called stop points. However, there is a range of salaries between the $17,000 and the teacher stop point that the teacher organization might settle for, depending on other concessions that accompany such lower salaries. Similarly, there is a range of salaries between the $12,500 and the administration stop point for which the administration might settle. These are *permissible ranges* for both sides. (See Figs. 7.4 and 7.5).

If bargaining is to be possible, there must be some overlap between permissible ranges of each side. The range of overlap is the *settlement range.* (See Fig. 7.6).

Much of the essence of bargaining is in three simple phases: (1) determination of the bargaining range, (2) calculation of opponents' permissible ranges, and (3) concessions and haggling to arrive at the settlement range.

"Calculating" or estimating the permissible range for the other side is an extremely difficult and risky undertaking. The difficulty derives from problems associated with estimating the relative value of a specific salary figure or other item to the opponent and the risk lies in the possibility of conceding more than might be necessary.

It is important to focus on the notion of the relative value of a specific salary figure. From the standpoint of administrator-bargainers, relative value refers to the overall importance of the salary figure as it is perceived by teachers and their leaders; that is, much more than the actual purchasing power of the dollar figure must be considered. In public education bargaining, perhaps more than anywhere else, teachers are often willing to lower their salary demands in exchange for other concessions. This means that other, companion proposals must be considered in calculating the relative value of a salary figure or other teacher organization proposal.

Another aspect that complicates estimation of the relative value of specific salaries or other items is compliance cost or total agreement cost. Such costs are not strictly dollars-and-cents costs. They are determined by the perceived total consequences, political or otherwise, of accepting or rejecting certain proposals or counterproposals. For teacher-bargainers this means that if a salary is on the low end of the permissible range, acceptance or agreement means some other important companion needs (as perceived by teachers) must be met. The same is true for administrator-bargainers: persons attempting to estimate total agreement costs for school boards must realize that those school boards must remain viable to broad-based constituencies at all times. Figure 7.3 illustrates a *possible* costing sequence employed by school board members.

The concepts discussed in the foregoing (bargaining range, permissible range, settlement range, costing, and others) are all central to the basic dynamics of collective bargaining in public education.

☐ Basic Dynamics of Collective Bargaining

Unfortunately, the marked differences between teacher organizations and school boards have been used in the past to explain the impetus to collective bargaining. But it is likely that a better grasp of the basic dynamics results from understanding *both* the common interests of and differences between the parties to bargaining.

Both school boards and teacher organizations are establishments. As such, they are interested in organizational survival for its own sake; that is,

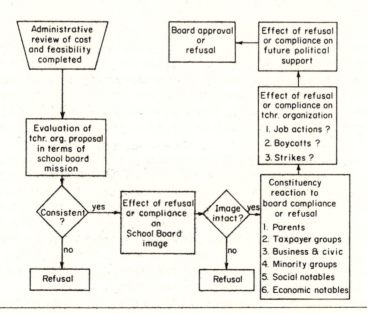

7.3. A hypothetical costing sequence for school boards.

there exists general motivation among members of each organization to perpetuate the organization and its power, quite apart from the legal mandates or avowed missions of the organizations. Remember that school boards often reflect the interests of certain power groups. The same is true of teacher organizations.

Another point in common between these two factions is interest in financial influence. Education budgets are usually the largest public budgets in American cities. Participation in decision making about financial matters of such magnitude is at the heart of the definition of political power.

A third point in common between the two organizations is that leadership in each affords high visibility that can lead to greater opportunities. Successful membership and service on school boards offers potential for entry into higher political offices, some as politically significant as seats in state assemblies or senates. For teacher organization officials, there are various well-paid positions in state teacher organization hierarchies as well as many executive secretary positions in large local teacher organizations.

There is a fundamental symbiotic relationship between the two factions. Intelligent school board members know that teachers need to vent their pent-up emotions on something, and the school board is that something. Teacher organizations provide an important service for school boards, that of channeling and controlling the collective ire of teachers. In return, school boards provide an important rallying point for teacher organizations, thereby helping to justify their existence.

An extremely important factor in common between the two factions is their clientele: children. Although the nature of the clientele limits the bargaining tactics available to both sides, it does serve two important purposes. It narrows the range of nonmoney matters to be bargained and makes it easier for the two factions to cooperate when it is necessary to mount publicity campaigns aimed at greater financial support for the schools.

Besides an awareness of these points in common, the observer of collective bargaining in education should realize that the intelligent leadership of each side recognizes these mutual interests. This means it is likely that each party incorporates these considerations into (1) criteria for predicting the moves and tactics of the other side and (2) the resulting role calculations on which its next moves will be based. Even when one party enjoys considerable relative bargaining power, that power is not always exercised. The mutuality of concerns sometimes forces restraint by the more powerful party simply because that party *needs* the other party for some or all of the reasons listed in the preceding paragraphs.

There are also several fundamental differences between school boards and teacher organizations. These differences are important because they, too, help explain some basic behaviors and tactical maneuvers during bargaining.

School boards and teacher organizations differ in their basic postures about collective bargaining. School boards usually adopt *defensive* postures and teacher organizations adopt *offensive* postures. Put another way, school boards appear to adopt attitudes supportive of the *status quo* and its attendant power, while teacher organizations perceive collective bargaining as a means of acquiring more power.

A second difference between the two factions is that of generalized and specialized constituencies. School boards must speak for and bargain on behalf of the welfare of the children, of all citizens, and citizens in general, while teacher organizations can identify various specialized subgroups with special needs as part of their constituencies. It is well known that certain teacher organizations have long championed minority causes when those causes lent momentum to their organizational causes. It is also common knowledge that some of the same teacher organizations took positions *against* the same causes, in direct contradiction to their original positions. The important point, however, is that teacher organizations have the advantage of advocacy of a narrower range of specialized interests.

Other differences between the two groups, all closely related to the dynamics of bargaining, are differences in perceived costs of opponents' demands, differences in available tactical alternatives during bargaining, and differences in visibility requirements. As with other differences, these can explain certain problems encountered in the give-and-take of collective bargaining.

Differences in perceived costs of opponents' demands are best explained with an example. A teacher organization demand for a 6 percent salary increase when only 6 percent is available can appear much greater than 6 percent, relatively, to a board of education. The board realizes that the teacher organization demand is in competition with other possible uses of the 6 percent—uses that the board is responsible for and under constant pressure about. Examples of other uses are items such as instructional supplies, building maintenance, paraprofessionals' salaries, and the like. Thus the 6 percent teacher organization demand looms larger in the eyes of the board members.

Differences in visibility requirements reflect the political character of school board membership and the reality that politically ambitious school board members must maintain a relatively high level of public visibility. The same is not necessarily true for teacher organization leaders. This need for visibility has direct effects on the dynamics of collective bargaining. It limits the tactical alternatives available to board members and forces closer adherence to the letter of the law. Board members must utter careful public statements about the bargaining issues or face charges of coercion of employees, but teacher organization officials have more freedom in making public threats about the same issue. Moreover, collective bargaining laws are focused primarily on the expected behaviors of school boards and their representatives. For example, the definitions of good faith bargaining in most state education bargaining laws are quite specific about what school boards cannot do, while stating relatively little about specific undesirable behaviors on the part of teacher organizations. Bear in mind these similarities and differences when observing the dynamics of collective bargaining in public education. These aspects can help explain behaviors, or, more important, they can sometimes help predict behavior.

☐ **BORN OF CONFLICT**   Collective bargaining occurs because of a basic conflict between two parties coupled with their recognized need to survive in their present operational context. The two conditions, left alone, would generate friction, open hostility, and other forms of strife — all costly where the life chances of children are at stake. The purpose of collective bargaining legislation is the provision of a framework for effective working relationships between the two parties that recognizes two conditions. The legislation is designed to permit both parties to survive in the institutional context.

☐ **TWO PERSPECTIVES**   Bargaining may be viewed, first of all, as a confrontation between factions designed to establish relationships that define the use of power. But such a definition requires consideration of power as an end in itself — a misconception as far as collective bargaining laws are concerned. There are times when power must be displayed, but always toward other ends. The teacher organization official who is losing control of his or her constituency must somehow become visible. Often, the only way to do so is through a display of power.

Another possible viewpoint of bargaining is that of *mutual needs satisfaction.* Teachers and their organizations need finalized contracts with provisions more or less comparable to those of neighboring school districts, because teachers' individual perceptions are based in part on what is necessary to achieve parity with other individual teachers elsewhere. Teacher organization leaders need finalized contracts together with reasonably competitive provisions to retain their leadership roles. Failure to achieve such provisions will arm the "young turks" of the organization with what they need to ascend to leadership through recall movements and other devices. Similarly, school boards and their administrators need both the bargaining process and the new contract to (1) remain credible to professional staffs within districts; (2) to remain credible to lay observers who know that state laws permit collective bargaining in education; and (3) refocus the energies of total school district staffs so that school boards can return to their rightful roles as shapers and makers of district policy.

The concept of mutual needs satisfaction can provide a model for analyzing the dynamics of collective bargaining. Although many frameworks for analysis are possible, one based on mutual needs satisfaction is consistent with the intent and spirit of most collective bargaining laws and the very essence of collective bargaining, because in effective bargaining, both sides win.

☐ **A NEEDS SATISFACTION MODEL**   An effective bargaining relationship can be conceptualized as the establishment and maintenance of a practical range of *needs satisfaction* costs. Put another way, teacher organizations must not hold out beyond the *practical* capabilities of school boards to satisfy *as those school boards calculate the costs of satisfaction*. Similarly, school board counterproposals and positions must not overtax the ability of teacher organizations to deliver what is held important by those organizations and their memberships.

Needs satisfaction costs must be defined. The term is subjective, varying quantitatively from one party to the other and from one bargaining period to the other. A teacher organization proposal for a 7 percent salary increase and an improvement in dental care, hospitalization, and vision care can serve as an example. Even if the 7 percent for the salary increase is available and the board has access to certain permissive overrides to pay for the benefits desired by the teachers, the board might include several other things in its calculation of the costs of compliance with the teacher organization proposal. Such costs might include possible loss of political support from other constituencies if they comply. Conversely, they might include a possible teacher strike as one cost of refusal.

Therefore, one extremely important activity that occurs during effective bargaining is the reduction of differences in *needs satisfaction cost estimates* between school boards and teacher organizations. That is, the bargaining act leads, or should lead, to near congruence in estimating bargaining concession costs. Teacher organizations learn to calculate board concession costs more accurately and boards and their representatives learn to estimate what teacher organizations *really want*.

A model based on *needs satisfaction* as the prime motivator to collective bargaining permits identification of several distinct stages or phases in bargaining: (1) assessment of opponents' needs, (2) evaluation of opponents' bargaining philosophies, (3) calculating needs satisfaction costs, (4) formulating bargaining tactics, (5) reduction of settlement ranges, and (6) settlement and contract finalization.

It is nearly impossible to capture the total dynamics of collective bargaining in public education by describing bargaining on an issue-by-issue basis. Issues are almost always commingled with other issues; that is, intelligent teacher organization bargainers combine issues in ways they believe will influence outcomes in their favor. The same goes for school board counterproposals. Hence, the discussion which follows will use the six-point framework above in combination with various examples in the hope that the dynamics of bargaining are made clear.

Assessment of opponents' needs. Once a teacher organization is established as the exclusive bargaining agent for the teachers of the school district, a date is set for opening bargaining talks for the upcoming school year. Although many collective bargaining laws are not specific about beginning bargaining dates, most require that they start reasonably early enough for completion prior to the start of the next school year. Other laws require starts early enough for incorporation of bargaining concerns into school district budgets.

After agreement on the ground rules of bargaining, teacher-bargainers usually submit a series of proposals. The proposals may be on any issues within the scope of bargaining as defined in the state. Ideally, such proposals contain information as to cost in dollars, relation of the proposal to current practices, and potential for improvement of current practices.

Irrespective of the number of teacher organization proposals, administrator-bargainers typically attempt to determine the total dollar costs of the proposals as submitted, feasibility of the proposals in terms of current school district practices, and the likely importance of the proposals from the vantage points of *both* teacher organization leaders *and* the teachers. The third point is significant when assessing the *true needs* of the teacher organization.

One should distinguish between the needs of teacher organization leaders and the needs of the teacher membership. The true needs of teacher organization leaders are likely to be tied to retention of power; specifically, to visibility because of competition for offices within the teacher organization or because of a growing, verbal, competing teacher organization. They must also provide effective responses to external pressures because of state teacher organization affiliations or higher teacher benefits and salaries in comparable nearby districts. On the other hand, the true needs of individual teacher members might be related to general dissatisfaction with salaries and benefits, dissatisfaction with district expenditure levels for instructional supplies, dissatisfaction with district evaluation procedures, or many other concerns. Note here the possibility that the focus of concerns of teacher organization leaders might be considerably different from those of the teachers they represent.

This suggests that proper assessment of the true needs indicated in teacher organization proposals might result from a composite evaluation that incorporates primary needs of teacher organization leaders, primary needs of teacher members, and interrelated needs of teacher organization leaders and teachers. Interrelated needs are those that are important to both, because teacher organization leaders must satisfy some of the primary needs of their teacher constituents to maintain power.

Although teacher organization bargainers will have to wait for the first round of counterproposals before attempting to calculate the true needs of the school board and its administration, the basic logic above should govern the process. Obviously, institutional peace is one primary need of school boards, irrespective of collective bargaining laws that force them to bargain in good faith. Most school board needs subsume under their requirement for institutional peace. Examples of other school board needs are for appearances of board unity, political visibility, satisfaction of pressure groups to which the boards relate; and, equally important, for dissociation from certain issues. There are other school board needs, to be sure, some of which are closely tied to the power status of their superintendents. (Review Chapters 2 and 3 and the sections related to superintendents' perspectives on collective bargaining and the power status of superintendents, respectively.)

There are no formulas for calculating the true needs represented by proposals or counterproposals. The process is more like estimation and involves knowledge of the total milieu of bargaining. The total milieu includes the factors cited in Chapter 3, as well as personality factors (ego needs, ambitions, etc.) of representatives of both sides together with precedents set by previous bargaining experiences.

Assessment of the opponent's needs is a critical factor in determining the bargaining tactics likely to be successful with that opponent. Additionally, such assessment shows various ways of stimulating the opponent to act and ways of modifying the intentions of the opponent.

Develop an index of the relative importance of an opponent's needs. The more basic the need, the greater the likelihood of success for the tactic adopted for dealing with it. While no rule for identifying the relative strengths of needs is offered, three distinct needs are always identifiable in bargainers of both sides—personal needs, group membership needs, and ego needs.

But assessment of needs is not sufficient grounds for determining successful bargaining tactics. It must be accompanied by an evaluation of the opponents' bargaining philosophies.

Evaluation of opponents' bargaining philosophies. A distinction should be made between bargaining *philosophies* and bargaining *attitudes.* Bargaining philosophy refers to an outlook about what the bargaining should yield for the bargainers and their constituencies. Bargaining attitude refers to how those bargainers approach the achievement of ends important to their philosophy.

A practical framework for determining the basic bargaining philosophies of participants and their aims involves two fundamental philosophical positions: bargaining as *maximization* or bargaining as *optimization.* (See McKersie 1965 for a comprehensive treatment of various perspectives on collective bargaining.) In the maximization approach, bargaining is viewed as an arena for achieving as many of their ends as possible *at the expense of the other side.* Bargainers view optimization as a process for achieving as many of their ends as practical *within* the long-range capabilities of the other side. An excellent analogy to the two basic outlooks may be found in nature. Some living creatures, forced to live symbiotically with other species, overextend the support capabilities of the other species. The result is usually extinction of one or both species. Other more successful living creatures make perfect adjustments to their natural support systems by remaining within the long-range capabilities of those systems.

Inexperienced bargainers often attempt maximization at the bargaining table. However, as they gain experience in bargaining, the same bargainers often change their basic philosophies to the concept of optimization.

Although the attitudes displayed by bargainers are related to their basic bargaining philosophies, they are not always exactly the same. Attitudes usually displayed during collective bargaining may be summed up as militant, defeatist, bartering, or cooperative. Thus a bartering attitude might be oriented to a maximization philosophy; that is, even though representatives attempt to barter during bargaining, the hoped-for exchanges are unequal in their favor.

Militant attitudes at the bargaining table are often found in teacher organization representatives and administrators during their first attempts at bargaining. These militant attitudes derive from maximization philosophies of bargaining, overcommitment to bargainers' constituencies, and unfamiliarity with the opposition that results in lack of confidence in those bargainers.

Defeatist bargaining attitudes result from the belief that their opponents are too powerful. These bargainers refuse to fight and give in to the demands of the perceived stronger party. The danger in such an attitude is that the self-perceptions of the weaker parties prevent them from using the mechanics of bargaining to demand something in return for concessions yielded.

Bartering attitudes develop from the perception that bargaining is essentially a quid pro quo process, that something must be exchanged for something else. Such a perception is accurate and consistent with the spirit of collective bargaining laws. The relative value of things exchanged is another matter, of course.

Cooperative attitudes are those present when there is confidence and trust between teacher organizations and school boards. Such attitudes are closely related to *optimization* philosophies. Teacher organization proposals generated by bargainers adhering to optimization attitudes incorporate attributes like (1) value to teacher organization, school board, children, taxpayers, and all school community elements; and (2) the capability of the school board to meet the terms of the proposals without sacrificing its mission.

These attitudes are often combined in actual practice. For example, cooperative and bartering attitudes sometimes combine quite successfully when those with bartering attitudes seek exchanges of equal value, instead of exchanges that are obviously unequal. Also, militant and defeatist attitudes are sometimes in combination: a militant attitude at the table often develops when school board members feel the collective power of teachers is too strong to resist.

During the first few meetings of the bargaining period, bargainers usually assess the philosophies and attitudes of their counterparts on the other side of the table. Clues to those philosophies and attitudes are usually revealed early—even during discussions of ground rules in which time, place, and time limits on meetings become major problems if bargainers of one or both sides evince militant attitudes. Bargainers observing such attitudes must formulate proposals or counterproposals that take into account those attitudes, while behaving in a way that encourages trust and confidence.

Calculation of needs satisfaction costs. For both parties, the calculation of the costs of satisfying the true needs of the other involves an analysis of each proposal in terms of its implementation impact. For example, administration bargainers calculating the cost of satisfying the needs manifested in a teacher organization proposal for, say, hourly pro rata pay for extra duty for teachers over and above seven events for the school year must (1) calculate the budgetary impact, (2) determine operational feasibility, (3) assess school board opinion about the proposal, and (4) estimate the costs of refusal.

There are times when administrators must resist such a proposal despite the availability of enough money and proven operational feasibility. At such times concerns about the political image of the school board often dominate; that is, the collective opinions of such school boards might be that agreement could damage their relationships with other segments of their constituencies. The same is true of teacher organizations. When teacher opinion is clearly against certain administrative counterproposals, teacher-bargainers must resist those proposals.

A hypothetical costing procedure was offered in Figure 7.3. A similar decision pattern would operate with teacher organization leaders, although the specifics might vary. In each case the costing procedure involves evaluations of consistency with organizational mission, impact on the established image of the organization, constituency reactions, and overall effects of compliance or refusal.

Needs satisfaction costs are relative; that is, they are determined by the situations and perceptions of those who evaluate them. From the standpoints of teacher-bargainers who introduced the extra-duty pay proposal in the example above, the relevant factors considered were budgetary impact and operational feasibility.

But bargainers who submit proposals and counterproposals without consideration of the power-retention interests of those who must react to those proposals are flirting with failure. While the extra-duty pay proposal is consistent with the mission of the school board that must react to it, that board might have taken a hard-line stance against extra-duty pay in the past, which means the proposal would conflict with its established image. Also, the board might be temporarily or permanently committed to a constituency (a taxpayer group, for example) that is opposed to extra-duty pay for teachers.

In keeping with the concept that a school board must weigh the overall costs of compliance or refusal, teacher organization reactions must be included in that calculation; that is, the board must think of the possibility of job actions by the teacher organization. The final decision is often one of which enemy the school board chooses.

Calculation of needs satisfaction costs is at the heart of effective bargaining. Effective bargainers are those who are able to approximate the needs satisfaction costs of the opposing bargainers so that proposals or counterproposals submitted are plausible within the framework of the costing outlooks of those receiving them. Put still another way, much of the movement toward closure of bargaining and contract finalization has to do with growth in the abilities of each side to approximate closely the needs satisfaction costs of the other side.

Formulation of bargaining tactics. The common tactics of bargaining have been discussed in this chapter. Of concern here are the relationships of bargaining tactics to opponents' bargaining philosophies and needs satisfaction costs.

An example may explain these relationships. Budgetary analysis in a large urban school district revealed the availability of 7 percent for salary increases. However, the teacher organization took a "12 percent or else" stance in its publications, public statements, and proposals submitted by its bargainers. During the bargaining sessions, administrators learned from various teachers that they wanted job action because when they settled for 5 percent the previous year, school administrators received 8 percent. Through private talks with the teacher organization president, administrators confirmed the job-action mood of the teachers. They also learned the president knew that only 7 percent was available but needed something with which to calm the teachers.

Hastily, the administrators formulated their tactics. They announced a new salary schedule for administrators that showed a 7 percent increase. This was followed by a school board announcement of a 10 percent salary increase for the superintendent, which was promptly refused by the superintendent who said that although he appreciated the "vote of confidence displayed by the salary increase," he could not "accept it in good conscience because of the limited resources available for teacher and administrator salaries in the district." The tactic "de-fanged" the teachers. This example illustrates the administrators' sensitivity to the teacher organization leaders' needs satisfaction costs, which were tied to retention of power. It also illustrates the optimization philosophy of the teacher organization president.

Tactics adopted in any situation should be based on analyses of opponents' true needs, their bargaining philosophies, and their needs satisfaction costs. The tactics that satisfy all three aspects are likely to be successful—all other things being equal.

Reduction of settlement ranges. After each bargaining team develops a reasonably accurate estimate of the permissible range of the opposing team for each issue, the overlapping permissible ranges (or the settlement ranges) are reduced through concessions by each bargaining side. For example, suppose the administrator-bargainers have learned through proposals, counterproposals, and verbal exchanges that the teacher organization permissible salary range for beginning teachers is roughly between $13,669 and $15,500. This means that teachers are not willing to go below $13,669 and would insist on $15,500 unless other companion demands are met. These companion demands could be any within the scope of bargaining, from increases in paid leave for urgent personal business or bereavement to additional paid leave days for religious holidays; increases in medical, dental, vision or other insurance coverage; improved sabbatical leave provisions; or any combination of these, as well as many others not mentioned here. Other companion demands could be those focused on working conditions—demands that might not carry price tags.

Although they are more difficult to illustrate, reduction of settlement ranges occurs in nonfiscal matters also. The haggling aspects of collective bargaining are most evident when settlement ranges are being reduced on each item of bargaining. However, the actual process is one of a series of proposed and actual trade-offs until a compromise is finally reached.

To understand the process of reduction of settlement ranges in bargaining, teacher salary proposals should be viewed as related to other concessions desired by teachers. It is possible to depict a relationship between teacher salary and concessions gained, as in Figure 7.4, where t_a is the *opening* teacher organization minimum salary (based on the first step for first-year teachers) and t_b is the *actual* minimum it will go, provided other concessions desired by the teachers are granted in bargaining. As the number of other concessions or companion demands increases, salary demands decrease, *approaching* the actual minimum, although the actual minimum is not usually known to administration bargainers.

Figure 7.5 illustrates a similar relationship from the perspective of administrator-bargainers. Administrator-bargainers start from a stated maximum for an opening first-year teacher salary, represented by sb_a. The *actual* maximum, not known to teacher-bargainers, is sb_b. As administrators gain other concessions, their permitted maximum increases, approaching their actual maximum.

The actual shapes of the curves in Figures 7.4 and 7.5 will vary, depending

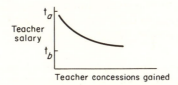

7.4. Teacher salary aspirations as a function of other concessions gained.

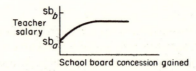

7.5. Teacher salary growth as a function of school board concessions gained.

on the specifics involved. The settlement range, then, is the overlap between the *permissible* ranges $t_a - t_b$ and $sb_b - sb_a$. This is illustrated in Figure 7.6, where the shaded portion represents the settlement range.

Each side attempts to estimate the permissible range of the other. But calculating the permissible range for the other side is difficult and risky because of the problems of subjectivity in estimating the total values of others and dangers of revealing an overestimation or underestimation. Because of these problems, much of the art of bargaining centers on tactics designed to force revelation of the permissible range of the other side without revealing an overestimation or underestimation in the process.

Such tactics operate over time. Time in bargaining is used in various ways. One use of time is withholding concessions so that their value increases over time. Another is the creation of doubt in the minds of opposing bargainers so that one's own settlement range is harder to estimate. Still another use of time is delaying in anticipation of an event external to bargaining that might change the perspective of opposing bargainers (a cutback in state funds, for example).

Perhaps the most important use of time in bargaining is learning what the other side *really wants*. Doing so takes time, for the trading of concessions — so necessary for reduction of settlement ranges — is slow, deliberate, and tedious, involving many proposals and counterproposals. Needless to say, each proposal and counterproposal must be priced and tested for operational feasibility as well as political acceptability.

Settlement and contract finalization. This phase is essentially one of locking-in all of the agreements arrived at. It is an extremely important phase, so much so that it is reserved for analysis in Chapter 12.

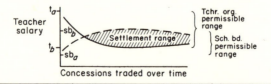

7.6. Settlement range for teachers' salaries as related to teacher and school board concessions traded over time.

□ Summary

Effective bargainers must have workable philosophies or bargaining techniques that may be translated into equally workable strategies and tactics. Such philosophies should address certain basic questions about the nature of bargaining—its proper function, the various perspectives, and most important, what it should yield for the participants.

Such philosophies may have variants, but the hoped-for outcomes of collective bargaining can be grouped under two headings: maximization philosophies or optimization philosophies. Maximization philosophies of bargaining are those holding that bargainers should "take-all" in bargaining; on the other hand, optimization philosophies are those based on the belief that bargainers should seek as much as the long-range capabilities of the opponent will permit.

Tactics are subsets of strategies. They are related to strategies in much the same fashion as short-range goals are to long-range goals. While the tactics and strategies of bargaining are limitless, some are commonly used. Among the more common tactics are "reaching for the moon," "looking to the future," "the third-party threat," "the use of public sentiment," the "hot issue" technique, and certain skillful uses of timing.

There are no rules for selection of the issues to be negotiated. Selection should be determined by (1) constituency interests and support, (2) educational philosophy, (3) legalities, (4) long-term effects on staff and student morale, and (5) extent of public support.

Bargaining range is the difference between the absolute minimum as perceived by one side and the absolute maximum as perceived by the other side. Settlement range is a more complicated concept, but it is essentially the overlap between the permissible ranges as those ranges are perceived by each side. One last significant phase in bargaining involves the reduction of settlement ranges on each issue until both sides arrive at a point of agreement.

CHAPTER 8

Important Basic Knowledge

THE NINE VITAL PRINCIPLES of effective bargaining delineated in Chapter 4 and practical bargaining philosophy, strategies, and tactics discussed in Chapter 7 were offered as requisites for the proper preparation of bargaining teams in public education. But teams steeped only in the behavioral dynamics of bargaining are like skilled musicians without instruments or craftsmen without tools.

Essential are a fundamental knowledge about the collective bargaining law in the applicable jurisdiction, detailed knowledge of current practices in the subject school district, similar details about selected comparable school districts in the area, and history of the collective bargaining relationship within the subject school district.

School districts are complex organizations, and it is difficult to absorb all the basic knowledge about them that is applicable to the collective bargaining situation. For this reason, the information must be organized or categorized in some way. This lengthy chapter is devoted to the following topics:

Legal Context of Collective Bargaining
Analysis of Personnel Policy
Financial Analysis
Analysis of Past Practices
Analysis of Comparable School Districts
Analysis of Bargaining History and Previous Agreements

It is hoped that the topics presented in this chapter will stimulate and direct the reader to the research necessary for effective bargaining; that is, within a practical study such as this, it is impossible to discuss every collective bargaining law in every state. The rationale for the topics selected derives from the hope that they will lead to the essential, applicable research.

□ Legal Context of Collective Bargaining

Collective bargaining in public education can be viewed as an outgrowth of collective bargaining in the public sector. The primary difference is the nature of the service rendered: firemen provide security against fires; police are responsible for safe streets, homes, and businesses; teachers are responsible for nurturance of children and transmittal of the wisdom of elders.

But public sector labor activity, specifically public sector bargaining, was based on private sector bargaining models. Because of this, combined with the nature and importance of services rendered by public employees, it has been necessary to modify public sector bargaining models. That necessity derives from the importance of protecting "the public interest" (set in quotations to convey the idea that the term is interpreted differently in various quarters). Defining the term public interest hinges on *how* and *when* the general public is hurt by the collective actions of public employees. The other dimension for such a definition is the *extent* of damage; that is, how much is the public interest threatened by police strikes compared to fire safety workers compared to garbage workers compared to teachers?

Clearly, withdrawal of services by these groups would affect the public interest adversely over time. But does that alone mean collective activity by these groups should be judged illegal? What of the individual rights of members of these groups to self-improvement, an aspect undoubtedly in tune with free enterprise and freedom of speech, two touchstones of democratic life?

There is no question as to the role of boards of education in protecting the public interest represented by the education of children. School boards are, by law, rightful shapers of public education policy, hirers of school administrators and teachers, decision makers for education budgets, and generally, protectors of the education aspect of the public interest. Of equal importance is the reality that board members are, by and large, elected officials, which means they represent the collective will of the people.

The foregoing surfaces two fundamental dichotomies: the public interest versus the collective power of teachers and, consequently, the legal mandates of school boards versus collective (and individual) teacher rights. There *is* a compelling fundamental public interest in public education; and teachers are guaranteed the right to strive to improve the quality of their work lives and life-styles. Balance is the key to the solution of these fundamental frictions. Somehow the rights of education professionals have to be balanced against the legal mandates of school boards. But the question is, how?

States have responded to this question with almost as many variations on education bargaining models as there are states. While it is outside the purview of a practical study such as this to speak to the details of these variations, it is important to understand the basic reasons for them. This is explained by Cresswell and Murphy (1980, 153):

> For a school board to sign and administer a labor contract, it must have the legal power to do so. Since the schools are creatures of state law, the ability of a school board to enter into such an agreement must be based in that law. This is the first and fundamental reason why there is variation

among the state legal structures when dealing with labor relations in the schools. . . .

It goes without saying that bargainers should be familiar with their specific state legal structures for bargaining. However, understanding the rationale for certain arrangements and their variations contributes to a better overall grasp of collective bargaining in general. Understanding the major characteristics of those arrangements requires a framework for discussion. An excellent survey of the legal framework of collective bargaining by Anthony M. Cresswell, Michael J. Murphy, and Charles T. Kerchner (1980) uses major collective bargaining contract items as a basic framework. Another framework employed by Doris Ross (1978) differentiates bargaining on the basis of several factors, including affected government levels, school district employees covered, union security arrangements, legalities related to strikes, and binding arbitration of disputes.

Consistent with the practical orientation of this book, a workable framework for discussion should be based on issues and items that generate the most conflict during bargaining and contract finalization proceedings. However, areas of conflict are likely to vary somewhat from area to area. Also in keeping with the practical intention of this book would be the *usability* of a framework for discussion; that is, such a framework should help readers formulate approaches for analyzing collective bargaining legalities in their jurisdictions.

Such an analysis could cover six major points: (1) the nature of the state education labor law, (2) the manner of determining bargaining units, (3) the scope of bargaining, (4) the union security provisions, (5) the impasse resolution procedures, and (6) the grievance resolution provisions. The analysis would have to be followed up with research about any applicable case law or findings of employment relations boards.

☐ **NATURE OF STATE EDUCATION LABOR LAWS**   State education bargaining laws vary, first, in the personnel covered. In states with education bargaining laws, variations are from the extremes of local bargaining only for K–12 teachers to bargaining for all education employees — teaching, supervisory, and other professional personnel as well as noncertificated.

The variety in approaches to education bargaining is to be expected and may, in the long term, translate to an advantage (Cresswell and Murphy 1980, 152):

> The lack of consistency among the states is less a problem than an opportunity. By observing a variety of approaches to such difficult questions as management rights in public schools, it is more likely that sound policies will be discovered and tested.

A survey of all fifty states shows four basic approaches to education labor law: (1) collective bargaining not permitted, (2) collective bargaining permitted but not required, (3) collective bargaining mandatory, or (4) collective bargaining or "meet and confer" relationships optional. California is in the fourth category, permitting collective bargaining *or* the meet and confer provisions of its previous education labor law (Winton Act), depending on the preferences of the majority of the teachers within each school district. (At this writing, employer-employee relationships in some districts in California are still governed by the provisions of the Winton Act. An example of a large district in this category is Clovis Unified.)

The specific labor relations remedy adopted by each state reflects a combination of factors, among them the intensity of organized private sector labor activity in the state, the length of time the state has been forced to deal with public sector bargaining, the evolution of case law in the state, and other political considerations. For example, in Pennsylvania (where strikes are legal under certain circumstances) public sector negotiations go back as far as 1939 (Cresswell and Murphy 1980, 150).

☐ **DETERMINATION OF BARGAINING UNITS**   This aspect of collective bargaining generates conflict primarily because it brings into direct confrontation the true strength of unionization with one of the primary strengths of management. Employee organizations rely on numbers to back positions taken on issues while management needs cadres of supervisory and quasi-supervisory personnel for its mission and assuring continuity of operation. Thus the question of who does or does not belong in employee organizations is a fundamental point of friction in collective bargaining.

States, too, have an interest in unit determination matters. That interest is a fundamental one, closely related to the reasons for the existence of collective bargaining laws; specifically, that employment relationships between school people will proceed with a minimum of problems. Because of this, some states have attempted to determine what types of personnel may belong to various employee organizations in school districts, either through collective bargaining legislation or rulings of employment relations boards (Cresswell and Murphy 1980, 161–65). But the problem is complex: district-to-district flexibility in role definitions and job descriptions is highly desirable, an aspect that limits the power of state legislation in unit determination matters while (sometimes) intensifying local frictions.

In the absence of clear-cut statements in collective bargaining legislation, several criteria are used by employment relations boards in unit determination findings. The first is the criterion of a group's "community of interest," meaning both occupational (skills and professional interests) and bargaining interests. A second criterion is whether an organization could represent a certain group (a teacher organization representing principals, for example) without conflict of interest. A third standard has to do with confidentiality; that is, could membership of one group in a larger group jeopardize the bargaining positions of an opposing group because of information leaks? Other criteria in state collective bargaining laws include established practice, effects of fragmentation, and efficient operation of schools.

State collective bargaining laws generally prohibit teachers and administrators in the same bargaining units and prohibit certificated and noncertificated employees in the same bargaining units. However, many cases are ultimately decided by state employment relations boards because of confusion about job titles and functions.

Typically, teacher organizations attempt to include as many certificated (credentialled) persons as possible in their memberships, especially when there are no exclusions stated in collective bargaining laws. Administrations or other employee organizations sometimes challenge these claims, resulting in representation elections.

Principals represent a special case or group of certificated employees because of the role conflicts that are built into their jobs. They must work closely with teachers. Yet they must be loyal to superintendents and central administrators from the dual standpoints of implementation of school board goals and dependence on those sources for rewards and job perquisites. Some state laws permit separate representation units for principals whenever principals bargain, and there is evidence that unions of school administrators are developing rapidly, possibly because of this (Holley et al. 1976, 361–69).

□ **SCOPE OF BARGAINING**   This area is the true battleground of collective bargaining because it is where the power of school boards to operate the schools comes into direct confrontation with teacher organizations and their quests for more power. Such quests for power are often clothed in justifiable — even self-righteous — garments like conditions of employment or procedures for evaluation of teachers. More than any other aspects (other than binding arbitration as a means of resolving grievances), these two phrases offer the potential for broadening the powers of teacher organizations. Both are plausible bargaining rights to most observers: there are many conditions of employment that teachers *should* participate in deciding and bargaining about. And shouldn't teachers participate in the procedures for their evaluations? Otherwise, how could evaluations be fair?

This second aspect, procedures for evaluation of teachers, holds as much if not more potential for acquisition of power by teacher organizations than the first. It is an area within scope in some jurisdictions (California Educational Employment Relations Act, Sec. 3543.2) and it is specifically excluded from the scope of others (Minn. Stat. Ann. Sec. 179.61–77, as last amended by Chaps. 127, 246, 247, L. 1974). This area has the potential for broadening the actual scope of bargaining because of its implications for teachers' roles in curriculum development. Instruction, teachers' primary area of responsibility, is an outgrowth of curriculum. Evaluation procedures must *necessarily* be based on instruction, specifically, on the instructional effectiveness of individual teachers. Traditionally, school boards have reserved the right to determine the goals of school districts, the logical first step in curriculum making. But teachers, seeking to participate in evaluation procedures, are likely to want to participate in much more than future instructional formulation for there is no logical way to exclude curriculum — goal setting included — from evaluation procedures. The point that separates the instructional aspects of teacher evaluations from curriculum and other related concerns may have to be decided in courts of law in the future.

Scope of bargaining speaks to three different bargaining subjects: mandatory, prohibited, and permissive. Mandatory subjects must be bargained; that is, management has no choice in the matter. Prohibited subjects are those on which the law forbids bargaining, and permissive subjects are the optional ones.

Mandatory subjects of bargaining. Subjects like salaries, hours of employment, salary schedules, and closely related conditions of employment are almost always mandatorily bargainable. By contrast, the states are split on other related employment conditions like pension and retirement plans, with some mandating and others prohibiting bargaining.

States vary with respect to the bargainability of the workload. Some reserve decisions about school calendars, hours, and workloads for management and others require bargaining.

Prohibited subjects. Generally, items of policy and policy determination are prohibited by state bargaining laws. Such items include hiring, supervision, job assignment, organizational plans, discharging employees, standards of service, recruitment, and others.

Permitted subjects. Items in this category tend to vary from state to state to a much greater extent than those in the previous two categories. In the absence of specific inclusions in scope, the bargainability of such items is decided by state employment relations board rulings or case law. It is likely that more items in this category will be bargained in the future, however, simply because the very nature of collective bargaining requires steady increments in concessions — especially those that do not erode management prerogatives directly. Some items in this category are class size, agency shop, preparation time for teachers, textbook selection, retirement benefits, and others.

☐ **UNION SECURITY PROVISIONS**   These are teacher organization concerns oriented to the maintenance of membership and basic income of the organization, together with certain lesser considerations like released time for bargaining for teacher organization officials, use of school bulletin boards, and the right to distribute literature in teacher's mailboxes. Common forms of union security agreements are "union shop," permitted in Pennsylvania, and "agency shop" permitted by the collective bargaining laws of some other states. Union-shop agreements require that teachers join the majority teacher organization (exclusive representative) a short time after employment and remain members for the term of the collective bargaining agreement. Agency-shop agreements require that all teachers pay to the exclusive representative a service fee equivalent to full dues of teacher organizations, but actual membership is not required. In *Abood vs. Detroit Board of Education,* 431 US 209, 97 SCt 1782 (US SCt, 1977), 81 LC, the court upheld the agency-shop provision in public employment. (In *Abood,* the plaintiff alleged that certain First Amendment rights were violated by the agency-shop provision. See Pulliam 1982.)

☐ **IMPASSE RESOLUTION PROCEDURES**   Impasse resolution is discussed in greater detail in Chapter 11. Thus, the discussion here is limited to its place in the legal context of collective bargaining. The laws of collective bargaining in public education are fairly consistent with respect to the resolution of impasse. Most states provide for specific steps: mediation, fact finding, and arbitration. A fourth provision of the law is that of injunction when justifiable, a tool available to management once employee organizations are on strike. As in the case of strikes, *threats of injunctions* are sometimes more potent than the injunctions themselves. In most jurisdictions, strikes are illegal. Even when they are permitted, certain requirements of due notice and exhaustion of impasse resolution procedures provided by law must be met first.

☐ **GRIEVANCE PROCEDURES**   Like impasse resolution procedures, grievance procedures are discussed separately (Chapter 14). Basically, grievance procedures insure proper implementation of the *contract as bargained.* They usually provide for several steps (levels) within the school district before resorting to third-party neutrals for settling disputes arising from teacher or teacher organization belief(s) that some terms of the bargained contract have been violated by the school district. If a grievance manages to reach the level of arbitration, the decision of the third-party neutral may be *advisory* or *binding,* depending on how the collective bargaining contract was negotiated.

Because of its power potential, binding arbitration of grievances constitutes one of the most controversial areas in all of collective bargaining — with teacher organizations advocating it and administrations and their boards resisting it. The power potential of binding arbitration derives from the impact of arbitrator decisions on subsequent contracts and future practices of school districts. School boards usually view binding arbitration as a threat to the powers vested in them by the law and their voters.

Most states make grievance resolution issues mandatorily bargainable because of the inherent difficulties in contract writing and the reality that contract aspects are often interpreted differently by the two sides. Binding arbitration as a method of settlement of contract disputes is usually left up to the parties to the contract.

Presently, grievance resolution procedures are written and implemented in a one-sided manner; that is, they are used primarily as teacher organization devices to insure proper contract administration by management – not the reverse. But a contract is a mutual entity; management could use the grievance mechanism as a weapon also. It is possible that certain external pressures, mentioned earlier, may eventually force management to use collective bargaining contracts to enforce certain accountability systems (Planning Programming and Budgeting Systems, for example) as well as other teacher behavior considerations.

Two examples of such behaviors are discussed under the headings of teacher ethics and teacher productivity. Conceivably, school boards could define ethical standards of behavior for teachers and force teacher organization endorsement of those standards as a condition of contract finalization. Teacher productivity, too, could be defined jointly by boards and teacher organizations during bargaining, despite many difficulties incidental to such definitions. For both broad areas, grievance procedures in contracts could become primary enforcement mechanisms for school boards.

☐ Analysis of Personnel Policy

Generally speaking, policies are designed to describe standard school district working relationships, procedures, and positions on any subject. Policies are developed and maintained so that all persons involved can move toward their objectives with a minimum of conflict or confusion. They are designed to keep school districts consistent in all aspects of their operation.

There are other reasons that school districts develop and publish policy statements. Policy, published and well-known to all concerned, can protect school districts in courts of law. Also, policy related to safety, similarly published and well-known to the personnel involved, can reduce insurance premiums if those policies are acceptable to the insurer.

Personnel policies, too, are designed for consistency. They govern the relationship of the school district with individual teachers and are inextricably related to bargained contracts; that is, a published personnel policy, for example, can be a basis for resistance to a proposal or counterproposal. Conversely, such a policy can virtually assure the success of a proposal or counterproposal if it can be shown that the new idea is consistent with existent policy or is intended to rectify an inconsistency in personnel policy.

Knowledge of school district policy is of paramount importance to both administration and teacher-bargainers: before policy can be changed, it must be known to both sides. Certain major aspects of personnel policy are of concern to the parties to collective bargaining.

☐ **ASSIGNMENT OF TEACHERS**   Most school districts will maintain policy documents that dictate the way teachers are assigned. Seniority is usually the standard when there is a conflict between two or more teachers about a given assignment. However, some districts include a provision for deviating from the seniority standard when the nature of the assignment, safety conditions, external regulations, or other conditions suggest that the deviation would be in the best interest of the school district.

State bargaining laws are basically consistent about teacher assignment, holding it to be a management right. However, there are some aspects involved in teacher assignment that are of prime interest to administration and teacher-bargainers, from the dual standpoints of bargaining and contract maintenance. These are: (1) consistency of assignment practices and (2) deadlines for assignment and reassignment. For example, administration bargainers must realize that inconsistency in assignment practices provides bonafide fodder for the introduction of new personnel-related proposals and counterproposals by teacher organizations and grievances related to inconsistent practices.

☐ **RECRUITMENT POLICIES AND PROCEDURES**   These are management rights in most jurisdictions. Teacher organization concerns related to them are usually addressed through the grievance mechanism. School districts usually maintain published policy and administrative bulletins on their recruitment policies and procedures to insure consistency of implementation. As in the assignment of teachers, both bargaining parties must stay abreast of these policies—teacher-bargainers to find inconsistencies and administration bargainers to avoid such inconsistencies.

☐ **EVALUATION OF TEACHERS**   This is perhaps the most important personnel-related area for both administration and teacher-bargainers, for two reasons: (1) more states are making teacher evaluation *methods* or *procedures* mandatorily bargainable, and (2) the minimum competency testing movement in many—if not most—states provides a side-door method of entry for teacher organizations to participate in the formulation of curricular policy. These two aspects are interrelated and deserve further consideration.

Collective bargaining laws in most states are silent on the negotiation of curriculum, the impact of new programs, or other curriculum-instruction concerns (Academic Collective Bargaining Information Service 1977, 7). But *teacher evaluation* must by its *very nature* be tied to curriculum and instruction, for teachers are the implementers of the curriculum: the bricklayer must be evaluated on the basis of bricks laid in workmanlike manner and the tool and die maker must be evaluated on the basis of an accurate, effective die or tool. It is likely that contradictions and conflicts between the rights of school boards to determine curriculum and the rights of teachers to participate in evaluation procedures (which must be based on instruction, the implementation of curriculum) will be resolved through case law in the future.

Of specific interest to both teacher-bargainers and administration bargainers are the following aspects of policy relating to teacher evaluation *procedures:*

1. Consistency of district policy with state law, including time lines, notification procedures, appeal procedures, and other due process requirements.
2. Too much subjectivity in teacher evaluation.

This second point deserves amplification. It is quite possible that subjectivity in teacher evaluations operates to the disadvantage of all — school boards, their administrators, teachers, and most importantly, the children. While such subjectivity permits mediocre and even inferior teachers to acquire tenure with minimal effort, the administrators are probably at fault. The situation is summed up by Hazard (1978, 361):

> Popular criticism of tenure laws tends to exaggerate the "protection" of teachers and the alleged inability of school boards to discharge incompetent but tenured teachers. Such criticism usually ignores the board's opportunity and responsibilities to select, screen, supervise, and evaluate the teachers *prior* to and during tenured employment. If the school board and its administrative agents choose to neglect their responsibility to supervise and evaluate the teachers' performance, their subsequent difficulty in supporting charges against teachers cannot be blamed on the tenure legislation.

It is possible that teacher organization leaders might be reluctant to advocate teacher evaluation formats wherein much if not most of the subjectivity is removed. Such reluctance might center on their belief that most teachers are protected against arbitrary dismissals because the burden of proof is on the school board during dismissal proceedings in most states (Hazard 1978, 361):

> The causes for dismissal of teachers are not easy to prove. Supervisors and administrators rarely maintain records adequate to support allegations of cause, and the burden to prove the cause rests on the board. Teaching competency, for example, has not been defined clearly. Reasonable people disagree as to alleged incompetency by a teacher in a given instance. The presumption of competency for a licensed teacher must be overcome by evidence presented by the board.

Teacher organizations seeking to capitalize on administrative weaknesses do so in the interest of solidarity and stronger memberships, a valid concern of teacher organizations. However, the concern is short-sighted; at risk is the actuality and the image of professionalism of the teaching profession (see Chaps. 2 and 4). Put another way, it is to the long-term best interests of teacher organizations to seek evaluation methods that indeed ferret out inferior teachers.

School districts often design evaluation formats that are ridiculously simple, with little or no focus on teaching quality and poor provisions for reporting of extenuating circumstances or, equally important, the objectives the teacher is (was) attempting to accomplish. Examination of these evaluation formats from many districts reveals evaluations based on a handful of personal attributes that are then ranked on an arbitrary numerical continuum by the administrator who observes the teacher. Absent in many cases are descriptions of the type of lesson involved, objectives, descriptions of the behavior of students, detailed accounts of teacher behavior, and descriptions of the relationship of the lesson to the overall curriculum plan. Both administrator-bargainers and teacher-bargainers should consider looking at other sources related to the evaluation of teaching (see Borich 1977).

□ **SALARIES**   Teacher organizations and administrators alike are in agreement on the merits of consistent, well-published salary schedules for teachers and other employees. Salary is mandatorily bargainable in all collective bargaining laws. Both bargaining teams should approach the table armed with all salary information possible, including statewide salaries and those of other states. Most importantly, they should have information on hand about salaries in neighboring districts and salaries in comparable districts.

Salary schedules have their rationale in personnel policy that seeks (1) to provide consistency in pay standards within a given occupational group, (2) to eliminate individual bargaining tendencies, (3) to provide a method for all personnel to predict their personal finances, and (4) to provide a consistent, well-known reward system for personal professional improvement.

The following are some principles for salary schedule adoption that may be used by both teacher organizations and administrations:

1. Salary schedules should be adequate to attract and hold good teachers
2. Salary schedules should be based on training and experience
3. Salary schedules should contain incentives for professional growth
4. Salary schedules should be revised annually

The following are some common types of salary schedules (Stoops et al. 1975, 628):

1. Position schedules wherein salaries vary from elementary, junior high school, to high school

2. Preparation schedules according to degrees held
3. Experience schedules according to years of teaching
4. Cost-of-living schedules based on consumer price indexes
5. Merit pay schedules based on teaching efficiency
6. Differentiated schedules based on level of responsibility

Fringe benefits are often mentioned right along with salaries, a practice referred to as "packaging" and should be commented upon.

☐ **FRINGE BENEFITS**   Fringe benefits are defined differently from school district to school district. State law will require certain ones such as retirement benefits. Others will be more or less common to all school districts. Health and dental insurance plans are examples. Still others are considered supplementary fringe benefits in some districts, such as group tax-sheltered annuities. Fringe benefits usually require school district contributions to several "pockets," including retirement plans, unemployment compensation insurance plans, health insurance plans, and others.

Many fringe benefits are mandated by state law and are usually paid in part from categorical restricted tax revenues levied by school boards at will, without the vote of the taxpayers. This means improved fringe benefits can sometimes be used to enhance the images of boards of education and teacher organizations alike.

Bargainers of both sides should be armed with the following information prior to considering fringe benefits for bargaining: (1) education code provisions related to employee benefits, (2) descriptions of fringe benefits paid throughout the state, (3) fringe benefits of nearby districts, (4) fringe benefits of comparable districts, and (5) analyses of current school district impact (rates) on the authorized revenue sources for fringe benefits.

☐ **CALENDARS AND WORK SCHEDULES**   States vary as to whether calendars and work schedules are management rights or mandatorily bargainable.

Calendars. This is a mandatory subject in some states and a management right in others. A conflict arises when collective bargaining laws require teacher participation in decisions on certain aspects of school district operation, then reserve to management the right to determine the school calendar. Some of these conflicts still rage and have yet to be resolved through case law.

Several points of interest are germane to both administrator-bargainers and teacher-bargainers. Among these are: (1) dates of bargaining sessions for the upcoming year, (2) dates and *spacing* of curriculum development and planning events, (3) extra-day in-service and professional development activities that may dictate salary considerations, and (4) calendar changes which in turn impact on other dates on the calendar.

All information related to the school year calendar is relevant at bargaining sessions. It is best for both sides to review a carefully documented series of negative events (conflicts, student problems, cancelled meetings, room conflicts, etc.) associated with one or several previous calendars before proposing new calendars purporting to avoid such events in the future.

Work schedules. These are closely related to calendars and conditions of employment. They are generally mandatory subjects of bargaining. Of concern are minimum days, professional development days, child-absent teacher workdays, supervision of extracurricular activities, and the like.

Work load. States are divided on the bargainability of work load. Some treat it as a management right and others permit bargaining. Despite other issues related to work load (in-service education requirements, parent conference days, and others), the recurrent central issue is class size. Teacher organizations have advocated smaller class sizes for many years, well before the advent of collective bargaining laws. Despite the obvious advantages of smaller class sizes in the areas of control, teacher-student relations, individualized instruction, and general teacher morale, the argument still rages. Administrator resistance to reduced class sizes is based on the tendency of reduced class sizes to increase costs dramatically, even prohibitively. Teacher organizations continue to advocate smaller class sizes for two reasons: (1) the obvious improvements they are likely to promote, and (2) the obvious political bargaining wedge that such advocacy gives toward other bargaining victories.

For many years administrators replied to demands for lower class sizes with a standard response: while the desire for lower class sizes is plausible and understandable, there has never been any conclusive evidence that lower class sizes make a difference in student achievement. Until very recently, this administrator position was true. However, some recent research has shed new light on the class-size issue.

Using achievement as the criterion for analyzing the effects of reduced class sizes, Cahen and Filby (1979, 492–95) of Far West Laboratories found that dramatic rises in achievement occurred when class size was lowered below 15 students. Small class sizes had slightly greater impact at the secondary level. Additionally, it was found that small achievement increases accompanied small reductions in class size. Subsequently, Glass and Smith (1978) reported findings that resulted in much stronger support for reduced class sizes as such class sizes produce increased academic achievement. Following this report, the same two researchers (1979, 27) reported that reduced class sizes had a "beneficial effect on the general quality of the educational environment."

At this time, the research techniques and (hence) findings of Gene Glass and Mary Smith have been attacked by Educational Research Service (1980, 239–41), an independent, nonprofit corporation, with the conclusion that the findings of the two researchers contain "no important implications for educational policy." The controversy still rages, with Glass (1980, 242–44) holding firm and defending both his original findings. Whether these research reports will have an impact on educational practices remains to be seen.

Even definitive, totally defensible evidence presented on behalf of reduced class size is likely in the forseeable future to be dominated by fiscal and political considerations. Some indication of this attitude may be seen in public pressure for accountability as manifested in the "Back-to-Basics" movement of the decade of the 1970s, with little or no attention being paid to class size.

Bargainers should familiarize themselves with the pros and cons of the class-size issue. More immediately, however, they should always bring to the bargaining table their analyses of the financial impact(s) of various class-size reductions.

☐ **GRIEVANCE AND APPEAL PROCEDURES**   Grievance procedures are the tools available to teacher organizations for controlling the implementation of bargained contracts. Both administration bargainers and teacher-bargainers should approach consideration of these procedures with extreme care. (See Chap. 14.)

☐ **PROBATION AND TENURE**   Tenure is basically defined and controlled by state laws. It is a legal grant of employment security that provides for sustained employment as long as the behavior of teachers is "good." Tenure laws specify the method by which tenure is acquired and the causes and procedures for dismissal. In most cases, tenure laws require that teachers can only be dismissed for on-the-job incompetency and prohibit arbitrary or capricious dismissals. States vary about (1) whether or not all districts within a state have tenure laws, (2) optional participation in state tenure, (3) whether administrators are covered, (4) whether or not the causes for dismissal are specified, and (5) the length and nature of the probationary period.

While it would appear that the existence of such tenure laws would preclude consideration of employment security at the bargaining table, certain related matters stimulate bargaining interest. Examples are subcontracting of teaching services with private contractors (who may use their own teachers), interdistrict agreements that often reduce the number of children served by the subject district, limitations on the length of time served by substitute teachers, part-time teachers, and other practices that reduce or threaten reduction of the ranks of teacher organizations.

☐ **JOB DESCRIPTIONS**   During the past decade the advent of accountability systems like Planning, Programming, and Budgeting Systems (PPBS) have made job descriptions an integral part of personnel records and task definitions. Both teacher-bargainers and their administration counterparts have an important stake in the details of job descriptions because they determine the makeup of bargaining units, define many working interrelationships and task-sharing, and are the key to many grievance proceedings.

The following are some working guidelines for developing job descriptions in public education:

1. They should be drawn from the objectives of the education professional
2. They should define the specific, recurring tasks of the education professional
3. They should state clearly the times for starting and ending the work day
4. They should state nonteaching tasks like lunchroom duty or yard supervision in detail, including specific hours and days
5. They should state clearly the authority of teachers whenever teachers are required to work with instructional aides
6. They should be developed by the teacher (or other education professional) subject to negotiation with and approval by the supervising administrator

The last point above is important. Various management-by-objectives schemes are based on goals that flow downward from controlling authorities like boards of education. For maximum effectiveness, the specific objectives and subsequent job descriptions must involve individual employees in their formulation: each administrator, teacher, instructional aide, parent volunteer, custodian, lunchroom worker—even students—must internalize the objectives they are attempting to accomplish.

☐ **SUBSTITUTE SERVICE**   The employment of substitutes is generally held to be a management right, although many states *permit* bargaining on the matter. But substitute teachers can have considerable impact on several bargainable aspects of school district operation. Among these aspects are: standards of services, performance, and productivity; teacher methods of disciplining students; the impact of curriculum changes; and grading methods.

☐ **GENERAL**   The foregoing are but a few of the many dimensions of personnel matters of concern to the parties to collective bargaining in public education. Examples of others are extracurricular duties, vacations and holidays, paid in-service activity, and salary schedule credit for in-service activity. Personnel policy is of utmost importance to bargainers, and effective bargaining requires a command of extremely broad information bases about school district personnel practices.

☐ Financial Analysis

Successful collective bargaining in public education depends in large part on an adequate information base, particularly in the areas of school finance, accounting, and budgeting. Proposals or counterproposals formulated on inadequate or incomplete information about revenue and expenditures are not only unintelligent, they are likely to result in rejection as well as embarrassment.

Despite the oft-repeated complaints of some teacher-bargainers about their difficulties in getting reliable fiscal information from their school districts, the information is readily available. In most states laws related to the disclosure of information about public school districts and prohibitions against secret board meetings insure access to the essential information for financial analysis of those districts. However, fiscal data often presented to the public or external agencies is not always in a format that lends itself to ready interpretation; to the contrary, it is often in format that defies intepretation.

This does not suggest that there are frequent attempts by administrators to "cloud" or "mask" information about the true financial picture of their districts. The budget is a functional document oriented to regular use. It is the basis on which the accounting structure is built. As such, its interpretation depends on an understanding of its uses, and anyone who wishes to analyze it must understand those uses.

Students of school budgeting should also be students of funding sources, curriculum and instruction, accounting practices, school board policy and history, employee salaries and fringe benefits, supply and plant concerns, and trends within the district.

The purpose of this discussion is to provide a brief informational backdrop that could help both administration and teacher-bargainers to develop financial analyses of their school districts in preparation for collective bargaining.

□ **INFORMATION SOURCES ON BUDGETING AND ACCOUNTING**   While the basic information for financial analysis is readily available, it will have to be "picked apart" and converted to usable form. It may appear that the sources presently discussed are more important to teacher-bargainers than administration bargainers. This is not necessarily true: administrators thrust into the position of justifying various actions of the boards they represent require a thorough understanding of the historical backgrounds and rationales for those decisions.

Proper financial analysis means going backward several years to learn, for example, why a certain budget item exists. If and when it appears that the original justification for the expenditure is no longer valid, teacher-bargainers have a possible basis for challenging the proposal or counterproposal. Likewise, administration bargainers are in better positions for explaining existent budget items.

Much of budget making is initially judgmental and incremental thereafter. Many line items in school district budgets have existed for many years, modified only slightly each year to accomodate inflationary increases or other minor changes. Such line items are defensible or subject to challenge according to whether the programs they support are or are not educationally sound and relevant as originally believed. Once programs are established, persons associated with them tend to defend them vigorously, often without qualitative reference to the content of the programs. Their desired ends often focus on getting the budget approved. (See Wildavsky 1974, 6–62 for a description of the strategies undertaken by those who formulate, modify, and defend federal budgets and subbudgets.) One reason for this behavior is that their jobs are sometimes at stake. Another reason is that boards of education — constricted by mountains of state regulations and levy limitations, together with the rigidity required by salary schedules and other mandatory expenditures — often attempt only minor adjustments in their budgets. (See James et al. 1966, 55–94 on the big-city budget-making process.)

Both parties to collective bargaining interested in proper financial analysis must undertake the painstaking job of research, of reading (some) old information from many sources, all related to the reasons certain school programs and subprograms exist.

Old school board minutes. These records are usually available from school districts for the cost of duplication. The researcher should look for statements by board members, administrators, and others about the inception or adoption of a certain program and its budget at the time of its passage. Often, school board members will make statements about supporting a given program conditionally as long as it meets certain criteria. Statements in opposition to a certain program made by the same persons are equally important. The researcher should examine these statements and try to relate them to the present program.

Old program proposals. Similar to the foregoing, analysis of current programs and their financial structures is more thorough when based on all aspects of the original rationale and makeup of the programs.

Newspaper accounts. Although newspapers often fail to offer accurate, verbatim accounts of school board proceedings, they are reasonably accurate in capturing the essence of statements made by board members, administrators, and others. Of importance to both administrator-bargainers and teacher-bargainers are the newspaper accounts of positions taken by the persons involved. Certain positions taken can preclude others later — or force still others later.

General purpose budgets. These are the master budgets for the school district in past years as well as the present year. Budgets in successive years should be studied along with the rationale or opposition statements in corresponding years so that the researcher gains a longitudinal picture of the decisions related to budget.

Categorical program budgets. These are the budgets for special programs. The researcher should be interested in the same aspects as those of general purpose budgets, with one *special* interest: the extent of consistency between budgeting standards in both budgets.

Statistical handbooks. These are usually published by school districts for public relations purposes. They are usually released annually at the start of the school year. Although they are often oversimplified, they are an important source of basic information related to distribution of school district funds, sources of the school dollar, taxation bases of school support, costs of supportive services, categorical programs and their funded amounts, enrollment information, tax rates, trends in assessed valuation, information on bonded indebtedness, and school calendars.

Newspaper notices. Most state laws require that certain types of school district transactions be posted in one or more newspapers of general circulation a number of days prior to the actual transactions. This usually applies to construction bids, maintenance contracts, bonding information, notices of sales of school property, and other school district business activity.

State budgeting and accounting manuals. These manuals prescribe guidelines for budgeting and accounting. While states vary in the amount of control they exert over these two functions, it is safe to say that virtually all states strive for consistency in budget format, budget deadlines, budgetary transfer procedures, and accounting procedures. Consistency in these procedures assures more efficient auditing.

General. There is no limit to source materials related to effective financial analysis of school districts. Any material will help, from a superintendent's foreword in a brochure describing a new kindergarten program to a very sophisticated program budget. The point is that the researcher preparing for collective bargaining should try to accumulate as much accurate information as possible for effective bargaining. Although most researchers will have access to budgetary information as it is released by the school district, the format in which the information comes leaves much to be desired for the promotion of in-depth budgetary analysis.

☐ **IMPORTANT BUDGET-RELATED ISSUES AND CONCERNS**   Before analyzing the financial picture of a school district, the researcher must be armed with certain information about the development of the district budget so that the research proceeds accurately. This information or separate criteria on which the typical school district budget is based, comes from:

1. District staffing policy as reflected in policy documents approved by boards of education

2. District salary policy for all personnel, from policy documents approved by boards of education

3. Accurate enrollment data, showing projections and trends, including average daily attendance and pupil-teacher ratios

4. District analysis of next year's funding sources, including local, state,

federal and other, together with projected amounts and changes from the previous year (or present year)

5. An analysis of present and anticipated insurance costs and coverage

6. Property tax and other taxation background, with emphasis on the relationship to assessments, including restricted taxes whenever applicable

7. Anticipated cost trends in nonsalary areas, together with the bases for the projections of costs

8. Projected retirements and dates

9. Anticipated changes in costs of district contributions to employee fringe benefits package

10. Reports of various district and community committees on district needs not met by the current budget

11. A report of the budget transfer experience of the present or previous year(s)

12. Transportation schedules and costs, present and projected

13. Budgetary guidelines for categorical programs

14. Inventory experience together with district inventory policy

15. Policy statements related to undistributed reserves or other contingency funds

16. Comparative cost information from surrounding districts

This list is not exhaustive. The point, however, is to put researchers into the best-informed situations possible. Note that the information must be generated for five years so that trends may be analyzed. Much of such trend analysis can proceed by getting budgetary and accounting information from the five preceding years. The researcher should also develop an information backdrop in standard budgetary and accounting practices. This can be obtained from several published sources. (Most state departments of education publish accounting manuals. For a standard budgetary format in use in most school districts, see U.S. Department of Health, Education, and Welfare 1960, 27–35.)

The unfolding of the budget as the year progresses is of utmost importance to researchers. Familiarity with accounting practices provides researchers with a prime device for monitoring the expenditure of the budget.

□ **ACCOUNTING: THE EXPENDITURE RECORD**   Accounting shows how the budget unfolds during the school year. It is the expenditure record and shows the activity in each budget category as expenditures progress, verification that the expenditure occurred for an approved item, unexpended amounts, and budget transfer activity.

Administration of the budget is controlled through accounting. Proper analysis demands attention to several dimensions: aspects of good accounting systems; principles for good accounting systems; and some practices in school district accounting, which will be discussed briefly.

Aspects of good accounting systems. Although there are various ways of maintaining records in accounting systems, only four kinds of records are necessary. They are (1) original records; (2) a voucher record for posting the distribution of expenditures that will be copied into the ledger later; (3) the ledger, or classified record that corresponds to the district budget; and (4) the receipts book, the ongoing account of revenues that come into the district, posted upon receipt.

Original records include all basic information involved in two broad kinds of data: revenues and expenditures *and* assets and liabilities. These original records can be anything written or printed that support the business transactions of the school district. Examples of such original records are cancelled checks, payroll lists, purchase orders, requisitions, invoices — just to mention a few of the more typical ones. These records should be maintained in the office of the administrator responsible for business operations, and they should be filed by category. Original records are necessary for substantiation of entries made in the ledger at a later date.

The voucher record is maintained by many, if not most, school districts as a method of keeping the record straight in the interim between the occurrence of original records and entry into the ledger. It is usually kept in the form of a book. It is basically a running account, kept in chronological order, of the debits and credits related to school district operation, together with a description of the location of the appropriate account in the ledger. This description is sometimes called a posting reference.

The ledger represents the accounting counterpart of the overall master budget of a school district. Whether a school district maintains one giant ledger or separate ones (the usual practice), those ledgers are organized on the basis of the same account groups as those of the budget. Ledgers maintained by school districts are important sources of information for tracking the business transactions of school districts for a given year.

The receipts book is essential because school districts need a considerable amount of detailed information about receipts. For each receipt, the following information should be shown in the receipts book: (1) the source of the receipt, (2) the identity (revenue or nonrevenue) of the receipt, and (3) the fund to which the receipt should be deposited. Regular school district income from taxes and appropriations is an example of revenue income, and insurance adjustment income, bond sales, and sales of school property are examples of nonrevenue receipts. Many variations are possible within the framework of sound accounting methods.

Principles for good accounting systems. Various agencies and sources have offered principles aimed at governing good school accounting systems.

The essential focus of these principles varies with the standpoint of those offering them. The National Committee on Governmental Accounting (Knezevich and Fowlkes 1960, 34–38) offers several principles requiring that good accounting systems:

1. Meet legal requirements
2. Use double-entry posting
3. Use a general-ledger accounting system
4. Standardize terms and classifications
5. Separate accounts related to current assets and liabilities from those related to fixed assets and liabilities
6. Use as few different funds as possible within legal and accounting requirements
7. Operate on the accrual accounting basis

In addition to these principles, several more are offered in a U.S. government handbook (Adams et al. 1967, 260), available on request. These principles are:

1. Financial record systems should provide operational information for the school board, the administration, the public, auditors, local, state and federal authorities, and school employees.
2. An adequate accounting system has both current and historical information available for decision making.
3. The accounting system should require accuracy and reasonable internal control.
4. A school accounting system should be consistent with generally accepted governmental accounting practices and consistent between one time period and another.
5. A school accounting system should be flexible; provisions should be made for taking care of changes with as little disruption as possible.
6. School accounting systems should be uniform.
7. School accounting systems should be as simple as possible and still fulfill pertinent requirements. A good accounting system will assist in improving educational processes, not hinder them.
8. A school accounting system should provide ready access to information about individual transactions as well as group or summary transactions.

The literature on principles of school accounting is abundant. Woven through it is stress on standardization and simplicity, accuracy, immediate accessibility, and operational usefulness. This last aspect, operational usefulness, is of utmost importance. Unfortunately, many school district budgets and accounting practices ignore the most useful information from the researcher's standpoint: the connection between expenditures and program. This connection—the real essence of Planning, Programming and Budgeting Systems—is the true basis for program improvement and should be a primary focus of collective bargaining research.

Little-known practices in school accounting. One basic charge given to administrators responsible for the budget and fiscal operations of school districts is that of keeping school finances viable and functioning for the entire school year. Simultaneously, many groups—teacher organizations included—tend to focus on certain line items in school budgets, especially those that appear to reduce the amounts of money available to the interests represented by those groups. The result is often encouragement of hidden stores of monies in certain accounts, available in the event of emergencies.

These practices are rarely illegal. Money must be available to cover unforeseen emergencies. Unfortunately, the militancy of external groups often congeals around the idea that money is withheld from general circulation within the school district, especially in the case of contingency-type line items, irrespective of the wisdom involved in the contingency items.

One favorite target is the superintendent's reserve, a legitimate, highly recommended budget category. The mere idea of as much as 5 percent of the total budget left to the arbitrary discretion of the superintendent often invites the ire of special interest groups.

Balance is important from the standpoints of both teacher-bargainers and administration bargainers. Teacher-bargainers who attack the superintendent's reserve as a totally inappropriate budget category often risk losing public credibility, as such a budget category is plausible in the minds of many lay observers. On the other hand, too much freedom in salting away money for contingencies can lead to ineffective utilization of available money. As mentioned above, administrators often resort to subtle means of preparing for contingencies because of these attacks by teacher organizations and other external groups.

Such subtle preparations for budgetary contingencies occur through the budget transfer mechanism, which accounts for most of the differences between adopted budgets and actual expenditure patterns. In some states, education codes permit budget transfers from one line item to another, limited by a percentage of the line item from which the budget transfer is made. Percentages permitted vary from state to state, and the usual practice is to require the approval of the county superintendent of schools. While both the transfer percentage limitation and the approval of the county superintendent are aimed at control, that control is often diminished because in many instances the budget transfer practice is permitted between the same line items repeatedly during the school year.

Many persons have observed the process during which school boards approve these budget transfers. Usually, at the start of board meetings a long

list of account numbers are read by one board member, often the board president or a board member responsible for a finance subcommittee of the board.
After the listing of numbers, a board vote follows. Many audiences attending
board meetings never realize that vital fiscal transactions are occurring.

Most of "these money-hiding" practices depend on the budget transfer
device. A few examples follow:

1. Budgeting teacher salaries on district averages rather than actual salaries. This depends on hiring inexperienced, low-salaried teachers as replacements.

2. Projection of extremely high costs of nonsalary items like expendable
supplies and equipment.

3. Budgeting full-year salaries for midyear retirements.

4. Overbudgeting contingencies for substitute and home instruction
teachers.

The key to an accurate picture of such practices is accounting. But the
only way to get a true picture of past accounting practices is through longitudinal analysis, so that both consistent practices and budget-program relationships are understood.

□ **TAKING A LONG LOOK AT BUDGETS**   One common mistake made by
those who would analyze the fiscal activities of school districts is that of
reliance *only* on budget information related to the present and upcoming
years. Adequate analyses must be based on a relatively long time span; five
years is suggested in the interest of effective budgetary planning. There is basic
consensus of opinion that it is possible to gain a realistic picture of the feasibility of an educational approach after such a time span. Moreover, the analysis should reflect the relationship between program effectiveness and budget
and show comparisons between adopted budgets and actual expenditures for
several years. These aspects deserve elaboration.

Analysis of budget and expenditure activity over a long time span is vital
to understanding trends in budgeting as well as accounting practices. For
example, five-year analyses of both budgeting and accounting practices can
reveal the existence of consistent hidden-money practices cited previously.

The relationship between program effectiveness and budget is central to
the positions that must be adopted by those who would defend or attack
budgets up for adoption. Items in a budget that have existed for a number of
years are often simply *presumed* to have had positive impact on the programs
they support. In many instances, the relationships cannot be established.

The budget transfer mechanism available to school districts permits great
differences between budgets planned and actual expenditures. Proper longitudinal analysis provides a basis for challenging such budgetary practices.

The various bases for challenges or defenses of budgets are educational, legal, ethical, comparative, or cost-effective. While the last four of these bases must ultimately be related to the first one, they deserve differentiation because relationships to educational rationale are sometimes remote and difficult to show.

Educational bases for challenges or defenses of budgets are those directly related to the failures or successes of school districts in meeting their goal of educating children. Such challenges or defenses must focus on the lack or presence of benefits accruing to children.

Legal bases are rare, but they do occur. They are challenges founded on the belief that the law has been broken.

Ethical bases for challenges or defenses of school budgets are founded on allegations that school district activities have violated or are inconsistent with: (1) commonly accepted practices; (2) commitments already made or promises given; and (3) the spirit of certain guidelines or regulations, even though there are no outright legalities violated. An example will explain: an ethical challenge is possible when a school administration has doubled its budgeted amount for conference travel and attendance while other budget items have been reduced.

Comparative bases for challenges or defenses of school budgets occur when school board policy in a given area differs markedly from standard practices in other school districts that are used as comparison districts for policy-making or salary purposes. A good example would be a school district reduction of fringe benefits after years of implementing a policy of fringe benefits comparable to those of the top ten school districts in the state.

Cost-effectiveness bases are those that derive directly from analyses of the extent given programs are economically prudent. Cost effectiveness in education is a technical concept (Haggart 1972). Applications of the technical sense of the term can enhance the effectiveness of challenges or defenses of school district budgets.

□ **A MODEL FOR FINANCIAL ANALYSIS OF SCHOOL DISTRICTS**   Adequate financial analysis of school districts requires painstaking research in three broad areas—historical rationales for program adoptions, analyses of program achievements, and analyses of trends and patterns in budgeting and accounting.

A historical rationale search involves looking backward at old board minutes and other documents that give a long-range picture of how certain programs came to be. A five-year search is proposed, although researchers may discover information that suggests a longer look backward. The objective of the historical rationale search is reconstructing reasons for the existence of certain programs so that the current effectiveness of those programs can be evaluated in accord with the reasons they were adopted originally. Specific statements made by board members and superintendents about their expectations for the programs adopted are significant. Of equal importance are statements in opposition to the programs, especially statements about conditional approval of the programs.

Analyzing program achievements is relatively simple and is based on the stated objectives of each program. Analysis is a matter of determining whether or not such programs met cognitive objectives and affective objectives. In most cases cognitive objectives (based in large part on pretest-posttest differentials of mean standardized test scores) are easy to measure. Affective objectives are those oriented toward enhancement of students' self-concepts. There are times when educators stress affective objectives following failure to achieve desired cognitive objectives. For a sharp-edged statement in resistance to such shifted emphasis, see the statement of Congressman Albert Quie in response to an evaluation statement made by an educator (House, *Oversight Hearings on Elementary and Secondary Education* 1972, 299).

Analysis of budgeting and accounting is concerned with three main interest areas: budget trends, budget transfers or the matchup between budget design and implementation, and outright legal violations. For analysis of budget trends, a five-year sequence is desirable for each budget line item. For budget transfer analysis, a second budget is developed that shows exactly how the money was spent each year.

The objectives of the three-dimensional analysis described above are:

1. Comparison of initial budgeting patterns with expenditure patterns, challenging budgeted items that have been consistently used as transfer accounts in previous years and uncovering deceptive practices
2. Determination of illegal practices
3. Analysis of budgeting trends for their comparison with program achievement trends in order to examine the relationships between programs and budgets
4. Comparison of achievement to stated expectations

☐ **GENERAL**   Effective financial analysis of school districts is as important for administrator-bargainers as it is for teacher-bargainers seeking bases for challenges; defenses of financial practices are best when framed in terms of educational benefits to children. Challenges or defenses so framed have the greatest public credibility.

The information on which challenges or defenses can be based is readily available. The problem is extracting it from its sources and converting it to usable format. Doing so requires many painstaking hours of research.

Preparation of bargaining teams depends on adequate knowledge of accepted budget and accounting procedures, as well as program evaluation methods. The budget-program relationship is the ultimate weapon for advocacy of proposals or counterproposals in collective bargaining.

Of vital importance to effective collective bargaining in public education are established school district practices, for their very existence can defend their continuation.

☐ Analysis of Past Practices

Past practices as used here refers to those school district practices that have been tested through repetition. They have cleared certain legal and political gauntlets and have thereby attained a defensible status. An example of this is the budget development process within large school districts in which standardization within the school district has stimulated the development of regular procedures. (See James et al. 1966, 56–59 for a discussion of the power of past practices.) Reliance on past practice is safe; budgets can be defended with explanations that "we've always done it this way."

Adherence to past practices in school districts is not limited to budget and accounting practices. Virtually all policy is determined by past practice, at least in part. The details of past practices have also withstood the scrutiny of the legal counsels of school districts — a consideration making past practices seem even safer to those whose job it is to implement school district policy.

A logical question that should arise is, "How does new policy get started?" The answer is quite simple. When a need arises, other closely related policies are used as bases for formulating the new policy. Its legalities are then examined and approved by appropriate legal counsel, after which school boards adopt the policy. Subsequent challenges and reactions force modification of certain aspects until there are no further challenges.

Both teacher-bargainers and administration bargainers should know the past practices of their school districts for two primary reasons: (1) disparities between policy and practices provide a basis for challenge for teacher-bargainers or must be defended by administration bargainers, and (2) proposals or counterproposals for policy change cannot be formulated intelligently unless past practices are known.

Prime sources for understanding past practices within school districts are written school board policy, corresponding administrative bulletins, grievance records, personnel records, warehouse records, and budget and fiscal records.

☐ Analysis of Comparable School Districts

From the standpoints of teacher-bargainers and administration bargainers, one of the most effective tools in all of collective bargaining in public education is the comparison strategy. Properly used, the comparison strategy can result in contracts that are acceptable to all.

The comparison strategy capitalizes on the following realities: (1) school boards base long- and short-range activities on certain policies as guidelines for maintaining consistency, often using the criterion of practice in other school districts; (2) school boards are political entities that often view excellent salaries and fringe benefits of employees as political assets, indicative of quality leadership; (3) teacher organization members are more likely to accept bargained provisions that compare favorably to existent salary schedules and fringe benefits in school districts they respect and see as comparable to their own; and (4) administrators are less likely to resist salaries and fringe benefits based on established schedules if and when revenues permit. The strategy is equally effective when used by administrator-bargainers or teacher-bargainers. Put another way, the comparison strategy can defend both teacher organization proposals and administration counterproposals with the same logic and effectiveness.

The effectiveness of comparisons made is directly related to the degree of *perceived* similarity between districts compared. Also, the geographical proximity of the districts will enhance the effectiveness of the comparison. Teachers, administrators, and school boards alike tend to accept more readily the validity of comparisons made with neighboring districts.

It is hard to point to every characteristic of school districts and their communities that can or should be used in making effective comparisons. Some of the aspects that should be considered when evaluating another district for possible use as a comparison district are:

1. Size of the community and the school district
2. Nature of the school district (urban, suburban, rural, mixed)
3. Socioeconomic level
4. Type of community (industrial, farming, etc.)
5. Occupations in the community
6. Educational problems (reading achievement, vandalism, truancy, etc.)
7. Educational level of parents and citizens
8. Living costs in the community
9. History of support for education-related issues
10. Growth or staticity of the community
11. Extent of organized labor activity in the city or area
12. Population mobility within the city
13. Health care available in the area
14. Nonpublic school salaries
15. Age of the community
16. Family makeup(s)

Comparisons can be particularly effective when tied to established school board policies based on gaining and/or maintaining a certain ranking in salaries and fringe benefits within a set of school districts in the area, state, or even the nation. These comparison districts selected by school boards are ones that meet criteria like those listed above.

Comparison tactics are often rendered hollow and ineffective if the comparisons — and their bases — are not plausible to both sides at the bargaining table. This means that bargaining teams must select comparison districts with great care, using every relevant argument to sell the selection to the other team.

One powerful argument for making a comparison is based on demonstrable similarities in "input-output" relationships between two or more school districts. If, for example, standardized test scores in reading showed an increase along with teacher salaries, benefits, and other perquisites in a comparison district, and a similar increase can be shown in the subject district, the comparability as well as a strong argument for salary increases and benefits is at hand.

The nearness of a district used for comparison reduces the amount of data needed to sell the comparison. Conversely, districts far away are harder to sell, requiring mounds of data to show similarities.

Planning is the key. Organizing for comparison tactics could be done by:

1. Analyzing neighboring districts for possible comparisons, applying those demographic aspects that enhance the case. Of special importance is student achievement in easily measured areas like reading and mathematics.

2. Analyzing school districts in the region, with emphasis on practices and pay schedules.

3. Determining average administrator and teacher salaries in the immediate area.

4. Analyzing school districts of similar demography throughout the state, with emphasis on practices, pay schedules and student achievement.

While not considered school district practice as such, the bargaining history between a school district and its teacher organization(s) must nevertheless be understood by bargainers of both sides. The obvious reason is that past mistakes must be avoided; less obvious but equally important is that both sides must understand how certain agreements and understandings *came to be* so they may bargain effectively in good faith.

☐ Analysis of Bargaining History and Previous Agreements

Bargainers of both sides must understand previous agreements (bargained contracts) *and* the strategies and tactics used to reach them. Teams must know every detail associated with step-by-step progression to the present contract;

comparisons of advantages and disadvantages of contracts from previous years; and rationales for both major and minor changes in contracts from year to year. In most areas of the nation, this information will not be hard to acquire because collective bargaining is relatively new and background information will thus be limited.

☐ **STEP-BY-STEP PROGRESSION TO THE PRESENT CONTRACT**   Simply stated, both sides of the bargaining endeavor seek to improve their contracts over those of previous years. Knowledge of the progression of changes through the years puts bargainers in excellent positions for evaluating the merit of any suggested change, however minor; reading the intent of proposals or counterproposals; predicting possible responses of the opponent to proposed issues; and calculating the retreat line of the opponent.

An example will help. In the late 1960s teachers in a large Midwest school district threatened a sick-out protest because of the principal-initiated teacher transfer policies of their school district. Three arbitrary transfers had occurred at three separate schools, two elementary and one high school. After Easter vacation that year, the issue died down without further demonstrations or opposition from teachers. Several years later, in the early 1970s, after collective bargaining laws were passed in the state, the teacher organization busily formulated a proposal on principal-initiated teacher transfers. The proposal was elaborate, providing for appeal and review procedures for teachers, together with requirements that considerable advance notice be given to both individual teachers and the teacher organization. The transfer policy developed was one of the best in the state and quite similar to a model provision developed by the state teacher organization. Strangely, the teacher membership voted against the provision, a reaction that confused teacher-bargainers and the executive board of the teacher organization. Backtracking, these teacher-bargainers found that teachers had been opposed to one aspect of the contractual provision, the "loose" statement that "principals may request transfer of teachers when they consider it in the best interests of the school." Teacher organization members wanted a stipulation that teacher organization representatives (building representatives) at each school be consulted by the principal prior to initiation of a request for a teacher transfer.

The point here is that the teacher organization leaders and teacher-bargainers would have been in much better positions to satisfy their members if they had researched the origins of the issue *in the district*. Inadequate research into the backgrounds of issues can put bargainers in positions of introducing issues that are duplications of effort, relatively unimportant or unnecessary, and reveal lack of basic knowledge to the opposing bargaining team.

☐ **ADVANTAGES AND DISADVANTAGES OF CONTRACTS FROM PREVIOUS YEARS**   Simply stated, improvement of bargained contracts depends on knowing what present contracts contain. Here, administrators have one distinct advantage, that of being forced to avoid potential grievances through execution of the letter of the contract. This experience can have the dual effects of surfacing detailed content of contracts as such content affects actual practice and relative merits of contract provisions as revealed by actual practice.

There are no absolute techniques for anticipating the long-range effects of certain contract provisions. The merit of such provisions can only be evaluated in practice. However, there are some ways of improving the likelihood that contract items will be workable in practice and acceptable to all concerned. The basic tool for evaluation is comparison of advantages and disadvantages of contracts from previous years. Some prime sources of information for such a comparison are listed below.

Grievance files. These files are prime sources of information about the adequacy of contract provisions. Recurring grievances in different schools in a given district suggest something about the inadequacy of a contract item. Sometimes the contract provision is simply ambiguous in meaning; at other times it is too difficult to implement.

Teacher organization opinion polls. Opinion polls, year by year, reveal much about the overall effectiveness of bargained contract provisions. High percentages of negative responses about certain provisions point to their rethinking and redrafting.

Surveys of principals. Since much of the burden for contract administration falls heavily on principals, they should be consulted as to the adequacy of contract provisions. Principals are in excellent positions to offer opinions about two additional important aspects of contracts—their effect on morale and their effect on the work life of the school.

□ **KNOWLEDGE OF RATIONALES FOR CONTRACT CHANGES** Reasons for contract changes are also important. Such reasons may involve duplication of education code provisions, conflicts between state and federal regulations, unreasonable implementation costs, undue interference with teaching, schedule conflicts, unpopularity with teachers, and many others. Bargainers are more effective when they know the reasons for contract changes. Not only are they likely to be perceived as competent by opposing bargainers, they will probably be more effective.

□ **Summary**

Bargainers need a comprehensive knowledge base about the school district in question. Such knowledge comes from several areas. Although it is not based on the school district, the first area of knowledge necessary is the collective bargaining law of the state. Parallel to the study of that law, bargainers should also study applicable case law as well as the rulings of state employment relations boards.

A second important area is personnel policy. This should include teacher assignment, recruitment policies and transfers, teacher evaluation, calendars and work schedules, workload, grievance and appeal procedures, probation and tenure, job descriptions, substitute teacher policies, and others.

Another knowledge base is financial. Such information requires financial analysis that is dependent on several sources. In addition to budgeting and accounting records, proper financial analysis means investigating old school board minutes, old program proposals, newspaper accounts of board proceedings and other board-related information, categorical program budgets, statistical handbooks, newspaper notices, state budgeting and accounting manuals, and other sources related to both the financial act and its rationale.

Past practice is an important source of information for the bargainer. Administrator-bargainers may use past practice to defend continuation of certain practices and teacher-bargainers may attack past practice if and when such practice can be shown to be ineffective, costly, or inconsistent with sound educational practice.

Both teacher organization bargainers and administration bargainers must be familiar with the comparison strategy in collective bargaining, together with the extensive knowledge base for use of that strategy. The comparison strategy derives its power from the tendency of school boards and administrators to base certain policies, practices, and activities on those which are common practices or typical practices in other school districts they view as quite similar to their own. Effective use of the comparison strategy requires access to mounds of data for defending the comparisons made.

Bargainers should know the present contract in great detail, of course. But they must also know how and why the contract evolved to its present makeup. Understanding this requires an appreciation of the step-by-step progression to the current contract; comparisons of advantages and disadvantages of contracts from previous years; and knowledge of the reasons for contract changes, year in and year out.

CHAPTER 9

Preparing Bargaining Teams

BECAUSE OF THE IMPORTANCE of bargained contracts to both parties to collective bargaining, the selection and preparation of bargaining teams must be undertaken with great care. Several aspects of the school district are affected: the work life of teachers and administrators, the educational potency of the school district, and the overall public perceptions of the district.

Also, the current slow trend toward greater openness in bargaining makes the personality characteristics of team members extremely significant. Of equal importance are the characteristics demanded by the very nature of the bargaining process. In addition to requiring considerable patience, ingenuity, and flexibility by the bargainers, the process mandates seemingly endless hours of preparation followed by many hours at the bargaining table.

This chapter is devoted to discussion of several aspects necessary for preparation of effective bargaining teams. Its topics are:

Selection of Bargaining Team Members
 Criteria for Selection
 Chief Spokespersons: Who, and How Much Power?
Bargaining Team Preparation
 Attitudes
 Record-Keeping
 Some Cautions

□ Selection of Bargaining Team Members

Some writers hold that collective bargaining in education is an adversary relationship between the two factions (Higginbotham 1975, 2). Whether one agrees with that premise, it is certain that collective bargaining holds the potential for changing many of the relationships in traditional school district practice. In any event, bargaining is ultimately reduced to self-serving interests, with each side striving to enhance its position.

Because of this potential inherent in bargaining, members of both bargaining teams must retain their perspectives on the bargaining process, irrespective of former or present relationships with members of the opposing team.

☐ **CRITERIA FOR SELECTION**   While it is impossible to mention all criteria that should be considered in selecting members of bargaining teams, some deserve special mention and explanation. Those criteria or individual characteristics are:

1. The ability to understand and respect all viewpoints represented by the bargaining team. This means that teachers at all grade levels should be understood and respected by team members. Administrator-bargainers must realize that various points of view of school board members must be respected.

2. Knowledge of the controlling state laws on collective bargaining.

3. Knowledge of the demography of the subject school district, school district budget, school board policies, history of the school district, curriculum and instruction practices of the district, and basic political dynamics of the school district.

4. Promptness and regular attendance at meetings.

5. The ability to control emotions at the bargaining table.

6. The ability to subordinate personal interests to those of the team.

7. Patience and endurance during the tedium of long bargaining sessions.

It is likely that administration bargainers will be appointed to bargaining teams. However, this is not always true for teacher-bargainers: some are elected. Tendencies of teacher organizations to elect members of bargaining teams are downright dangerous. Election often surfaces teams that will act contrary to the best interests of the organization. Teacher-bargainers should be appointed and the appointment should be followed by ratification by the board of directors and the total teacher membership if possible. The importance of appointment and ratification cannot be overstated; as such, both deserve discussion.

Appointment of teacher-bargainers is pivotal because of the characteristics required of good bargainers. Elected bargainers often win their elections largely because of popularity, but popularity is not always an attribute related to skill in bargaining.

Two types of needs are immediately recognizable in persons engaged in collective bargaining — group membership needs and personal needs. Group membership needs are those that derive from identification with the mission of the organization represented by the bargainer. Personal needs are basic to human behavior. Some personal needs are also group membership needs.

Using the needs identified by Maslow (1954) as basic factors in human behavior, it is possible to categorize them in terms of the collective bargaining context:

Group membership needs	*Personal needs*
Safety and security	Physiological (homeostatic)
Love and belonging	Esteem
	Self-actualization
	Needs to know and understand
	Aesthetic

The grouping above is somewhat arbitrary since most of the needs are interrelated. For example, esteem needs could very well be closely related to group membership needs for some people. For others, esteem needs are very personal and not at all related to group membership needs.

Pertinent to selection of bargaining team members is the extent to which certain needs *motivate* individuals. Persons motivated by esteem and self-actualization needs, for example, may not be effective bargainers if those needs dominate individual behavior to a greater extent than do group membership needs.

After appointment of bargainers, the ratification process is important for two reasons. First, it suggests that the selected bargainer speaks for the *total* membership of the teacher organization and second, it suggests that the selected bargainer is not part of a clique within the teacher organization leadership.

☐ CHIEF SPOKESPERSONS: WHO? AND HOW MUCH POWER?

The power and authority to act should be given to the members of each bargaining team in writing. Such authority should state that final agreements are subject to review by higher authority.

Selection of chief spokespersons should be based on ability and ability alone. Ability encompasses many personal attributes that are quite hard to define. The basic motivation of the individual selected should be considered, consistent with the above discussion. But the primary area of expertise in such a leader is the ability to manage conflict (Likert and Likert 1976).

Leadership ability is a second criterion. Those qualities should be positive ones, centered on the ability to keep the bargaining process moving effectively toward completion. Although impasse is an important strategy sometimes, chief spokespersons should be committed to avoidance of breakdowns in communication when possible. Firmness is absolutely essential in a chief spokesperson. Such firmness should be displayed in an unemotional manner; objections to proposals or aspects of proposals should be delivered convincingly, accompanied by a rationale. But firmness and the ability to stand by a position taken should not project outright hostility, because hostility has the potential for destroying agreement momentum.

The ability to effect meaningful interpersonal relationships is another criterion for selection of chief spokespersons. Such individuals must possess qualities that seem almost contradictory and simply not possible in one person. Carl Rogers (1965, 49–65) offered some key attributes of persons effective in interpersonal relationships. Those attributes are positive regard, unconditional regard, empathy, and congruence. All qualities are essential for persons engaged in the heat of collective bargaining.

Both school administrations and teacher organizations must avoid sending a chief spokesperson to the bargaining context with "an axe to grind" with the opposing side. Such a person can quickly reduce bargaining sessions to name-calling, accusations, and other actions that make the true give-and-take of effective bargaining extremely difficult, if not impossible, to attain.

The power extended to chief spokespersons is important also. Generally, the power granted must afford as much latitude in decision making as possible while retaining firm control.

The chief spokesperson must have the power to censure other team members because:

1. The opposing team could misinterpret the true team position
2. There is the ever-present possibility of accidentally revealing the true team position whenever one or more team members are "out of control"
3. The opposing team must never be permitted to question the authority of the chief spokesperson

The chief spokesperson should be responsible for the training and overall preparation of the bargaining team. Preparation encompasses many aspects, some of which were discussed in Chapters 7, 8, and 9.

☐ Bargaining Team Preparation

In addition to the principles, strategies and tactics, and knowledge bases discussed in Chapters 4 and 7, preparation of bargaining teams for effective bargaining requires factual data about the school districts involved. The amount of essential factual data is so great that division of labor is required for its adequate coverage. Such factual data should include:

1. The collective bargaining law of the state
2. School district policy documents
3. School district administrative bulletins
4. Basic statistics
   a) Five-year trends in assessed valuations
   b) Average daily attendance
   c) Bonded indebtedness
   d) School year calendar (present year)
   e) Enrollments (present and five-year trends)
   f) Expenditures

g) Income
h) Racial and ethnic data, students
i) Racial and ethnic data, teachers
j) Teacher data by sex
k) School locations
l) Tax rates
m) Special projects (Bilingual Education, Vocational Education, etc.)
n) Sources of the school dollar
o) Salary schedules (certificated and classified)
p) Employee benefits
q) Replacement costs for books, supplies, and equipment
r) Administrator job descriptions
s) Teacher job descriptions
5. Settlement histories of all school districts in the area
6. Settlement histories of other school districts in the state when those districts are meaningful for comparison purposes
7. Curriculum and instruction concerns
8. Grievance history of the school district
9. Previous understandings between bargaining teams
10. Newest developments in state or national bargaining

This factual data is in addition to the various analyses suggested in Chapter 8. Fortunately, most school districts maintain ongoing records on much of these data for many other purposes such as public relations and reporting to external agencies.

Two more aspects of bargaining team preparation should not be overlooked by the chief spokesperson. One is the bargaining team attitude in the collective sense and individual attitudes as they influence the group. Another is training in record keeping.

☐ **ATTITUDES**   Most attitudinal aspects were discussed in Chapter 2. One more deserves further discussion; it was excluded in Chapter 4 because it is not one of the nine vital principles of effective bargaining. Rather, it is an attitude that must be discouraged.

One of the most dangerous attitudes taken to the table by some bargainers is the "winner-take-all" attitude. Although collective bargaining laws mandate good faith bargaining, they do not mandate agreement. Hence, coercive behaviors at the table or statements intended to berate members of the opposing team have no place in the effective bargaining context. Moreover, an overall team attitude oriented to winning without conceding will surely doom that team to failure.

Each chief spokesperson must emphasize that effective bargaining involves a quid pro quo, a mutual exchange, a gain for both sides. This is sometimes difficult to convey to team members who are first-time bargainers. One means of conveying the mutual exchange concept to team members is that of explaining several proposals or counterproposals from the opposing team as a set of concessions aimed at a set of hoped-for returns. If and when the chief spokesperson or other team member is able to predict the desired gain of the other side, the mutual exchange concept is made clearer to the team members.

The extreme attitudes that operate in some collective bargaining situations were discussed in Chapter 7 and should be reviewed. Positive attitudes toward bargaining, together with an awareness that the opposing team must have incentives for continued bargaining are two keys to proper bargaining team attitudes. Such an overall attitude will result in a team that is effective and not vulnerable to ploys used by some opposing teams.

☐ **RECORD KEEPING**   In the absence of skilled secretarial help, one member of each bargaining team should serve as secretary. This person should be skilled at recording the important details and interchanges, although it is virtually impossible and impractical to keep verbatim notes. While tape recorders provide an alternative, they should not be used for one powerful reason — the presence of tape recorders tends to stifle open interchange and expression of ideas.

The importance of accurate notes cannot be overemphasized. Such notes often reveal subtle but crucial changes in the opponent's positions on issues. These notes can also capture the various reactions of opposing team members to an idea. Equally important, they help to keep track of tentative concessions, withdrawn proposals, or old issues that might resurface and complicate matters.

Teams bargaining for the first time should receive the benefit of some "don'ts" that derive from experienced bargainers.

☐ **SOME CAUTIONS**   Although each situation will dictate slightly different procedures, some general cautions should be observed. Unless these are considered, a bargaining team might inadvertently give certain advantages to the opposing team. These cautions are:

1. Don't forget to present your credentials.
2. Don't agree to fixed schedules for bargaining sessions too far in advance because it is difficult to know how much preparation will be required. Inability to meet a schedule or agreed-upon session can arm the opposing team with a prime public relations weapon. Meetings should be planned ahead without loss of flexibility.

3. Don't fail to notify the opposing team *in writing* well in advance whenever cancellations are necessary.
4. Don't agree to tape bargaining sessions.
5. Don't be late for meetings. The negative publicity can be disastrous.
6. Don't forget to include the following aspects of proposals or counterproposals introduced:
   a) Cost information
   b) Feasibility
   c) Value that accrues to children
   d) Relationship of a proposal or counterproposal to a currently unsatisfactory practice
   e) The legal aspect that supports entry into scope of bargaining
   f) The state or national precedent, when applicable
   g) The comparative aspects of the practice based on nearby districts and their practices
7. Don't hesitate to clarify all proposals when asked to do so.
8. Don't agree to package offers on the spot. They should be considered carefully because they often force abandonment of other important aspects.
9. Don't abandon or drop a demand unless something is gained in return.
10. Don't forget that bargaining is a confidential relationship.
11. Don't forget to develop clearly stated ground rules for dealing with the media, holding press conferences, and releasing news.

Some additional aspects of bargaining team preparation deserve consideration, although they are not cautions in the usual sense. These aspects center on the dangers inherent in the makeup of some bargaining teams.

☐ **RESERVATIONS ABOUT CERTAIN TEAM MEMBERS**   School districts vary in size and the capabilities they bring to the bargaining table. Large districts not only have access to diverse staff resources, they can buy the services of skilled bargainers. Small school districts are generally the opposite: the bargaining team sometimes consists of the superintendent, two board members, and two principals.

A new trend among small school districts is the formation of consortia to buy the services of skilled bargainers who can then divide their time(s) among those districts. Present indications are that this trend will continue. Teacher organizations, too, have access to skilled outside bargainers from state teacher associations or independent outside agencies. There are pros, cons, advantages, and disadvantages inherent in facing certain bargaining team members.

School board members are often participants in bargaining in very small districts. From the standpoint of such boards, it is not a good practice—especially where public observers or media representatives are present. Arguments against this practice are:

1. The presence of board members on bargaining teams can interfere with the openness of exchanges between administrators and teachers
2. There are situations in which board members can be forced into what amounts to commitments
3. Teacher-bargainers can assume the right to interpret statements made by board members as board positions
4. Changes in positions (by board members) from one bargaining session to the next can be used by teacher-bargainers as a basis for accusations of failure to bargain in good faith
5. The ego-bound board members can be made to look like they are badgering or pulling rank on teacher-bargainers, especially when observers are present

Bargaining superintendents are often found in small districts. Although bargaining superintendents are generally at a disadvantage (for reasons similar to those of bargaining board members), they are an improvement over bargaining board members. This is true because one layer of retreat remains; that is, bargaining superintendents can delay agreement on issues by saying that before closure on any issue or set of issues it will be necessary to consult with their school boards.

There are some advantages enjoyed by bargaining superintendents. In small districts, superintendents of long tenure can often persuade teacher-bargainers on certain issues by using their long-lived, cooperative relationship in the past. Also, a superintendent acting as a one-person bargaining team can sometimes generate public support and sympathy to nullify teacher efforts during job actions and other teacher organization activities.

Professional negotiators are used in many school districts throughout the nation. There are both advantages and disadvantages associated with them. Their advantages are (1) intimate familiarity with the laws on collective bargaining, (2) knowledge about the dynamics of collective bargaining, and (3) emotional detachment from the process. Some disadvantages of professional negotiators are: (1) unfamiliarity with the interpersonal and political dynamics within a school district, and (2) lack of concern with the education of children. While professional negotiators rely heavily on the "stonewalling" tactic, their presence affords one prime tactic to teacher organizations: portrayal, through media and other avenues, of these professional negotiators as cold, detached persons who know nothing and care nothing about quality education for children.

State and national school boards associations can provide school boards the names of professional negotiators in a given geographical area. Before retaining such professionals, boards or their administrators should address the following concerns:

1. Services offered
2. Fees, including expenses and billing policy
3. Negotiator's expectations of the board and administrators
4. Availability for negotiations and follow-up when necessary
5. Previous experiences with school districts

☐ Summary

The proper mix of personal attributes of bargaining team members cannot be overstated, for they influence the nature of the final contract that in turn affects several significant aspects of school district operation. The most important outcome is the quality of education within the district.

This means that bargaining team members must be chosen with extreme care. The criteria for selection of bargaining team members should include overall knowledge about the school district, the laws and dynamics of bargaining, certain personal attributes like promptness and regular attendance, emotional control, and—equally important—respect for the viewpoints of others, including members of the opposing team.

The chief spokesperson is by far the most important bargaining team member. In addition to possession of outstanding leadership qualities, the chief spokesperson must be able to orchestrate and control the preparation, attitudes, and activities of the bargaining team members. This argues for the granting of clearly defined authority for the chief spokesperson. Parallel to this, the chief spokesperson must handle such power evenhandedly. Moreover, the chief spokesperson must be capable of diligent application of the team's time and effort to achieve the best collective bargaining contract possible.

In keeping with this, the chief spokesperson should seek to influence positive attitudes in the minds of team members. The winner-take-all attitude should be avoided, for it contributes to an overall negative bargaining climate. Bargaining must be viewed as a quid pro quo, a gain for both sides.

The chief spokesperson is also reponsible for seeing that adequate records are kept for all bargaining sessions. In the absence of a paid secretary, one team member should serve as secretary.

There is a tendency in small districts to have both superintendents and board members on bargaining teams. If possible, such practices should be avoided because the presence of these individuals often induces a negative climate in bargaining.

PART 4

At the Table

CHAPTER 10

Bargaining Procedures

WHILE IT IS DIFFICULT to generalize about the specifics of collective bargaining encounters, certain procedures are common. They are offered to give the inexperienced bargainer and/or the interested reader an idea of the typical procedures adhered to in collective bargaining in public education.

This brief chapter includes discussion of the following topics:

First Meeting
Proposals and Counterproposals: The Essence of Bargaining
Proposals Categorized
Analyzing Proposals and Counterproposals

□ First Meeting

The first meeting of bargainers and their opponents will be different from all subsequent meetings. This means that if a contract exists already, certain basic things usually dealt with during first meetings will have been taken care of.

During first meetings, both sides should establish ground rules that will govern their bargaining relationship and avoid confusion. Although the number of ground rules should be minimized, they should address:

1. The time and place(s) of the meetings. Meeting places should be convenient for both sides and should be located near chalkboards, copy machines, and separate, private rooms for caucusing. Coffee and snacks should be available if at all possible.

2. The time limits on the meetings. There should be some provision for flexibility, especially in the late stages when teams are close to agreement.

3. Procedures for handling proposals and counterproposals.

4. The conditions under which other observers or resource persons will be permitted to attend the meetings. The usual rule centers on persons who can clarify substantive aspects of issues.

5. Procedures for raising new issues after the first round of proposals and counterproposals.

6. Confidentiality and releases to news media. Bargainers should agree to notify each other well in advance of media releases.

7. The definition and method of reaching tentative agreements.

□ Proposals and Counterproposals: The Essence of Bargaining

Usually, teacher organizations propose at the first bargaining session, after ground rules are established. Typically, administrator-bargainers offer nothing more than requests for clarification, with no hints as to whether they agree or disagree. On occasion, administrator-bargainers will ask for the teacher organization rationale as justification for certain proposals.

Under ideal conditions, both team spokespersons should offer brief presentations that express optimism for mutually satisfactory outcomes in bargaining. These utterances are consistent with the principle of "Developing Agreement Momentum," discussed in Chapter 4.

School board proposals are usually discussed in the next bargaining session. Such school board proposals are *not* counterproposals to teacher organization demands; counterproposals are dealt with in subsequent sessions. During the presentation, the chief spokesperson for administrator-bargainers summarizes each school board proposal to make its intent clear to teacher organization bargainers. Finally, both parties attempt to agree on agendae for subsequent meetings, with administration bargainers trying to delay discussion of economic items because these economic items constitute the basic incentive that makes teacher organizations bargain. Put another way, early agreement on economic items puts school boards at a disadvantage in two ways: increased teacher organization resistance to nonmoney items proposed by the board and inability to package noneconomic gains desired by the board with economic offers.

Counterproposals offered by administrator-bargainers are often no more than original teacher organization proposals with language changed so that administrations can live with them. The timing of such counterproposals is tactical, depending on the specifics of the bargaining scenario. After complete exchanges of proposals and counterproposals, the process is essentially one of whittling down long lists of demands and counterdemands.

Of utmost importance is clarification about what constitutes tentative agreement, mentioned earlier as one of the ground rules that must be established at the first meeting. The usual practice is to finalize such agreements and have representatives of both sides initial them.

Bargaining procedure may be summarized as being in several phases: initial proposals, counterproposals, temporary adoption of specific items, trade-offs and compromises, tentative agreement, and agreement by both sides.

While the actual procedure will vary from context to context, the usual procedure is to leave agreements verbal until the tentative agreement stage, which is completed when the members of each side initial the agreement. At this point, bargainers of both sides should have access to legal help in reviewing the legal language of the tentative proposals. Most state laws do not control the specific details of bargaining. However, these laws do control the specifics of impasse resolution. This aspect is discussed in Chapter 11.

☐ Proposals Categorized

Proposals and counterproposals have different intentions. Some are mutually enhancing to pupils and teacher organizations, others are aimed at achieving certain desired ends of the teacher organization, still others are designed to help administrations project positive images. The various reasons for proposals and counterproposals, together with some examples, are considered below.

Pupil-benefit proposals. There are many times when teacher organization proposals and administration counterproposals have child advocacy as a sincere concern. At other times, the obvious child advocacy is intended to enhance the image of the party introducing the proposal.

An example of a sincere pupil-benefit proposal introduced by teacher-bargainers is one that seeks to modify testing practices in a given district so that criterion-referenced tests replace standardized tests. Advantages gained would be (1) closer matchup between objectives taught and objectives measured, (2) curriculum objectives more closely oriented to the experiential backgrounds and daily life experiences of students, and (3) more freedom and local discretion in the organization and planning of curriculum through teacher participation in the design and selection of tests to be used. Although curriculum matters are usually school board prerogatives, such a teacher proposal could be admissible to bargaining in states where teacher evaluation procedures are admissible — because testing is, or could be, a necessary aspect of teacher evaluation procedures.

However, there are teacher organization proposals that use child advocacy as a cover-up for certain self-serving interests of the teacher organization. Similarly, there are administration counterproposals that are aimed at the same end.

Organizational image proposals. These are often identical to pupil-benefit proposals. The image of child advocacy tends to enhance the images of both parties to bargaining. Other organizational image proposals focus on projecting an image of leadership in the affairs of the school district. While it is the legal bailiwick of the school board in the long run, teacher organizations continue to — and *should* continue to — generate proposals attempting to spearhead change. Although many such proposals are likely to be rejected, especially those in the curriculum area, the attendant publicity is to the advantage of those teacher organizations.

Administrators often capitalize on this strategy, too. An example is a proposal for a "Cinco de Mayo Day" celebration. Such a proposal or counterproposal, based in the multicultural education curriculum rationale, can enhance an administration image of child-advocacy and forward-thinking leadership, concerned with human rights. The image generated is doubly potent if teacher organizations had a chance to introduce such a proposal but failed to do so. This situation could occur only when school calendars are bargainable, of course.

Scope-widening proposals. State collective bargaining laws vary with respect to scope of bargaining. Even when scope is specifically delimited, it is possible for teacher organizations to propose aspects in certain admissible areas of bargaining that in turn have impact in nonadmissible areas.

The broad area of teacher evaluations can serve as a prime example of this. Teacher evaluation formats and procedures are permitted in scope in some states; curriculum is not. However, it is impossible to formulate effective, adequate teacher evaluation formats and procedures without considering curriculum; after all, instruction is but the implementation of the curriculum.

While tactics and strategies have been discussed earlier, two important scope-widening tactics employed by teacher organizations deserve mention:

1. Introduction of a proposal intended to dramatize the exclusion of teacher organizations from scope in a certain area in which the public believes they should participate.

2. Incorporation of philosophical language into proposals, to the fullest extent possible. Administration and school board agreement on such proposals has the subsequent effect of opening bargaining in areas addressed by the philosophical language.

Trade-off springboard proposals. These proposals or counterproposals may be in any area bargainable. They are usually issues that are desirable in a long-range sense, but present conditions make them impossible to achieve. They are most effective when clothed in other rationales that are acceptable to most reasonable observers and promise the capability of improving the educational program.

When those two conditions are met, it is difficult for opposing bargainers to reject them outright or counter with meaningful criticisms. Also, counterproposals in these areas tend to *admit to their educational validity.*

An example of such a proposal is (and was) the "elementary preparation period" issue. Although many districts now have elementary preparation periods as part of standard policy, for many years the annual requests for elementary preparation periods were trade-off springboards for teacher bargainers: the issue is (was) a just one, it makes sense to all concerned, and it is (was) directly tied to child welfare.

Such issues tend to die natural deaths. Repeated use of them in bargaining results in internalization by teachers; that is, teachers begin to demand them as rights. The end result is that teacher organizations must deliver on them.

Organizational security proposals. These proposals are aimed at strengthening teacher organizations relative to the size and strength of competing teacher organizations or in some aspect of ongoing bargaining with the school district. An example of the former is an "agency-shop" proposal. An example of the latter is a proposal giving the teacher organization the right of final approval of agreements with colleges or universities related to student-teacher programs within the subject district.

Whether proposals originate with teacher organizations or school administrators, they must be analyzed. While there are no specific rules for doing so, organized approaches to doing so can help with analysis.

☐ Analyzing Proposals and Counterproposals

Simply stated, each side must analyze proposals and counterproposals in terms of impact on their organizations. Doing so requires considering many variables, some difficult to explain. However, proper organization can minimize the problems incidental to analysis.

Once all proposals or counterproposals are submitted, the following steps for analysis are important:

1. Organize proposals on the basis of areas to which they relate; counterproposals should be organized on the basis of the proposals to which they relate

2. Identify each proposal or counterproposal on the basis of what the opponent *really intended* the proposal to communicate (refusal, further discussion, stalling for time, etc.)

3. Cross-reference all counterproposals or proposals that impact on others and identify the common ground, together with the overall implications (cost, board response, teacher organization response, implementation costs and difficulties, etc.)

4. Reclassify all proposals or counterproposals on the basis of overall desirability

5. Attach costs to each item or total costs to each proposal or counterproposal

6. Rerank all proposals, incorporating cost, intent of the opponent, cross-referenced impact, and impact on persons external to the bargaining process

7. Evaluate ranked proposals or counterproposals with respect to your organizational goals, both long-range and short-range

8. Develop an acceptability index for each counterproposal or proposal

9. Eliminate unacceptable proposals or counterproposals from the list

10. Look for areas that permit bases for new proposals or counterproposals

The foregoing should be thought of as a "loose" model, for all steps will not be applicable to all situations. Such a model must be modified, depending on local circumstances. Also, it must include people involved, previous bargaining history, legalities, and logistics.

The following concerns must be addressed when evaluating teacher organization proposals or administration counterproposals:

1. Intent. Is it sincere, or is it aimed at some other strategy?

2. Is it clearly stated or ambiguous?

3. How does it (a counterproposal) compare to the original proposal?

4. How does it compare to standard practice in the area?

5. Is it educationally sound?

6. Is it actually an elaborate refusal?

7. Is there evidence or a suggestion of refusal to bargain in good faith?

8. What other proposals or counterproposals does it cross-reference?

9. Would acceptance of it create desirable or undesirable precedent?

10. What would the school board response be? Other administrators? Teachers? The general public?

11. Should it be discussed with members of other teacher organizations? Other administrators in other school districts?

☐ Summary

While the specifics of the bargaining process will vary from situation to situation, some procedures are similar in most places. The procedure is essentially one of proposal and counterproposal, followed by clarifications, time-lapses, and finally temporary agreement. Temporary agreements become tentative agreements conditional on approval of the controlling authorities of both sides. These tentative agreements are followed by final agreements.

Bargainers must go to the table armed with ample basic information as well as certain attitudes that promote favorable climates at the table. These positive attitudes must be displayed no matter who the opponents are.

The actual procedures of bargaining are simple, but the strategies and tactics of bargaining are very complex. They are designed to create an advantage in the bargaining relationship. This advantage is the essence of all collective bargaining.

Most state laws are silent on the actual bargaining procedure, but well-organized bargaining teams will strive for order in the proceedings. The first meeting should be devoted to defining and establishing the basic ground rules, simple understandings like the time, place, and time limits of meetings, conditions under which observers will be present, understandings about relations with media, as well as the definition of what constitutes agreement.

There are many types of proposals and counterproposals, depending on what the bargaining team is trying to accomplish. These proposals range from those oriented to pupil benefit to those that openly attempt to enhance the position of the organization making the proposal.

Chaos can be avoided if bargainers attempt to develop a hierarchy of importance for proposals or counterproposals received. The result should be simplicity and a better overall perception of what the opponent is trying to achieve. Such a perception should result in more effective strategies for responding to the proposals or counterproposals.

CHAPTER 11

Resolution of Impasse

IMPASSE MAY BE DEFINED as hiatus in bargaining that results from failure in communications. When it occurs, the opposing sides find it hard to compromise. The result is stalemate.

Many factors contribute to impasse, depending on context. The reasons teacher-bargainers resort to impasse may range from something (seemingly) as insignificant as a minor improvement in a vision care plan to a major change in procedures for teacher organization speeches to a board of education. No matter how trivial or significant the issue, some basic power principles are almost always involved.

These power principles are at the core of impasse. O'Connell and Heller (1976) studied nineteen school districts in New York State and found that the basic reasons for impasse centered on one conflict: teachers' desire for increased participation in decision making versus school boards' desires for retention of power. Closely related findings were also reported by Hill (1973), Hicks (1973), and Jones (1969).

When impasse occurs, the outlook for finalization of a contract is bad— for many reasons. One of the strongest of these reasons is psychological, with each team attributing the breakdown in bargaining to the attitudes and philosophies of the other.

The primary aim of bargaining laws is institutional peace. Thus the levels or "tiers" for the resolution of impasse are provided by law, giving both parties the chance to develop working relationships and resolve conflicts without disturbing the mission of public education.

This chapter is devoted to discussion of the various aspects of impasse and its resolution. Its topics include:

Impasse in Collective Bargaining
Mediation
Fact-finding
Arbitration
Strategy Alternatives

While collective bargaining laws vary in specifics, most provide three levels designed to protect the public interest in minimizing or eliminating disruptions in the education of children that sometimes happen during bargaining. The three commonly known levels—mediation, fact-finding, and arbitration—represent increasing degrees of third-party influence, legal involvement, and publicity.

Before discussion of the aspects of impasse and its resolution, it is important to distinguish between *interest* disputes—the subject of this chapter—and *rights* disputes—discussed in detail in Chapter 14. Interest disputes are those centered on the subjects that may be bargained in a given jurisdiction. Put another way, interest disputes develop *before* contract finalization. Rights disputes surface when the bargained contract is implemented. A second way of distinguishing the two types of conflict relates to their coverage or scope; that is, while the range of matters involved in interest disputes is governed by the applicable collective bargaining law, the range of matters involved in rights disputes is determined by the letter of the negotiated contract between the parties. The essential differences between the conflicts are shown in Figure 11.1.

☐ Impasse in Collective Bargaining

The immediacy of impasse is dependent on factors related to the situation and the persons involved in the bargaining process. Some teacher organizations never resort to impasse; others resort to it at some point during every annual bargaining session. Administrator-bargainers, too, vary in viewpoints about impasse: some see it as something to be avoided, and others see it as a strategy alternative under certain circumstances.

Impasse is an undesirable alternative. Even though most state collective bargaining laws provide mechanisms for its resolution, the intent and spirit of

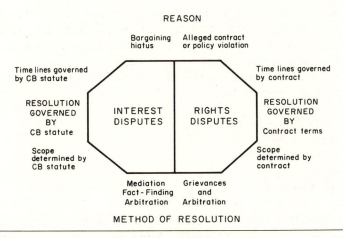

11.1. A scheme illustrating basic differences between interest and rights disputes.

those laws center on avoidance of impasse. Because of this, most impasse
resolution processes provided by state laws are aimed at a quick return to
regular bargaining.

☐ **REASONS FOR IMPASSE**   While reasons for impasse vary, the following are some of the common reasons for it in public education bargaining:

1. Teacher organization bargainers are often suspicious about the com-
   prehensiveness of the information base they use for bargaining because they are aware of the power of administrators to limit their
   access to meaningful information—especially financial information.
   Impasse results from their hopes that a third party might surface relevant information.
2. Impasse is a face-saving device for teacher-bargainers, a way of dis-
   guising that the bargaining confrontation has failed to yield results.
   Put another way, impasse is a means whereby teacher organization
   leaders can temporarily maintain credibility with their teacher constituents despite failures to make gains in bargaining.
3. The act of declaring impasse is another way of putting the blame on
   the other side, when the party declaring the impasse is sure that the
   total staff and public perception would be against the other side.
4. When one party or the other is clearly opposed to the use of a third
   party.
5. When the teacher organization has overcommitted itself with promises
   and there has been a new disclosure about reduced revenues or legal
   limitations. In such instances, impasse provides a convenient face-
   saving alternative.
6. When the act of declaring impasse can be well-publicized, and the
   party declaring impasse feels that it has the stronger case in the eyes of
   the staff and general public.

☐ **COLLECTIVE BARGAINING LAWS AND IMPASSE**   Most collective bargaining laws in public education permit either side to declare that the bargaining process is at impasse. These state laws vary with respect to the conditions
under which impasse can be called. They differ also on time lines for impasse;
that is, some laws mandate declaration of impasse if agreement is not reached
after the passage of a certain amount of time.

Another important difference in these laws is enforcement rigidity. Put
another way, some laws offer mere guidelines for impasse resolution while
others require strict adherence. Strict adherence to impasse resolution provisions in some states derives from the existence of budget development time
lines mandated by the education codes of those states. School district budgets

are dependent on many revenue sources and conditions, so stalled bargaining situations are, in effect, stalling other aspects of school finance.

One of the prime techniques for resolution of impasse in collective bargaining is mediation, which is the first level of impasse resolution.

☐ Mediation

Mediation is a process that employs a third party who attempts to get the two bargaining teams to resolve the issues that prevent final agreement. By meeting with the opposing parties separately, the mediator tries to bring opposing parties together on the issues involved.

The mediator is not concerned with the values involved in the dispute; that is, he or she is not necessarily guided by the educational or moral considerations or the overall justice of the matter. This is a primary point that bargainers must recognize: above all else, the mediator is simply trying to resolve the dispute.

The laws about the powers and duties of mediators are fairly consistent throughout the states. Most laws contain the following provisions concerning mediation: (1) mediation is a confidential process; (2) mediation is advisory only, which means that mediators have no real authority; and (3) mediation results in a set of recommendations for settlement, given to both bargaining teams.

☐ **THE PROCESS OF MEDIATION**   Mediation in states with collective bargaining laws is controlled in most instances by the state agency that monitors public employee labor disputes. The name and specific role of this agency varies from state to state. In California, it is called the Public Employment Relations Board; in Iowa, the same name applies; but in Massachusetts the agency with the same function is called the State Board of Mediation and Arbitration.

The sequence below describes the basic steps in the mediation process in most states:

1. The bargaining team requesting mediation files either a letter or proper forms with the designated employment relations agency.
2. One or more mediators are selected by the employment relations agency and notified of the task. This mediator contacts the bargaining teams separately and sets up appointments so that the mediation process can start.
3. The mediator meets with the teams separately so that procedure can be discussed and understood.
4. The mediator then meets with both teams to review the state law on mediation and determines the position and underlying rationales of each

team. Then, each team presents its case without interruption, with the team that requested mediation presenting first; and after clarification discussions, the mediator *may* ask for rebuttals from each team.

5. The mediator meets with each bargaining team individually, often proposing alternatives to the positions of each. If the bargaining parties appear ready to accept a compromise solution, the mediator will try to lock it in.

6. An alternative to the compromise above, used by some mediators, is the tactic of recommending a solution — forcing each party into the position of rejecting it. This has the effect of "revealing hidden cards" to some extent, an effect that can result in compromise. Other tactics used by mediators to move bargaining teams closer to compromise are improvement of the tone and communication of the meetings between two teams by demanding cessation of profanity and other emotional outbursts, acting as an emotional outlet in separate meetings between the teams, bringing teams together occasionally for further clarification and/or finalizing verbal agreements when possible, keeping costs prominent in the minds of both sides if and when it works to speed up progress toward settlement, and transmitting communications (even bluffs at times) that might stimulate compromise.

7. State laws vary, but if it is apparent that mediation is failing, either the mediator, either team, or the state agency might declare an end to mediation; or,

8. The state employment relations agency might appoint a new mediator if both teams indicate that one might lead to progress; or,

9. The state employment relations agency might appoint a fact-finder.

□ **THE ROLE OF BARGAINERS DURING MEDIATION**   There is a certain precarious balance that bargainers must observe during mediation. This balance must be maintained between (1) the basic trust vested in a mediator so that she or he is potentially effective and (2) releasing information to the mediator that might hurt the tactics and strategy of the overall bargaining team effort. Specifically, administrator-bargainers or teacher-bargainers should:

1. Give the mediator a complete history of the bargaining up to the mediator's entry into the situation. Stress the attempts tried previously, but be willing to try them again with the mediator as a third party.

2. Reveal methods used by their organization to arrive at the data-based conclusions undergirding their positions, including cost calculations; class size calculations; calculations used to compare district data with that of other districts; and analyses of the school district's revenue sources and potential sources of revenue, including matching funds or other funds that the board of education may have failed to vote for.

3. Refrain from displays of power; mediation is a compromise activity.

4. Avoid press releases while mediation is in progress.

5. Be receptive to solutions that are alternatives to written contract solutions.

6. Be willing to spend long hours in mediation.

These actions will go a long way toward successful mediation. However, there are a few cautions that should be borne in mind by bargainers of both sides. "Packages" are fine and they are quite necessary (at times) in successful mediation. But make sure that certain vital items are not thrown away or excluded from the package. Also, be sure that while certain priorities are revealed, the retreat line of your side is not. Remember: the mediator is interested in one thing — a solution.

☐ **WHEN MEDIATION FAILS**   Mediation may be thought of as the first tier of a three-tiered process provided by most state collective bargaining laws for resolution of impasse in bargaining. It is not public; that is, public opinion is not a factor bearing on the positions of the parties. The second tier of the impasse resolution procedure in most collective bargaining laws is fact-finding.

☐ Fact-finding

Like mediation, the intent of fact-finding procedures is helping bargaining parties reach agreement. It is conducted by a person assigned by the employment relations agency of the state. In some states, fact-finding is carried out by a panel of persons, usually three. Laws differ also about the method of selecting fact-finding panels: in some states, the appointment is by the state agency; in others, both parties can participate in selecting persons on fact-finding panels. Stated simply, the intention of fact-finding is to provide a neutral third-party opinion as to what a contract settlement should be, together with a rationale for that conclusion. Fact-finding results are usually made public, an aspect that can — and does — force the parties out of their rigid positions.

☐ **FACT-FINDING AND COLLECTIVE BARGAINING LAWS**   Fact-finding is handled differently in various states. While it is impossible to discuss all of the state-by-state variations, some major differences prevail.

1. Some states have laws that provide for a fact-finder whose identity is the responsibility of the appointing state agency.

2. Some states provide for a panel of fact-finders and each party selects the individual members by various methods.

3. Other states provide for a three-member team, one selected by each party and the third member selected by the other two fact-finders.

4. Some states require the issuance of recommendations over and above "the facts," and others do not.

5. Almost all states permit publication of the fact-finding report.

6. Results of the fact-finding are advisory in most states, but in a few it is binding.

7. Fact-finders are usually legally authorized to subpoena witnesses, records, and other information. They are also authorized to take sworn testimony.

□ **THE PROCESS OF FACT-FINDING**   Whether the state mandates fact-finding immediately after the failure of mediation or leaves the decision to request it to the opposing parties, the basic steps in fact-finding are:

1. The employment relations agency of the state selects a fact-finder from a list of qualified persons or provides such a list to the bargaining parties to select one by mutual agreement

2. The selected fact-finder contacts both parties to set up a hearing, and at this time the fact-finder may request information of each bargaining party that could shed light on the essential conflict, including

   a) All demographic data on the school district, such as student enrollment, per-student expenditures, state and local revenues for several consecutive years, plus similar figures for the anticipated school year

   b) First proposals made by the teacher organization and administration counterproposals, before mediation

   c) The bargaining history of teachers with the school district

   d) The bargaining history of the current session, including the number of meetings

   e) The mediation history of the current session

   f) Items that were tentatively accepted by both sides

   g) A list of controversial items, together with the positions of each team on each item, including:

      (1) Cost factors

      (2) Comparative data (with other school districts)

      (3) Impact of teacher salaries on new revenues for the preceding five years

      (4) Impact of administrators' salaries on new revenues for the preceding five years

      (5) Impact of noncertificated salaries on new revenues for the preceding five years

      (6) Impact of fringe benefits on their specialized revenue sources for the preceding five years

       (7) All cost data for the current year

       (8) All cost data for the projected (upcoming) year

   h) Unexpended account balances in noncategorical funds for the preceding five years, including projected account balances for the current year

   i) Distribution of teacher salaries according to the position on the salary schedule for the present year and the projected year

   j) Cost-of-living data for the area in which the school district is located for the preceding five years

   k) The tax levy history of the district for the preceding five years, including general levies and restricted taxes

   l) The total tax limits as prescribed by law

3. Initial meetings with the fact-finder to explain the process and the criteria used in arriving at recommendations will usually be separate

4. The team requesting fact-finding usually makes the first presentation at the joint meeting of both teams with the fact-finder; this presentation is usually under oath attesting to the truth of the information presented

5. Meetings can involve a great deal of cross-examination of presenters, although the procedure varies with the fact-finder

6. Fact-finders often ask for written rebuttals of opposite team presentations or clarification of presentations made earlier by a team

7. Fact-finders often will turn to mediation if it appears that teams are capable of resolution of differences (especially if there are indications that both sides might not want a published fact-finder's report and its recommendations released) and remember it is possible for teams to continue bargaining while fact-finding is in progress

8. Fact-finders issue their reports to each bargaining party and to the employment relations agency of the state, which reviews the recommendations of the fact-finder

9. After an intentional delay (to intensify pressure on the two parties for a last-minute contract settlement), the report is made public

10. Except in jurisdictions where fact-finding may be binding, the parties may

   a) Accept the recommendations of the fact-finder

   b) Renew direct bargaining efforts, using the recommendations of the fact-finder as a framework for settlement

   c) Request arbitration

☐ **THE FACT-FINDING REPORT**   While it is difficult to generalize in this regard, the fact-finder's criteria center on fairness, comparative standing, and fiscal capability. The report may be a compromise (splitting the differences) with a set of recommendations that favor one side or the other or an entirely new set of recommendations.

☐ **THE COSTS OF FACT-FINDING**   Despite the existence of state employment relations agencies, some collective bargaining legislation requires that both parties share fact-finding costs. The intent is to discourage a hasty, capricious resort to fact-finding and to encourage serious participation in the process.

States vary with respect to costs. Some pay all costs of fact-finding, some pay none. Still others pay part of the fact-finding costs and require that the bargaining teams split the costs of the remainder.

☐ **FACT-FINDERS EMPHASIZE SOLUTIONS**   This point was made earlier but deserves restatement. Fact-finders are interested in solutions; so much so that some will resort to mediation. Their interest in solutions is so strong that some fact-finders actually believe the ultimate measure of effectiveness of the fact-finding process is *removal of the necessity for issuing reports and recommendations.*

☐ **THE ROLE OF BARGAINERS DURING FACT-FINDING**   The best role for bargainers to adopt during fact-finding is cooperation with the fact-finder. This means submission of all information he or she might require for the development of a report. Meanwhile, bargainers should:

1. Respect the confidentiality of the relationship with the fact-finder and refrain from public releases or statements until the report is released
2. Strive to explain all rationales undergirding their positions
3. Be prepared to protect the image of their organizations when and if a report and recommendations are released to the press by the fact-finder by
   a) Developing published defenses of the organization position on an issue-by-issue basis so that disparities between the bargaining position of the organization and the fact-finder's recommendation are clearly understood
   b) Developing written press releases, couched in lay terms, explaining the reasons for the organization position on an issue-by-issue basis
   c) Releasing the same information to other organizations in the community
   d) When and if the findings lean toward the opposing organization, refrain from public criticism of the fact-finding process, threats, statements attacking the competence of the fact-finder, and statements about arbitration or future strategies

☐ Arbitration

Like mediation and fact-finding, the intention of arbitration is to assist bargaining parties in circumventing job actions or other disruptions in educational services. Such third-party interventions are aimed principally at avoiding the ultimate weapon of organized teachers — the strike.

In most states arbitration is the last step available to bargainers trying to finalize a contract settlement. It is also the least used method of resolving differences, principally because the mechanisms preceding it — mediation and fact-finding — often produce results that preclude arbitration.

Arbitration is basically a method whereby a third-party neutral reviews all aspects of a bargaining conflict and renders a decision, called an award, which details the future procedures to be followed on each issue. An arbitration award may be likened unto a decision in a civil court. The extent to which arbitration is binding depends on the legalities as spelled out in collective bargaining laws.

☐ **THE TYPES OF ARBITRATION**   Two fundamental arbitration procedures should be differentiated. The first, oriented to the resolution of impasse in bargaining, is called *interest arbitration*. The other, oriented to resolution of differences that arise out of conflicts incidental to contract implementation, is called *rights arbitration*. The concern here is with interest arbitration only; rights arbitration will be discussed in Chapter 14.

Interest arbitration is either binding or nonbinding. This means all awards must be complied with in binding arbitration. Compliance is optional, however, in nonbinding arbitration, sometimes referred to as *advisory* arbitration. In such nonbinding arbitration, the award is usually dependent on the acceptance by both parties.

Depending on whether arbitration was ordered by a court of law, an outside agency, or entered into voluntarily by both parties, it is either *compulsory* or *voluntary*. Voluntary arbitration is quite rare.

☐ **THE ARBITRATION PROCESS**   In most jurisdictions the processes of arbitration and fact-finding are quite similar. The general process of arbitration involves the following *basic* sequence of steps, which may vary from situation to situation:

1. The bargaining teams request arbitration services jointly. These are usually provided by the employment relations agency of the state. Requesting arbitration will usually force both parties to agree to accept the contract provisions offered by the arbitrator when the law requires it. In some states, arbitration is automatically mandated when previous forms of third-party assistance fail.
2. The method of selection of arbitrators varies, depending on the state. Usually, however, the state agency provides the bargaining parties with lists of names of approved arbitrators, together with instructions to

eliminate names that they do not want involved in arbitration.

3. The selected arbitrator contacts each bargaining team and informs its spokespersons as to what information will be necessary at the initial hearing. The initial hearing is for purposes of
   a) Familiarizing both bargaining groups with the law related to arbitration.
   b) Familiarizing both bargaining groups with the criteria for awards.
   c) Entertaining opening presentations by both sides.
   d) Requesting rebuttals (sometimes) to the opening presentations made by each team.
4. In states where "final offer" arbitration is the law, the arbitrator will be required to choose the last best offer that he or she considers most reasonable, based on the presentations and evidence offered.
5. Awards made are sent to each bargaining party and to the state employment relations agency.
6. On issues not subject to arbitration, a contract is finalized and signed by both parties.

☐ **GENERAL OBSERVATIONS ABOUT ARBITRATION**   Currently, many disputes and unresolved aspects of arbitration are in debate in some quarters. One of the prime issues is the relationship of binding arbitration to public sector collective bargaining (Zachary 1976). Some hold that binding arbitration encourages resistance of teacher organizations to the resolution of differences through mediation or fact-finding (Dubel 1977).

Another issue still debated with fervor concerns the value of "final offer" arbitration, sometimes referred to as "binding fact-finding." Some factions prefer it while others—including many arbitrators—do not. The rationale for opposition to this procedure derives from the belief that while it rewards the most reasonable party, it seriously restricts the compromise-making role of the arbitrator.

Various well-known job actions, considered next, are discussed as strategy alternatives from the perspectives of administrators and teacher organizations.

☐ Strategy Alternatives

Job actions are strategy alternatives resorted to by teacher organizations when impasse resolution procedures provided by collective bargaining laws fail to yield hoped-for outcomes. At the present time, certain job actions are considered illegal.

At this period in the development of labor legislation in education, many impasse resolution provisions of collective bargaining appear ineffective in inducing the cooperation of the bargainers. Whether or not the law can force school boards to offer contracts to teacher organizations or prosecute them for legal violations remains to be seen.[1]

Job actions involve disruptions of service to one extent or the other. Examples of job actions are:

1. "Sick-outs," when teachers use sick leave or personal leave, in concert, on the same day so that the normal school day is disrupted
2. "Work-to-the-rule" actions, which are group refusals to perform any duties not specifically required by the contract
3. Boycotts of business establishments or other connections associated with school board members
4. Pickets of board members and/or school board meetings
5. Strikes

Such job actions vary in effectiveness. Their ability to achieve the desired ends of teacher organizations depends on several factors, such as:

1. Unanimity of teacher support
2. Support of other labor organizations within the school district
3. The time of the year
4. Direct impact on services to children
5. The power of the element of surprise
6. Public support established for teachers or school administrations

There are no ways to guarantee the success of job actions. Many factors outside the control of teacher organizations influence success or failure. Moreover, the legal charge of boards of education centers on protection of the rights of children, which forces school boards to attempt to keep schools open during job actions — irrespective of the rightness of the teacher organization cases that catalyze the job actions. Put another way, teacher organizations can often be made to look like they are against the best interests of children during job actions.

The ultimate job action is the strike, and it is not a desirable alternative. However, experiences in recent years indicate that many more teachers are willing to strike. Strikes by teachers are permitted in Hawaii, Oregon, and Pennsylvania, provided the exclusive bargaining organization calls the strike; impasse procedures have been tried; notice has been given of the intention to strike or after a certain number of days have gone by since fact-finding results were publicized; and school boards have had chances to petition the state public employment relations board.

---

1. In the case of the Modesto, California, Teachers Association versus the Modesto Board of Education the sequence of events, since teachers were ordered to cease their seven-day strike of March 4–12 1980 and return to teaching, is especially interesting (see *Modesto Bee*).

Strikes by teacher organizations are usually aimed at pressuring school boards by exposing the issues to community scrutiny. Teacher organizations hope to get the community support necessary to achieve their ends, even to the extent of stimulating recall movements against board members.

Before and during teacher strikes, boards of education usually: (1) adopt strike manuals as part of policy — an overt move to discourage and/or break the wills of strikers; (2) try to keep the schools in operation — success in doing so is a key weapon against the strike; (3) attempt to get court injunctions to end the strike; (4) exercise the penalties provided under state collective bargaining laws; (5) hire replacements (usually temporary) at highly competitive salary levels and increase substitute teacher pay to equally high levels, both tactics aimed at breaking the wills of striking teachers; and (6) intensify public relations activities to project the idea that schools are functioning normally, despite the strike.

☐ **ROLE OF BARGAINERS DURING AND AFTER STRIKES**   Once a strike is in progress, the efforts of bargainers of both sides should focus on: (1) publicity aimed at presenting (both) viewpoints to the educational community and the general public, (2) protecting the images of each side, and (3) maintaining communications with the other side, if possible.

After the strike, many — if not most — of the efforts of both sides must focus on repairing the damage done by the strike. Much of this damage is in the area of working relationships between striking and nonstriking teachers and striking teachers and administrators, especially at school sites.

If a new contract or a modified contract results from the strike, teacher-bargainers usually seek to incorporate *no-reprisal* provisions. Such provisions should contain stipulations that (1) teachers can return to their same jobs, (2) teachers and teacher-bargainers will be protected from retaliation by the board or administrators, (3) personnel files will not contain entries related to individual teacher participation in the strike, and (4) striking teachers close to retirement will receive credit for full service.

☐ Summary

Impasse is hiatus in bargaining because of the failure of bargaining parties to communicate effectively with each other. The issues, per se, are sometimes secondary reasons for impasse.

Provisions made for resolution of impasse in states with collective bargaining laws usually follow the sequence mediation, fact-finding, and arbitration. Time aspects and other specifics vary from state to state.

In all states the collective bargaining laws and their specific provisions for impasse resolution are aimed at circumventing various job actions by teacher organizations. The most feared—and destructive—job action of all is the strike.

Strikes are prohibited under collective bargaining laws of most states. Wherever they are legal, certain conditions must be met before teacher organizations can strike.

There are strategies and proper roles for bargainers in and during all phases of impasse resolution. Most roles center on cooperation with third-party neutrals and staying within legal boundaries.

□ **CHAPTER 12**

Contracts

ENERGY DEVOTED TO DEVELOPMENT and implementation of bargaining strategies and tactics is of utmost importance to both parties. However, that energy can be wasted without comparable attention to securing well-written contracts. Failure to do so is analogous to the situation wherein a hitter strokes a bases-loaded, two-out home run, fails to touch all the bases, and is called out by the umpire – nullifying all of the runs.

Put another way, it is counterproductive to mobilize and polarize the entire educational community of a school district and then fail to lock in the gains or changes because of a poorly written contract. This happens often in collective bargaining in public education. (There is evidence of dissatisfaction in this area, especially from principals, who contend that their roles are often constricted because of poor contract language. See National Association of Elementary School Principals 1982.)

Reading some teacher contracts as well as books on contract language developed by administrator and teacher organizations is informative. However, because of the limited purview of this book, the discussion on contracts will cover certain topics only.

Contract Language
Areas of Conflict in Contracts
Leave No Stones Unturned
Importance of Legal Help

□ Contract Language

Since the bargained contract is the primary basis of the working relationships between persons in the district, it should be well-executed to protect the interests of all. School boards and administrations interested in implementing management schemes (PPBS, MBO, and others), for example, should view properly executed bargained contracts as bases for enforcing such schemes; after all, it *is* possible to write bargained contracts that extract performance commitments from teaching professionals. While analogies to collective bargaining contracts in private sector bargaining should be made with care because of certain evaluation complexities, school boards are on solid ground when requiring such performance commitments in return for concessions made in bargaining. Similarly, well-written contracts with effective grievance procedures — coupled with competent, consistent monitoring of contract provisions by teacher organizations — can do much to guarantee pleasant working conditions for teachers. Both aspects, contract maintenance and grievance procedures, are discussed in Chapters 13 and 14 respectively.

Irrespective of the surface manifestations of conflicts in contract finalization, all differences can be traced to one true reason: power. It is to be expected that school boards will attempt to retain as much traditional power as possible by insisting on precise (nonphilosophical) language related to teacher prerogatives. At the same time, teacher organizations seek to expand their prerogatives and scope of bargaining through contract clauses and phrases that invite additional interpretations and permit new considerations. No end seems to be in sight; the conflict rages and it is likely to continue. In some instances it centers on organizational security; in others, wages and benefits are focal; and in some other circumstances, teacher job security over and above the provisions of state law is the area of conflict. (See Masters 1975.)

State collective bargaining laws vary especially in scope of bargaining. There are many aspects in which teachers have legitimate interests even when those aspects are excluded from scope. The class-size issue is a good example. Some states hold it to be strictly a management prerogative, but it is (logically) of paramount importance to teachers and their organizations — especially since the recent intensified parent and community demands for improved measurable achievement gains on standardized tests.

As collective bargaining laws vary from jurisdiction to jurisdiction, so do primary areas of conflict during contract finalization proceedings.

☐ Areas of Conflict in Contracts

For purposes of discussion, the areas of conflict described below are divided into two broad groups, teacher-initiated issues and board-initiated issues. The more common areas of disagreement are included.

☐ **TEACHER-INITIATED ISSUES**   *Agency shop.* Besides binding arbitration of rights disputes or grievances, this item is at the root of much of the conflict during contract finalization proceedings. Some state collective bargaining laws permit agency shop (see Chap. 8). Although union shop is permitted in one state, it is not permitted in others.

Thus agency shop is a matter for bargaining and its existence in a contract is the result of relative bargaining power. It is dear to teacher organizations because it can assure steady membership and organization income during the life of the bargained contract. It is often opposed by school boards and their administrations as unfair to individual teachers and difficult to enforce. Other administrators contend that all teachers should have the right to work without interference.

However, in the final analysis such administrator resistance to agency-shop provisions translate into powerful bargaining fodder in other areas of contracts. Teacher organization interests in agency shop forces concessions elsewhere – and great concessions they are.

Most agency-shop provisions advocated by teacher organizations are aimed at (1) automatic dues deductions for teacher organization members by the school district payroll office; (2) automatic deduction of equivalent fees for nonmembers under the rationale they are represented by the teacher organization nevertheless; (3) exclusions for nonmembers who object on religious or personal grounds, provided they pay equal amounts to tax-free, nonreligious, nonlabor organizations that are charitable. Apart from the direct organizational security aspects, such provisions are intended to have all teachers feel teacher organization presence, while making participation in other teacher organizations very costly.

It is to the advantage of administrator-bargainers to make agency-shop provisions very dear to teacher organizations during every bargaining session. This means the provisions must be bargained anew during each session. Even during the term of the contract, there are some management devices that are used primarily to force bargaining during the next contract period. One such device is a management requirement that *all* teachers fill out new payroll deduction authorizations at the start of each school year, even when the collective bargaining contract is a continuing one.

Binding arbitration. In most cases, primary teacher organization interest in binding arbitration centers on teacher or teacher organization rights disputes under existent contracts. Binding arbitration is usually limited to certain portions of bargained contracts, agreed upon by both parties.

Binding arbitration as a final resolution of grievances is dear to teacher organizations and – understandably – strongly opposed by boards of education and their administrators. The conflict results because of the power potential of binding arbitration in influencing contract interpretations and more importantly subsequent bargaining and contract interpretation.

One common variation on total binding arbitration is that of binding arbitration applicable to specified contract clauses. Such variations are usually offered in areas where boards of education do not perceive the potential for erosion of power. Binding arbitration is discussed in greater detail in Chapter 14.

Length of contracts. State laws vary as to the length of contracts. In the case of long-term or continuing contracts, teacher organizations attempt to bargain reopener clauses for specified items, usually salaries and fringe benefits. Administrators typically insist on great detail in reopener clauses to avoid vagueness that might generate a contract dispute or imply broader reopener options.

Negotiation of successor contracts. Teacher organizations attempt to establish time lines for bargaining next year's contract during present-year contract finalization procedures, especially in the absence of specified time lines in collective bargaining laws. Administrators often attempt to resist this with the rationale that the time lines for collective bargaining laws are implied by other deadlines that must be met.

Organization recognition. This is an extremely significant aspect of contract content. The rationale undergirding membership in employee organizations is that of community of interest; that is, collective bargaining laws seek to assure that persons in teacher organizations are strongly related to total teacher interests. Teacher organizations attempt to include as many job classifications as possible, for obvious reasons. As is to be expected, administrator-bargainers attempt to limit the types of job descriptions included in teacher organizations.

Areas of conflict center on contract language that includes certain quasi-supervisory positions in teacher organizations and contract language that includes certain noncertificated persons in teacher organizations whenever state bargaining laws do not exclude such noncertificated persons from teacher organizations. Collective bargaining laws usually provide for unit clarification when necessary.

Preambles. Preambles are written to introduce the bargained contract and set its tone. Teacher organizations try to insert statements that lend themselves to broad interpretations, like, "the members of the teaching profession are uniquely qualified to advise their school boards in the formulation of educational policies and standards." Administrators resist such clauses and phrases. Their basic resistance comes from the interpretations possible in grievance proceedings or courts of law.

Provisions contingent on increased revenues. Logically, teacher organizations attempt to protect their interests in the event of additional monies that might accrue to a district. The usual strategy is contract wording that forces school boards to reopen bargaining on those new monies in excess of those on which the present contract is based. Administrations will counter this with fully-bargained clauses seeking to close the contract so that no considerations of new revenues are permitted.

Grievance procedures. These are hotly contested issues during contract finalization proceedings. (See Chapter 14). The basic conflict during finalization of grievance procedures centers on power; that is, properly developed grievance procedures provide teacher organizations with the most effective device of all for protection of teachers during regular workdays and workweeks. Conflicts arise from several aspects of grievance procedures: (1) conditions that constitute a grievance, (2) time limits, (3) steps in grievance procedures, and (4) the extent to which arbitrated grievances should be binding on the board.

Statutory savings clauses. These simple statements put forth by teacher-bargainers seek to make sure the contract is not interpreted to mean that any provisions cancel provisions of the law. These clauses are intended to guarantee that the rights bargained in the contract are (at least) over and above those provided by law; that if the provisions of law offer more than the specific contract provision, those legal provisions are applicable.

Rights of the teacher organization. Teacher-initiated provisions under this heading are those that seek to strengthen the ability of the organization to do its job of protecting teachers and strengthening their individual and collective abilities to teach. These provisions protect teacher organizations. Some provisions of this type are:

1. Full access to information necessary for protection of the interests of teachers

2. Use of school buildings for organizational meetings

3. Released time of organization representatives for bargaining, grievance hearings, or other related activities

4. Use of facilities, including mail boxes, offices, bulletin boards, and school equipment

Orientation programs for new teachers. Teacher organizations must recruit new members constantly. The best way is organization-sponsored orientation programs. Administrations sometimes counter with carefully worded no-solicitation provisions that make recruitment of the new teachers (through other than private avenues) a violation of the contract.

No-subcontracting provisions. Such provisions seek to bar boards of education from subcontracting educational services with private firms or other groups that could (would) compete with teachers. Specifically, these provisions seek to require teacher organization approval before boards enter into contractual relationships with outside vendors for actual teaching services within school districts. Administrations try to resist such no-subcontracting provisions by citing precedent showing the success of external subcontracting of educational programs elsewhere; holding that external subcontracting is a board prerogative; and documenting organized support for external subcontracting from community groups, especially minority groups concerned with measurable achievement in categorical programs like Chapter I.

Teaching load and teaching hours. Teacher-advocated provisions in this broad area are procedures for "clocking-in"; starting time; leaving time; lunch periods; preparation periods; extra-pay provisions; total time; mandatory meetings, including general faculty meetings; and field trips. Of these, the **most** controversial have been preparation periods, especially elementary preparation periods; extra-pay provisions; and the number of mandatory meetings per month.

School year calendar. Conflict between teacher organizations and administrators centers on misinterpretations of teacher prerogatives and management rights. Many administrators contend that the calendar should not be negotiated. On the other hand, there are many reasons why teachers should be involved to the fullest extent possible. An example is a calendar modification for minimum days wherein teacher in-service sessions are conducted in the areas of human relations or school community relations. How could such events be successful without teacher participation in planning?

Class size. Teacher organizations attempt to specify class-size maximums in every type of class in the school district. These maximums are determined by teacher-pupil ratios for the district as a whole, with variations in weighting for selected kinds of classes. Weights given are directly proportional to the kinds of problems anticipated, thereby reducing class sizes for situations where there are several students who pose management or teaching problems for teachers.

In states where class size is within the scope of bargaining, administrators often counter with counterproposals that:

1. Permit latitude in anticipation of declining enrollments
2. Permit latitude in meeting special needs of certain experimental projects
3. Exclude matters related to class size from grievance procedures

Staffing. Teacher organizations have a vested interest in the number of specialists (guidance counselors, reading specialists, nurses, and others) provided by the school district. For this reason they make proposals that insure minimum numbers of such specialists. These proposals are often resisted by administrators in the name of one consideration, administrative flexibility.

Substitute teachers are a special staffing category. Usually, teacher organizations attempt to influence certification of substitutes, coverage (substitutes for all certificated positions instead of merely for classroom teachers), and pay rates for substitutes.

Nonteaching tasks. Teacher contracts vary with respect to the amount of attention paid to nonteaching duties. This is an area traditionally used as bargaining fodder by teacher organizations. Some items in this broad category are group curriculum preparation activities, secretarial support for nonteaching tasks, teachers transporting students, and supervision of certain student events.

Administrators tend to seek as much latitude as possible in this broad area, so that board prerogatives are preserved. Administrators attempt contract language that stresses past practice and incorporates "such activities as may be determined by the board" into the basic job descriptions of many teachers.

Conditions of teacher employment. These contract provisions advocated by teacher organizations seek to protect teachers in certain vital areas. Administrators attempt to resist them with the rationale that they are management rights. Some of these concerns are:

1. That all teachers hired shall be credentialled by the state
2. That noncertificated personnel are not permitted to replace teachers even when state education codes permit
3. That placement on the salary schedule meets certain conditions, like adequate credit given for prior experience and credit given for service in special organizations or overseas
4. That contracts with individual teachers are issued by a certain date, detailing as many specifics as possible

Salaries and fringe benefits. These are pay considerations. The following basic provisions are usually sought by teacher organizations:

1. Basic salary statements, including salary schedules
2. Cost-of-living provisions, including how differences will be paid
3. Adult school pay
4. Summer session pay
5. Additional compensation rates for teachers who hold higher degrees or their equivalents
6. Longevity increments
7. Terminal leave payments
8. Hourly pay rates for short-term teachers
9. Salary schedule adjustments for in-service training or college and university postgraduate training
10. Transportation allowances for teachers when appropriate
11. Pay for unused sick leave for retiring teachers
12. Pay allowances for military service

Teacher assignments. This area is almost always in dispute. Many administrators (and certain collective bargaining laws) hold teacher assignment to be a management right; however, certain aspects are clearly of concern to teacher organizations. These areas are adequate notice of the assignment, negative impact on teachers required to travel between schools, and changes in schedules and class assignments.

Teacher transfers and reassignments: voluntary. Teacher organization interests in voluntary teacher transfer policy are:

1. Methods and dates for posting assignments
2. Dates of notification of teachers
3. Methods of applying for vacancies
4. Methods of requesting transfers when no vacancies are posted
5. Publication of information on transfers
6. Methods of determining placements together with justifications
7. The role of teacher seniority in determining placements, along with situations when seniority is not used
8. Methods of resolving transfer conflicts

Administrator-bargainers tend to resist teacher organization prerogatives in voluntary transfer policy, despite the fact that this broad area is in the scope of some collective bargaining laws. This resistance reflects their desire to retain flexibility for their school boards. Usually, administrators attempt to retain flexibility by including contract phrases like "in the best interests of the district as determined by the board of education." Also, these administrators will generally seek provisions (through counterproposals) giving them alternatives in the event of changing needs.

Teacher transfers and reassignments: involuntary. This is a sensitive area in contracts, primarily because of the stance taken by teacher organizations against capricious, arbitrary transfers. Teacher transfer policy is of keen interest to teacher organizations when monitoring the implementation of bargained contracts.

Teacher organizations usually attempt to include certain clauses in involuntary teacher transfer policy. They are:

1. Notice of impending transfer, including:
   a) Adequate documentation of reasons, together with evidence that administrators involved have exhausted alternatives in helping the teacher adjust to the present teaching assignment
   b) Ample notice time
2. Criteria for involuntary (administrator-initiated) transfer designed to prevent (or make extremely difficult) arbitrary, capricious actions by the administrator in charge
3. Appeal provisions, including detailed steps and time lines
4. Reassignment priority
5. Preeminence of voluntary transfers over involuntary when appropriate and feasible

As in the case of voluntary transfers, administrator-bargainers usually attempt to retain their flexibility to the fullest extent possible. They generally counter with clauses like "when dictated by special program needs" or "when unusual circumstances mandate." These phrases are typically coupled with "in the best interests of the district" and "as determined by the board of education."

Promotions. Since many collective bargaining laws preclude membership of administrators in teacher organizations, teacher positions that represent promotions are quite limited. They are usually quasi-administrative in the areas of curriculum development, community liaison, or leadership of aspects of special categorical programs. These positions typically pay a salary differential. Teacher-bargainers usually try to include the following safeguards in bargained promotion policy:

1. Date of posting, with particular attention to:
   a) Notices posted in schools
   b) Dates posted ahead of selection date
   c) Notice to the teacher organization
   d) Provisions for waiver of application dates under unusual circumstances
   e) Procedures for notifying teachers during the summer or when they are on leave
2. Application procedures
3. Details of the notices
   a) Qualifications for the position
   b) Duties
   c) Rate of pay
   d) Where the job will be performed
   e) Selection procedures to be used
4. Methods of announcements of appointments
5. Preference to teachers currently employed, when this is not in violation of law

Promotion policy is another sensitive topic when closing contracts. This is due in part to certain external pressures (Affirmative Action programs, for example) on school districts and a natural tendency of administrators to retain as much arbitrary latitude as possible.

"Notice" provisions do not usually generate problems. Rather, problems are encountered over preferences given to teachers currently employed, changes in qualifications during the time openings are posted, and withdrawals of postings.

Faculty councils. These are on-site committees of teachers, organized for teacher input into decision making and policy development about improvement of the daily work life of all teachers. Teacher-bargainers attempt to include the following dimensions in such policy:

1. A general statement of the purpose of the councils
2. Methods by which the councils will be selected
3. The relationship of the councils to principals' decision-making prerogatives
4. Dates by which councils will be selected
5. Frequency of meetings
6. Selection of chairpersons
7. Size of the councils
8. Term of office of the members
9. Methods of operation of faculty councils

Sensitivity in this area of contract talks derives from administrators' perceptions of faculty councils as groups that have the potential of encroaching on the principals' decision-making prerogatives. Also, many administrators see faculty councils as potential arenas for "mini-negotiations" (school-site bargaining), setting precedents that in turn influence district master contracts:

Teacher protection. This area involves considerations related to the physical safety of teachers while performing their duties. At times, teachers—even elementary teachers—are vulnerable to physical attack by students, parents, or outsiders. While the law provides for protection of teachers, it does not always detail the specific actions to be taken by school administrators. Teacher organizations often seek additional protections and avenues for redress that exceed those provided by law.

There are some specific protections that teacher organizations attempt to include in comprehensive contracts:

1. Permission (to individual teachers) to use reasonable force for self-protection while retaining the legal protection of the school board
2. Legal protection paid by the school board when the teacher has acted prudently and according to district administrative bulletins
3. Reimbursement for losses incurred during the assault, including damaged clothing, lost pay, artifacts, and damage to automobiles
4. Costs of medical, surgical, and hospital services incurred
5. Tort liability coverage for all teachers in amounts adequate to protect them from loss due to civil suits against them in connection with their employment

Supervision of student teachers. Teacher organizations usually take the position that since student teachers have direct impact on the daily work life of teachers, teacher participation in the formulation of policy on the use and deployment of student teachers is justifiable. Such teacher organizations generally attempt to:

1. Define the amount of teaching experience necessary before a teacher supervises a student teacher

2. Make student teacher supervision strictly voluntary

3. Provide for released time for student teacher supervisors to meet with university or college supervisors

4. Limit the extra assignments imposed on student teacher supervisors

5. Require well-defined responsibilities for student teacher supervisors

6. Insure that all materials and supplies are adequate

7. Preclude use of student teachers as substitute teachers under all circumstances

8. Insure adequate background information on prospective student teachers for use by the supervising teacher

9. Require adequate orientation for all parties involved

Discipline of students. Because it is closely related to previously discussed teacher protection interests, teacher organizations are concerned about student discipline. These teacher organizations typically seek contract provisions to improve student discipline policy through clarification and to specify the responsibilities of administrators, coordinators, and other supervisory and quasi-supervisory personnel. These contract provisions also attempt to force supervisory personnel to react to discipline problems when teachers so request.

Specifically, such provisions:

1. Clarify the specific job descriptions of all supervisory personnel in the area of discipline
2. Make the teachers' request the *only* necessary requirement for:
   a) Professional attention of the principal, vice-principal, counselor, psychologist, or other appropriate person centered on the problem student
   b) A conference between all professionals involved to solve the problem
3. Give teachers the authority to suspend students for a certain number of days, with additional authority to refuse class admittance to the student until a conference is held with parents and other appropriate professionals

Personal and academic freedom. These are contract provisions aimed at giving additional protection to teachers in their jobs. Basically, such provisions seek to insulate teachers from intimidation on the basis of the *personal* life-style(s) of individual teachers when such life-styles are not related to classroom effectiveness and discipline or discrimination on the basis of political or religious activities that do not violate laws.

☐ **OTHER TEACHER-INITIATED ISSUES** There are many other areas of conflict in contract closure. Many are items introduced by teacher organizations for the express purpose of creating "trade-off" possibilities; others are genuine but future goals of teacher organizations; still others are aimed at publicity for the teacher organization.

The issues deserve brief mention. *Just cause provisions* are protections for teachers over and above those guaranteed by the education codes of the state, insurance against arbitrary or capricious dismissals for both tenured and nontenured teachers. *Teacher criticism* provisions are protections against open or public embarrassment of teachers by parents or students on school-related matters. *Teacher organization prvileges and rights* are those designed to insure the functioning of teacher organizations within school districts without interference, including (1) use of school buildings, (2) access to district information necessary for bargaining, (3) use of school equipment, (4) mail facilities, (5) bulletin boards, (6) office space, and (7) released time for certain teacher organization officials. *Parent complaint* provisions are those seeking to protect the teacher's dignity against parent complaints, justified or not. They usually require immediate notification of the complaint, confrontation with the irate parent, and a hearing before the board of education before action can be taken against the teacher. *Teacher facilities* provisions seek to define the conditions of employment in a physical sense, including classroom equipment, rest rooms, communications systems, closet space, parking facilities, special clothing when necessary, and others. *Maternity leave* provisions seek protections for pregnant teachers by defining the conditions under which they must leave and return to work after the pregnancy. Some have sought maternity leave with pay for teacher members, but there are no widespread trends toward acceptance to the pay provision.

☐ **ADMINISTRATOR-INITIATED ISSUES** There are some issues that are likely to be introduced by administrators during contract finalization talks. As representatives of school boards, administrators tend to introduce issues that seek teacher organization commitment to the primary charge of those school boards: keeping schools open and operating effectively. Other administrator-initiated issues are oriented to limiting the breadth of teacher-initiated issues by making specific their provisions and rewriting issues which seem too philosophical and "loose."

Specifically, administrators tend to seek the following provisions in bargained contracts:

1. Clauses seeking teacher organization commitments against strikes, sickouts, or slowdowns
2. Protections against teacher organization endorsements of candidates for local school boards

3. Commitments that the teacher organization will support teacher attendance and participation in open houses, parent nights, and other related activities without additional compensation
4. Teacher organization support and activity in the passage of district bonding elections, tax overrides, and other activities related to the financial base of the school district
5. Teacher organization help in getting state school support bills through the legislature
6. Commitments that the teacher organization will encourage its members to attend and participate in necessary in-service workshops
7. Commitments that the teacher organization will
   a) Seek to build a district image of constructive service to the children of the community
   b) Try to develop public support for the district
8. Commitment that the teacher organization will attempt to help the district solve personnel problems as they arise and keep grievances as low-keyed as possible
9. Commitment that building representatives of teacher organizations will be removed from their positions if and when it is established the representative is attempting to generate conflict and without reason
10. Clauses that assure
    a) School district right to waive seniority provisions in justifiable circumstances
    b) District right to schedule after-school–parent-teacher conferences
    c) Teacher organization encouragement of teacher responsibilities in maintenance of pupil records; supervision of halls, playgrounds, bus loading, lunchrooms, etc.; preparation by teachers of instructional materials, study assignments and lesson plans; advising student clubs, supervising field trips, monitoring and supervising school events, etc.; and supervising student teachers

Certain other administrator-initiated issues are often woven throughout the language of collective bargaining contracts.

Academic freedom. This type of administrator effort is designed to restate certain teacher-initiated items on academic freedom to include board prerogatives for dismissal or removal of teachers who fail to meet the criteria of continuity in the educational process, material commensurate with the maturity level of the students, and consistency with the goals of the curriculum. Such counterefforts also seek to restate the legality that responsibility for the curriculum is with the superintendent and discourage indoctrination of students by teachers who use the academic freedom argument to defend their challenged actions.

Management rights. This is essentially a "savings" item on behalf of boards and their administrations. Management rights clauses restate the power of boards to control and direct their school districts. Basic contract language in such provisions depends on phrases like "rights of determination of the school board" of the "best interest" of school districts. Management rights clauses may be found in any contract area.

Publicity. Contract language proposals concerning publicity, introduced by administrators, often try to control the conditions under which publicity about bargained contracts or the bargaining process is released. Such provisions usually hold that neither the teacher organization nor the administration will speak to the press relative to the bargained contract or parties will always issue joint press releases. An added provision concerning the bargaining period for the next year is often sought. Such a provision would force both parties to issue statements to the press that "no progress has been made," "satisfactory progress has been made," or "no comment."

Fully bargained provisions. These provisions in contracts state there will be no additional issues bargained, whether they are bargainable or not under the collective bargaining laws of the state. Such provisions have the effect of locking up the contract, except for categorical (usually salary-related) reopener clauses.

☐ Leave No Stones Unturned

In the interest of covering everything important in bargained contracts, both administrator-bargainers and teacher-bargainers should use "example agreements" or "model agreements" produced by their respective statewide organizations. Although many of these documents repeat certain provisions of state codes (items that are already law), it is in the best interests of bargainers to wade through these duplications so that nothing is overlooked. Usually, such model agreements are consistent with the collective bargaining laws of the state, but they should not discourage hiring an attorney.

☐ Importance of Legal help

Bargainers of both sides should make sure they have access to an attorney with experience in labor law. Indeed, it would be better to have one familiar with the legalities of collective bargaining in education as well as case law in this broad area.

Administrators usually rely on the advice of competent jurisdictional counsel (county or city attorneys). However, under certain circumstances these administrators find it advantageous to consult lawyers steeped in labor law — specifically, public sector bargaining law.

☐ Summary

Bargained contracts should be executed with extreme care. Such care is equally important to both sides of the bargaining endeavor.

There are many potential areas of conflict during contract finalization proceedings. Some of these are teacher-initiated and others are administrator-initiated. In both instances, conflict derives from interest in the acquisition and retention of power.

Typical teacher efforts during contract finalization proceedings focus on issues like organization recognition, negotiation of successor contracts, contingencies for increased revenues, grievance procedures, statutory savings clauses, teacher organization rights, orientation programs for new teachers, no-subcontracting provisions, teaching load, teaching hours, school calendar, class size, staffing patterns, conditions of teacher employment, nonteaching tasks, salaries and fringe benefits, teacher assignments, teacher transfers, promotions, teacher safety, student discipline, academic freedom, and others. On the other hand, administrators tend to focus their efforts on restatement of management rights clauses, no-strike provisions, publicity release conditions, fully bargained provisions, and generally those aspects that make the language of the contract more specific. Understandably, administrators strive to reduce the amount of broad, philosophical language in bargained contracts.

It is a good idea for both sides to engage attorneys to write and edit the final contract. This requires several meetings by both sides for clarifying intentions. Following those meetings, both bargainers — school boards and teacher organizations — adopt the final contract.

PART 5

Making the Contract Work

CHAPTER 13

Contract Administration

PROPERLY WRITTEN CONTRACTS ensure advantages for both school administrations and teacher organizations. But contracts are mere paper entities unless they are implemented properly. Implementation of contract provisions is the responsibility of both parties to collective bargaining in public education.

This chapter is devoted to some of the prime aspects of contract maintenance. It involves these topics:

Significance of Contract Administration
Some Areas of Conflict in Contract Administration
School Administrators and "Building Units"
Past Practice and Contract Administration

□ Significance of Contract Administration

Contract administration involves the processes of interpretation, implementation, and enforcement of collective bargaining agreements. It is the means by which the objectives of the contractual relationship are fulfilled. To that extent, it is as important as the entire bargaining process that yielded the contract.

Since grievance procedures are the means by which contract violations are monitored, it is possible that a certain number of alleged violations could be decided by arbitrators in either binding or advisory arbitration proceedings. After arbitration, it is likely that many of the contract interpretations issued by the arbitrator will establish certain practices that in turn will become bases for future bargaining. For this primary reason, neither side should be negligent in administering the aspects of bargained contracts for which they are responsible.

Both school administrations and teacher organizations should:

1. Have a central authority for ensuring uniform interpretations of contract items

2. Remember that contract administration relates only to the bargained contract and not to all issues within the bargaining scope

3. Publish the contract and provide copies for all employees if at all possible

4. Give copies of the contract to news media and community groups

5. Avoid establishing practices contrary to or inconsistent with the contract

Conflicts will arise in contract implementation because both parties tend to interpret contracts to their respective advantages. Thus it is in the best interests of each side to maintain ongoing liaison with the other in a good faith effort to minimize confusion in contract interpretation, although errors in contract interpretation sometimes operate as devices for effective future bargaining for teacher organizations. Also, such errors help teacher organizations to maintain presence at school sites and develop bases for grievances.

☐ Some Areas of Conflict in Contract Administration

Many conflicts in contract administration at school sites develop because of the impact of the strict language of the contract on the leadership style of the principal, and subsequently, the relationship between the principal and the teachers. Principals contend that collective bargaining contracts have changed the role of the principal from that of a maker of decisions to an interpreter of decisions. (Some principals hold that collective bargaining contracts tend to (1) stifle personality-based leadership, (2) project a flunky image of the principal, (3) stifle innovation, and (4) shift teacher loyalty from the school to the teacher union. See National Association of Elementary School Principals 1982.)

Generally, the prime areas of conflict in school site contract management are:

1. Class size provisions that limit the flexibility of principals
2. Rigidly contracted duty hours for teachers
3. Classroom discipline
4. Changes from the previous bargained contract for which no in-service training has been provided for teachers or principals
5. Inconsistencies in administration
6. Changes in school policy that affect teachers

Obviously, some conflict is generated by the presence of union representatives at the school site. Such conflict derives from:

1. Teacher organization needs for visibility because of rival teacher organization membership at the school site

2. Teacher organization tendencies to test the language of newly bargained contracts

3. Teacher organization "grieve it" campaigns, aimed at generating advantages in the upcoming bargaining sessions

Much, if not most, contract interpretation conflict occurs at school sites; there are definite ways of minimizing this conflict.

□ School Site Administrators and Building Units

"Building units," "local units," or "building representatives" of teacher organizations have as their basic function the ongoing liaison between teaching staffs and principals on all matters related to bargained contracts. These units vary in makeup, ranging from those composed of several teacher organization members with one member as spokesperson to one representative. No matter how they are organized, building units serve as resources for teachers in implementing their bargained contracts.

The intent and spirit of a collective bargaining contract is always focused on enhancing professional relationships at school sites. Consequently, representatives of both sides should strive to maintain positive working relationships rather than hostile, suspicious ones. Damaged professional relationships can have negative effects on children.

Principals have vested interests in the proper execution of bargained contracts for several reasons: (1) pressures from superiors aimed at avoiding grievances, (2) maintenance of effective working relationships with teachers, and (3) sustaining teacher accountability. At stake is the total climate of the school.

It may be argued that teacher organizations have a much greater stake in contract administration. Contract violations form bases for grievances by teachers. Grievances, taken to arbitration, can bring contract advantages for teacher organizations when arbitration awards result. Or, even when arbitration is advisory only, the findings of arbitrators tend to influence bargaining in subsequent sessions.

One more teacher organization interest in contract maintenance deserves separate discussion. Besides creating bargaining advantages and contract gains, barrages of grievances have the effect of establishing and maintaining teacher organization presence and power as perceived by teachers.

□ **MAINTAINING THE CONTRACT**   The basic relationship of the building representative and the principal should be cordial if possible. But that relationship should not be so relaxed as to permit gaps in the implementation of the bargained contract.

Good working relationships cannot be overvalued. Although there are constant pressures on principals for proper implementation of bargained contracts, they should remember that teachers' confidence in school administrators is a consideration that should transcend bargained contracts.

Principals should

1. Familiarize themselves with every aspect of their district collective bargaining contract
2. Make sincere efforts to implement every aspect of contracts in a fair, impartial manner
3. Be friendly but firm in implementing contract terms at the school site
4. Seek clarification from appropriate district administrators when confused about contract terms
5. Keep appropriate district administrators informed of all attempts to conform to and/or exceed the provisions of the contract
6. Inform teachers and other employees of their rights to present grievances for adjustment *without* the intervention of the building representative
7. Allow building representatives and other teacher organization representatives to have reasonable (or agreed-upon) access to
   a) Bulletin boards
   b) Mail boxes
   c) Rooms for meetings consistent with terms of the agreement
   d) Means of communication when reasonable
   e) Employee work areas consistent with terms of the agreement
8. Know and respect grievance procedures, executing them to the fullest when required to do so

Principals should not

1. Impose or threaten to impose reprisals on any employee
2. Attempt to bargain or negotiate at the school site
3. Convey the impression of opposition to collective bargaining or to any individual associated with the teacher organization
4. Let themselves be intimidated by overzealous teacher organization representatives
5. Be afraid to take disciplinary action because of the existence of a collective bargaining agreement
6. Circumvent or abandon school standards to enhance personal popularity or avoid confrontation
7. Be arbitrary, capricious, or discriminatory
8. Resolve any grievance

a) In a manner that is inconsistent with the terms of the contract
b) Until the teacher organization is fully informed and has a chance to respond
c) Without informing appropriate district administrators

All administrators in school districts should be responsible for detailed knowledge of bargained contracts. This is accomplished best in most school districts through regular in-service meetings focused on contract administration. Other administrators have specific contract administration responsibilities. Examples are:

1. Central administrators who plan and direct teacher activities in curriculum development
2. Field-based administrators (attendance supervisors, parent-community liaison administrators, and others) who work with teachers regularly
3. Administrators responsible for executing higher level grievance procedures

Building representatives are responsible for teacher advocacy (within the framework of the bargained contract) at school sites. They are also obligated to give teachers accurate contract information. Although their basic roles are liaison and information, there are times when they are likely to be quite aggressive in relationships at school sites.

Teacher organizations launch "grieve it" campaigns at certain times. Such campaigns are calculated to establish teacher organization presence in the minds of teachers and create bargaining advantages in subsequent bargaining periods.

But building representatives must protect their individual images as well as those of their teacher organizations. Many principals have the support of most of their staff members; unless building representatives are careful they can find themselves on the losing side of faculty opinions.

Building representatives should

1. Never allow meetings with principals to be casual or nonregular
2. Never get angry in open meetings; the respect of teachers is at stake
3. Always create the impression of their availability to teachers, even for tiny, seemingly insignificant details
4. Always follow-up on the concerns of every teacher
5. Treat nonunion teachers with respect
6. Avoid appearances of badgering principals
7. Be helpful and cooperative in school duties; a role of building representative should not conflict with the role of teacher

8. Verify an alleged contract violation before proceeding with grievances or other actions

9. Treat grievances and other complaints as confidential matters

☐ Past Practice and Contract Administration

Written contracts are documents signed by representatives of both parties to collective bargaining. Despite the best intentions of both, it is impossible to include every clause and/or phrase that will capture all possible situations in the day-to-day public education context. Even when situations are anticipated by the bargainers, certain aspects of those situations will not be.

Many daily occurrences in school operation can cause frictions between persons who implement contracts and those subject to their terms. Such differences of opinion often result in grievances, many ending in arbitration.

When there is no contract terminology to cover a situation, the arbitrator's job is difficult because they attempt to interpret contract language as it appears the parties meant it at the time the contract was signed. Left with no contract language, arbitrators often rely on past practice between the parties as a criterion of contract intent.

For persons of both sides concerned with writing effective contracts, custom and past practice are major aspects of employer-employee relations. Custom and past practice provide the basis of behaviors related to matters not included in written contracts. Both aspects often lend themselves to the interpretation of ambiguous contract language during arbitration or in courts of law. Moreover, these aspects may indicate that otherwise clear language in a contract has been informally (either intentionally or unintentionally) changed by the mutual action or agreement of the parties to the contract.

There are implications here for bargainers of both sides. For teacher-bargainers, it means that desired new practices must be specifically written into the contract in unambiguous language. For administrator-bargainers, it means current practices in every imaginable area must be reviewed before finalizing contract language, so that current unsatisfactory practices are written out and satisfactory ones are not.

☐ Summary

Proper contract maintenance or implementation of bargained contracts is as important as the entire collective bargaining procedure. Teacher organizations should prepare teachers at school sites and other locations to insist on proper execution of every contract provision. When contract provisions are violated, teachers should be encouraged to exercise their rights to grievance proceedings. Similarly, all administrators should be versed in the details of bargained contracts in their districts to avoid or minimize grievances by teachers. For both sides, in-service sessions on the details of bargained contracts are useful.

Principals must respect all provisions of bargained contracts. Similarly, principals should be cautioned about the importance of maintaining good working relationships with building representatives of teacher organizations.

Administrator-bargainers and teacher-bargainers responsible for contract finalization must understand the importance of custom and past practice if and when grievances are taken to arbitration. Custom and past practice are relied upon heavily by arbitrators when attempting to interpret the intentions of the parties to the contract. Bargainers must make sure that current practices not included in contract language are those they can live with. Similarly, undesirable practices must be written out of the contract with clear, nonambiguous language.

☐ **C H A P T E R   1 4**

Resolution of Grievances

EFFECTIVE CONTRACTS can be nullified quite easily if both sides are lax about monitoring the implementation of those contracts. The prime avenue of redress for those who believe their contractual rights have been violated is the grievance mechanism built into bargained contracts.

Although there is a tendency for school administrators to view grievance procedures as time-consuming encumbrances that interfere with the orderly operation of schools, such a viewpoint should be discouraged. Whether used or not, the mere existence of grievance procedures can enhance the overall confidence of teachers in the significance of their roles in school districts. And the fact that grievance procedures were seldom resorted to during the school year serves as a silent signal that school operation was satisfactory as far as the bargained contract was concerned.

This chapter is devoted to discussion of grievance resolution. Its topics are:

Grievances Defined
Grievance Procedures
Grievance Arbitration
Grievance Resolution: Strategies and Tactics

☐ Grievances Defined

Grievances are complaints based on alleged violations of bargained contracts. Specifically, grievances are expressions of dissatisfaction of parties to contracts about the employment aspects governed by the contracts under which they work. Put another way: in education bargaining, grievances are formal complaints based on teacher and staff beliefs that the terms of the bargained contracts have been violated.

Bargained contracts cannot and do not cover every aspect of school district operation. Some aspects are not even mentioned in bargained contracts. Grievances, then, are based on issues that are the subjects of bargained contracts. Dissatisfaction arising out of aspects not based on the bargained contract are complaints. Put another way, all grievances are complaints, but not all complaints are grievances.

The distinction between complaints and grievances is important to bargainers of both sides. Grievances defined strictly on the basis of the bargained contract excludes many complaints that may be closely related to the substance and content of bargained issues. Grievances defined broadly can include just about every aspect of employment. Thus great care must be taken to define grievances during contract finalization procedures.

Even though specific definitions found in bargained contracts often omit it, definitions of grievances imply the condition of adverse effect on the grievant. Some school districts incorporate this condition into the language of the contract and others do not (Ostrander 1981, 9–12).

Some districts operate two systems, one for processing simple complaints not related to bargained contracts and another for handling formal grievances based on the specifics of bargained contracts. The processing of simple complaints will vary from district to district, from informal procedures to formal procedures. However, grievance resolution is a more sophisticated process, dependent on the procedures set forth in the bargained contract.

□ Grievance Procedures

Grievance procedures in public education bargaining relationships vary according to several factors, among them the size of the school district, the degree of informality possible between the bargaining parties, and — perhaps most important — the prior grievance experiences between the parties. In initial contracts, however, size of the school district appears to be the prime determinant of grievance procedures.

Most grievance procedures are formal, consisting of a point of origin, steps of appeal, and methods for final resolution as outlined in the bargaining agreement. Often both teacher organizations and school district representatives prepare manuals for handling grievances by the building representative and principal respectively.

Informal procedures — encouraged by the language of the contract to remove the reason for the grievance — are very important. Generally, the aggrieved teacher and the building representative discuss the grievance with the principal. If it is not answered satisfactorily, the formal, contractual grievance procedure is resorted to.

The coverage of the grievance procedure may be limited by specific designations in the contract. Certain topics may be excluded from the grievance procedure or the grievance procedure may be confined to such topics as stipulated in the contract. This situation, perhaps more common in education bargaining, is the typical one and is called a *closed* grievance procedure. The rarer situation, wherein there are no limitations on what may be grieved, is called an *open* grievance procedure.

Essentially, all grievance procedures are composed of three parts. First, the grievance is initiated at the teacher-principal level. Second, appeals through one or more steps are taken to top management of the school district. Third, appeals to arbitration are settled by an impartial umpire—the arbitrator—whose decisions may be advisory or binding, according to contract language that in turn must be within the framework of the jurisdiction's education bargaining laws.

Some contracts incorporate five-level grievance procedures. Usually these procedures involve two additional steps: (1) an intermediate-level supervisor, a step between Level I and Level II described above; and (2) with the school board, a step between Levels II and III described above. In five-level as well as three-level grievance procedures, typical contracts require that the process must move to the next higher level if no decision is rendered after the passage of a specified number of days or if the employee is not satisfied with the decision.

Figure 14.1 offers three typical grievance procedures in terms of the personnel involved. Representations of school district size associated with each procedure are very general; that is, in any specific instance steps may be fewer or more.

The advisory arbitration model in Fig. 14.1 is a variation on the other

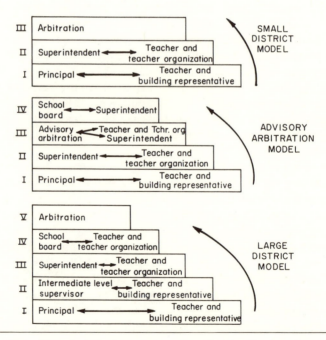

14.1.   Three typical grievance procedures in education bargaining.

two. It is sometimes used in collective bargaining agreements without binding arbitration. In such cases the third step, advisory or nonbinding arbitration, is followed by an appeal by the superintendent of schools to the school board when the superintendent wishes to challenge an advisory arbitration finding. If the superintendent fails to appeal such an advisory finding after the passage of a specified number of days, the superintendent is (usually) required to implement the arbitrator's decision.

Typically, collective bargaining agreements stipulate that individuals may represent themselves or be represented by their organizations. Group grievances are those alleging the issue(s) in question affects an entire class of employees, which has the effect of making school district policy the essential focus of the grievance(s).

Understandably, many teacher organizations attempt to encourage group grievances, while administrators attempt to control group grievances by (1) reserving the right to separate grievances placed by two or more individuals through a good faith contention that those grievances involve substantively different considerations; and (2) limiting the number of grievances that can be filed by the teacher organization during a given school year or during the contract period.

While grievance procedures may vary considerably from jurisdiction to jurisdiction, certain aspects should be incorporated into written contracts.

☐ **CRITERIA FOR EFFECTIVE GRIEVANCE PROCEDURES**   Bargainers of both sides should examine collective bargaining contracts from other sources to avoid omitting aspects that may fit their particular needs. Also, they should attempt to incorporate the following qualitative aspects into their grievance procedures. Generally, grievance procedures should:

1. Encourage problem-solving behavior
2. Involve progressively higher levels of authority
3. Be governed by a theme of fairness
4. Have a rationale based on employee confidence and morale
5. Be based on contract violations only
6. Lend themselves to resolution at lowest possible levels when possible
7. Contribute to better knowledge of district regulations and policies
8. Result in specific remedies

Since collective bargaining contracts are developed jointly by teacher organizations and school administrators, they involve two vastly different viewpoints. Such viewpoints often result in variations in interpretation of contract language. The role of grievance arbitration is, in large part, reduction of the ambiguity of contract language (Ostrander 1981, 12).

☐ Grievance Arbitration

Grievance arbitration is a third-party mechanism for settlement of contract disputes outside of courts of law. It is known as "rights" arbitration and is based on the details of bargained contracts.

Arbitration takes place after all previous steps of the grievance procedure have been adhered to and there is no solution satisfactory to both parties to the contract. Grievance procedures usually end up in arbitration because of conflicts in (1) contract interpretations, (2) contradictions between two or more items in a contract, (3) contract silence on certain issues, and (4) changed conditions to which the contract may not apply directly.

Specifically, grievance arbitration is a process whereby a third-party neutral is employed to settle a dispute between two parties to a bargained contract. It is a quasi-judicial proceeding and is designed to result in an award based on the findings of the neutral third party after a comprehensive review of the case. In nonbinding arbitration, the result of such comprehensive review is simply an advisory decision made by the arbitrator to the school board involved.

Various aspects of grievance arbitration, including arbitrability, purposes of arbitration, selection of arbitrators, criteria for arbitration awards, and arbitration procedures should be examined. Intended here is an overview of the process. (For a detailed analysis see References.)

☐ **ARBITRABILITY**   Arbitrability refers to whether a matter should be subject to arbitration. Questions of arbitrability arise because of allegations that the arbitrator has no jurisdiction over a dispute between a teachers' association and a school board because of the letter of the contract or because grievance procedures have not been utilized properly. In most cases, school boards raise questions of arbitrability before the substantive merits of the grievances are examined by the arbitrators.

Whenever both parties are unable to agree to let the arbitrator decide the arbitrability of a matter, the courts are resorted to. These courts decide such matters by issuing injunctions against arbitration in some instances or ordering it in others. On occasion the courts will ask the chosen arbitrators to decide arbitrability. The rationale for this derives from the simplest logic, that the arbitration procedure is (already) established voluntarily by both parties (Zack 1974, 2).

> The theory for granting the arbitrator jurisdiction over the question of arbitrability is that this issue is itself a dispute between the parties to be resolved through the procedure voluntarily established by them.

Questions of arbitrability are usually on substantive or procedural grounds. Substantive questions derive from the contention that the matter is outside the authority of the arbitrator. Procedural questions are based on the allegation that the grievance machinery has not been adhered to. Arbitrability is assumed unless one of the two parties to the contract challenges it. Such a challenge requires proof by the challenger.

Arbitrators involved in questions of arbitrability are usually involved in subsequent grievance arbitration. This happens because both parties recognize the tremendous expense involved in getting a new arbitrator for the case itself. Also, the familiarity of the arbitrator with the case tends to reduce the costs of the case. Arbitration costs play a large role in the tactics of grievance resolution.

□ **ARBITRATION COSTS**   As with arbitration itself, the costs of arbitration are bargainable. Various arrangements are possible, ranging from equally divided costs to costs paid by the "losing" party.

Arbitration costs are significant in a tactical sense. Administrator-bargainers are aware that grievances taken to arbitration can result in bargaining advantages for teacher organizations in upcoming sessions, irrespective of whether the grievance arbitration is advisory or binding. They also acknowledge that arbitration costs are more difficult for a small teacher organization to absorb. For this reason some administrators push for arbitration when the outcomes promise relatively little for teachers and their organizations and when the finances of teacher organizations are such that prolonged arbitration and its associated costs might be difficult to handle.

□ **PURPOSES OF ARBITRATION**   Arbitration is intended to avoid work stoppages and other disruptions related to conflict over a contract. This is the prime purpose, of course, but there are other reasons rooted in long-range teacher strategy. These are discussed later in this chapter.

Another important purpose of arbitration is contract interpretation. During contract finalization, it is possible for two parties to use the same language and mean entirely different things. Arbitration provides an important test of the meaning of contract provisions in such instances.

□ **ARBITRATORS AND THEIR SELECTION**   An arbitrator is a third-party neutral who is acceptable to both sides. This individual is retained to resolve contract-related conflicts. Because of this, bargainers of both sides should make certain that contract language includes details about the method of selecting arbitrators. Both sides should be familiar with criteria for evaluating competent arbitrators.

Arbitration proceedings may be presided over by individual arbitrators or a board of arbitrators. Individual arbitrators may be ad hoc or permanent. Ad hoc arbitrators are hired by both parties for one case. Permanent arbitrators are individuals usually named in collective bargaining agreements as persons who will hear all cases during the term of the contract. As with individual arbitrators, arbitration boards may be ad hoc or permanent. They are composed of two or four persons, with one or two persons selected by each side. Decisions arrived at by such boards are by majority vote.

When arbitrators are not named in contracts, they may be selected after agreement by both parties by contacting and applying to various associations of arbitrators at state or national levels. They may also be selected from local sources.

Arbitrators should be steeped in collective bargaining laws and have reputations for impartiality in legal matters. Many organizations of school administrators and teachers maintain dossiers on all arbitrators who operate in their states. Such dossiers give relevant information on the backgrounds and arbitration "track records" of these individuals.

Ad hoc arbitrators are resorted to in the absence of contract provisions that designate permanent arbitrators. While in some cases the contract language will limit ad hoc arbitrators to hearing only one case at a time, in other situations they will hear a number of grievances at one session. The primary disadvantage of ad hoc arbitrators is that one side or the other might lack confidence in them. Thus bargainers should be thoroughly familiar with the personal backgrounds and awards records of arbitrators.

Permanent arbitrators are those whose names are written into bargained contracts, meaning that both sides have confidence in them. For this reason, grievance arbitration involving permanent arbitrators is likely to proceed smoothly. Other advantages of permanent arbitrators are:

1. Time savings from elimination of the necessity of selecting arbitrators on a case-by-case basis
2. Both parties are sensitive to and aware of the style of the permanent arbitrator
3. Permanent arbitrators provide decision-making continuity, helping to reduce the number of future conflicts on contract items
4. Permanent arbitrators tend to discourage weaker grievances because both parties know the arbitrator's previous positions on related items
5. Permanent arbitrators are familiar with the intergroup dynamics between the two parties
6. Certain time savings result from elimination of discussions of backgrounds of some issues

There are some disadvantages to permanent arbitrators. They are:

1. The permanent status of an arbitrator tends to invite more issues for arbitration because of lower relative cost
2. Both sides are committed to the philosophies of one arbitrator for the duration of the contract, possibly stifling other creative approaches to problem-solving

Qualifications of arbitrators. There are no specific qualifications for arbitrators in terms of academic preparation or legal requirements. The only requirement is that both parties are willing to be bound by the decisions of a given individual whenever binding arbitration is the case. Even when arbitration is advisory only, the meaningful criterion for the arbitrator involved is the respect of both sides.

For teacher-bargainers and administrator-bargainers, two qualities should be foremost in the selection of arbitrators. Those qualities are overall experience in the field of collective bargaining in education and previous satisfactory experiences with an arbitrator reported by their appropriate statewide or national organizations.

There is no sure method of guaranteeing a favorable arbitrator. By their very nature, successful arbitrators have withstood scrutiny that has helped to establish their reputations as impartial individuals. This does not mean that arbitrators fail to mirror certain philosophies. They do. Both sides should determine those philosophies by studying the awards handed down by certain arbitrators over a period of years to get a feeling for what can be expected from them. Arbitrators are guided by certain criteria in formulating awards and decisions.

□ **CRITERIA FOR ARBITRATION AWARDS**   Generally, arbitrators issue their written decisions together with supporting rationale after all the evidence is in. Written opinions are extremely important because the rationale undergirding various decisions tends to spill over into other portions of collective bargaining contracts not being arbitrated. Put another way, the existence of written decisions can discourage other grievances that may be capricious. More importantly, the rationale used by the arbitrator establishes that the decision was arrived at judiciously. This helps to maintain the confidence of both parties in the process.

Arbitrators vary in the way they analyze and weigh evidence and testimony. While it is hard to understand the relative merits of criteria used by arbitrators in determining awards, some primary considerations are:

1. The specifics of the contract and the intentions of both parties at the time the contract was signed
2. Fact as distinguished from hearsay
3. Motives of witnesses and plausibility of their allegations
4. Contradictory testimony by several witnesses
5. Prior experiences of both parties with contract items under consideration
6. School district practices that appear contradictory to other related contract items
7. Contract language of other agreements between school boards and other employee organizations in similar or the same areas of interest

8. Contract ambiguities, in which case arbitrators attempt to (Ostrander 1981, 5):
    a. Base awards on contract language as written, established by facts revealed at the hearing
    b. Draw on past practices of the parties to the agreement
    c. Base awards on good general practice
    d. Use precedents established by other arbitrators, courts or federal regulatory agencies
    e. Establish a standard of his or her own
9. Previous arbitration awards in the same contract category
10. Past operational relationships between the school board and teacher organization(s)
11. Previous problems encountered by both sides in adapting contracts to practice

Both bargaining parties should understand that arbitrators' awards are not primarily oriented to what is right, wrong, or fair; rather, these awards are based on arbitrators' opinions of contract language and intent as they relate to evidence and testimony presented at grievance arbitration hearings. Of equal importance is that the awards are influenced in some measure by the limits of the powers of the arbitrators; that is, arbitrators *may not* embrace considerations not specifically authorized. This means that neither party to bargaining should expect substantial modifications or alterations of the basic contract to result from any one arbitration proceeding.

☐ **TYPICAL ARBITRATION PROCEDURES**   Actual arbitration procedures will vary somewhat from situation to situation and jurisdiction to jurisdiction. However, there is a *basic* sequence of steps in the process.

1. Making the decision to arbitrate
2. Selection of the arbitrator
3. Preparation for the hearing
4. The hearing
5. The award

Both aspects, the decision to arbitrate and selection of the arbitrator, have been discussed. Following are brief accounts of preparation for the hearing, the hearing, and the award.

Preparation for the hearing. Both bargaining parties should make every effort to agree as to the issues to be arbitrated as well as the sequence involved. This requires meetings prior to arbitration. Such meetings can serve two purposes: (1) when specific issues to be arbitrated can be decided upon in advance, the result can be a significant saving in arbitration costs; and (2) the process of deciding issues to be arbitrated provides a last chance to resolve each issue short of arbitration.

Data collection is another essential prehearing step. While both sides should have data supporting their respective positions on the matter to be arbitrated, teacher organizations must also present evidence that the grievance was justified and no redress was offered to the aggrieved teacher. Administrator-bargainers are responsible for data that contradicts both points.

Generally, both sides should include the following data in preparation for arbitration hearings:

1. All reports and statements of witnesses to the incident that prompted the grievance.

2. The reports or testimony of other persons (doctors, police officers, firemen, teacher aides) should be collected, organized, and analyzed. One key is consistency or inconsistency of testimony, depending on viewpoint. When certain individuals are unable to attend hearings, sworn affidavits should be taken.

3. The minutes of all meetings, proposals, and counterproposals should be available to both sides and sequenced in an order that permits ready interpretation.

4. Organization charts, work rules, job descriptions, medical records, police records, teacher attendance records, and any other supporting data related to the grievance should be on hand.

5. A prior record of the selected arbitrator on similar issues should be developed so that each party to the grievance proceedings can anticipate the style and other characteristics of the arbitrator.

6. Analyses of statements of witnesses should be performed in the interest of eliminating ineffective ones. It is sometimes best to have a smaller number of consistent, noncontradictory witnesses.

Perhaps the primary task prior to the hearing is preparation of the argument. Teacher organizations must support charges and defend them while administrators must defend against the charges. Arguments should be pointed, without extraneous aspects unless those aspects can be related to the main argument. Moreover, those arguments must be based on the collective bargaining contract, or, whenever appropriate, past practice. The argument should state the requested remedy.

The hearing. Arbitrators vary about the formality they demand during the hearing. After introductions, most arbitrators will explain the sequence of events that follow. The basic sequence is like that of a civil trial: agreement on the boundaries of the issue being arbitrated, opening statements, examination and cross-examination of witnesses, and closing arguments. The arbitrator usually asks for the sequence of appearances for witnesses introduced by both sides. If there has been considerable tension between parties (and attendant poor communication), the arbitrator will sometimes insist on greater formality in the proceedings.

The party that took the first action toward arbitration (the teacher organization, usually) begins presentations first. Once an order is established, it holds throughout the hearing until time for closing arguments. Closing arguments are offered in reverse order so that the party who opened the hearing has the last word.

Opening statements are optional. The arbitrator will not usually insist on opening statements, although it is best for each side to offer them unless doing so might reveal some argument strategy. From the standpoint of teacher organizations, opening statements offer excellent opportunities to establish the rationale(s) for the grievance, especially when the grievance is based on alleged contract misinterpretations.

The manner in which evidence is displayed will vary from one arbitration proceeding to the next. Arbitrators usually let the parties decide whether oaths should be administered to witnesses. Such oaths are often waived if both parties agree.

As is the case in courtroom proceedings, witnesses are first examined directly by the party that took the first action toward arbitraton, followed by cross-examination of that same witness by the opposing party. Cross-examination is basically restricted to *content* surfaced during direct examination of the witness. A second opportunity for direct examination of the witness is then extended by the arbitrator. This is followed by a second opportunity for cross-examination of the same witness. This process is repeated until both spokespersons (or counsel) feel that the witness has nothing more to offer. The next witness is introduced and questioned in the same manner.

After all witnesses for the first party have been examined and cross-examined, the second (opposing) party is given an opportunity to make an opening statement if none was given at the start of the proceeding. After the statement, the direct-examination–cross-examination procedure described above proceeds for witnesses introduced by the second (opposing) party.

Exhibits may be introduced at the start of the proceedings or separately as various witnesses are introduced. When there is an objection to the introduction of an exhibit as evidence, the arbitrator rules on admissibility.

Arguments may be oral or written, depending on the preferences of each side. Written arguments are more time-consuming. Oral arguments are more common than written ones.

The content of closing arguments centers on points each party believes support its case. Often cited in argument by one side or the other are (1) contract items and language; (2) exhibits; (3) sworn testimony of witnesses (especially police officers, firemen, and other public servants); (4) instances of contradictions between witnesses for the opposing side; (5) previous arbitration awards in similar situations; and (6) evidence of established past practice.

The arbitrator sometimes asks for posthearing briefs prior to the award. These are usually submitted within a specified time after the hearing and are designed to show each party's separate interpretations. Each party sends copies to the arbitrator and exchanges copies. The content of posthearing briefs is limited to the content of the case under arbitration; that is, new material not subjected to direct and cross-examination cannot be introduced.

The award (or advisory decision). The award of the arbitrator must be rendered within thirty days in most instances. The nature of the award or advisory decision is limited by the terms of the contract between the parties. It is also limited by the remedy specifically requested by the aggrieved party. Awards may contain recommendations by the arbitrator, but these may be rejected in part or whole by the parties.

☐ Grievance Resolution: Strategies and Tactics

Generally, teacher organizations seek to expand the scope of collective bargaining and school administrators attempt to narrow scope. Apart from specific grievances, these behaviors of the two bargaining parties are at the core of grievances and their resolution. The two sections which follow explain some of the major strategies and tactics involved in grievance resolution.

☐ **ADMINISTRATOR STRATEGIES AND TACTICS IN GRIEVANCE RESOLUTION**   There are certain positions and attitudes typically taken by administrators about grievance resolution procedures. These attitudes are apparent most often during contract finalization proceedings, in which administrators attempt certain tactics, described below.

Limitations on definitions of grievances. Administrators prefer limiting definitions of grievances to violations of collective bargaining contracts. This excludes simple complaints from definitions of grievances.

Time limitations for processing grievances. Understandably, administrators attempt to get as much time as possible for processing grievances. Also, additional time tends to encourage alternate solutions.

Individual versus group grievances. Administrators prefer individual grievances. They attempt to reserve the right to utilize their good faith efforts to separate grievances that are not related to the same basic consideration and limit by contract the number of grievances teacher organizations may introduce during the term of the contract.

Number of steps in the grievance process. Administrators prefer to have grievance procedures match the steps in the chain of command of the school administration (chain of supervision within the school district). This lengthens the grievance process and exposes the aggrieved teacher to more supervisory persons who have the chance to influence a change of heart by the teacher.

Binding arbitration. Generally, administrators are against binding arbitration for resolution of grievances. This attitude can be traced to positions taken by their school boards: many, if not most, school boards see binding arbitration as a device for encroaching on their policy-making prerogatives; that is, these board members view the binding arbitration process as one that permits an outsider (the arbitrator) to make future policy through the device of an arbitration award. Understandably, many of these board members view agreement to binding arbitration as (essentially) abdication of the charge given them by the voters.

Even when administrators and their boards reluctantly agree to binding arbitration, they usually seek to limit it to certain contract clauses and exclude others. These administrator attitudes carry implications for teacher organization strategy and tactics related to grievance resolution.

□ **TEACHER ORGANIZATION STRATEGIES AND TACTICS IN GRIEVANCE RESOLUTION**   The primary purpose of grievance procedures in collective bargaining agreements is ongoing monitoring of contract implementation. While the grievance mechanism provides a long-range strategy for broadening teacher prerogatives in bargained relationships, no strategy should sacrifice that primary purpose.

Ongoing teacher organization strategy typically seeks to expand the definitions of grievances. As these definitions are expanded or broadened, so are the arenas into which teachers may (possibly) bargain because awards favorable to teacher grievants often translate into new contract interpretations.

Consequently, teacher organization interest in grievance procedures centers on the possibility of such procedures reaching the arbitration stage. Although the award provided by the arbitrator is limited by the submission terms of the parties, the remedy sought by the aggrieved teacher, and the general terms of the contract, the award can and does often influence subsequent bargaining. Findings of arbitrators in previous arbitration proceedings are in the minds of bargainers as they formulate proposals and counterproposals. While not always the case, teacher-bargainers will find administrator-bargainers more receptive to proposals that are somewhat consistent with decisions of arbitrators. Put another way, it is easier to plow through new turf if an arbitrator has opened the way already; the teacher-grievant who was dismissed unfairly and subsequently reinstated by an arbitrator paves the way for future teacher-grievants.

The foregoing encourages two primary tactics related to the use of grievance machinery as a long-range strategic tool to increase teacher organization power within school districts. Those two tactics are "grieve it" campaigns and "arbitrate anyway" tactics.

"Grieve it" campaigns. These are drives by teacher organizations to alert

teachers to the necessity of ongoing contract monitoring as well as the long-range strategy described in the preceding paragraphs. Such grieve it campaigns should not be capricious, retaliatory efforts launched during contract bargaining periods because teacher organizations risk public credibility and support when it appears that a serious collective bargaining mechanism provided by law is being exploited and such campaigns during bargaining periods can make other bargaining activity by teacher organizations appear insincere. Grieve it campaigns should be carefully planned. Certain points must be stressed to teacher members during such campaigns, such as:

1. Teachers should have no reservations about using grievance procedures because they are permitted by collective bargaining laws for teacher protection
2. Grievance procedures should be aimed at policies and procedures, not people and personalities
3. Teachers should request a specific remedy based on a specific contract violation
4. Grievances should be resolved at lowest possible levels

When contracts call for binding arbitration of grievances, teacher organizations sometimes attempt to reserve the right to consider the merits of individual teacher grievances. The concern of teacher organizations in such instances is whether advancement of such grievances to arbitration will enhance the overall bargaining position of the teacher organization in the future.

From the perspective of teacher organizations, the decision to arbitrate is wise even when arbitration is advisory only. For example, in many urban areas private sector collective bargaining and widespread unionization is the rule rather than the exception. In such areas, arbitration — binding or advisory — can focus pressure on school administrations and their boards.

"Arbitrate anyway" tactics. The alternate possibilities of winning or losing awards are not the only considerations that must be taken into account by teacher organizations when deciding whether to arbitrate. There are times when those organizations must push for arbitration even when they are certain to lose. Examples of such situations are:

1. When failure to submit the matter to arbitration would threaten the overall confidence of teachers in the grievance process
2. When the arbitration procedure would put school administrators on notice about contract maintenance
3. When teacher organizations need greater visibility because of smaller, competing teacher organizations in the same district

However, most decisions to arbitrate are rooted in the possibility of winning arbitration awards. Some considerations in this regard are:

1. Whether the evidence will be strong enough to win the award

2. Whether the costs of arbitration are justified by the possible economic and political gains involved

3. Whether the spillover from the award will have positive impact on other contract-related items in the next bargaining period

4. Whether the won-lost record of the teacher organization in arbitration can withstand additional losses

☐ Summary

Grievances are contract-related disputes. Grievance procedures incorporated into bargained contracts are designed to provide monitoring of contract violations. Basically, these procedures are designed for resolution at lowest possible levels.

Grievance procedures vary from school district to school district as to the number of steps and the time limits for each step. The most common procedure is the three-level one.

When grievance procedures at lower levels are exhausted, the alternative is arbitration. Arbitration may be binding or advisory, depending on the collective bargaining contract. Whether arbitration is binding or not must be stipulated in the contract because most collective bargaining laws permit binding arbitration with the consent of both parties to the agreement.

Arbitration is a quasi-judicial process wherein a reputable third-party neutral is hired to decide on the merits of the case and render an award or an advisory decision. The purpose of arbitration is circumventing work stoppages and other job actions. However, there are subtler, more powerful long-range reasons for arbitration from the standpoint of teacher organizations.

The primary interest of teacher organizations in arbitration centers on (1) proper contract monitoring, (2) expansion of prerogatives under the present contract, and (3) creating certain advantages in bargaining during the next bargaining period. Because of this, teacher organizations often launch grieve it campaigns aimed at intensifying grievances, any or all of which have the possibility of resolution through arbitration. Even when arbitration is advisory only, many of the possibilities above still exist.

Administrators attempt to protect the powers of their boards through various means. They attempt to (1) limit the definitions of grievances in collective bargaining contracts, (2) extend time limitations for processing grievances, (3) resist group grievances by separating them when possible, (4) limit by contract the number of grievances that teacher organizations may introduce, and (5) oppose binding arbitration outright or limit it to certain contract items.

CHAPTER 15

A Futuristic Note

THE RELATIVE YOUTH of collective bargaining in public education has been a recurrent theme in this book. This newness of the field continues to influence certain events. But other events, external to public education bargaining, are likely to alter the very nature of the bargaining encounter.

Unfortunately perhaps, teacher organizations have operated on the basis of raw power, with little apparent awareness of the impact of public opinion. But it is likely that external events will bring teacher power into head-on confrontation with public opinion in the very near future. And because of the power of the public to withhold support of tax-supported services, teachers will lose that confrontation.

These external events are the back-to-basics thrust by parents and their organizations, the protracted recession of the early eighties, and the taxpayer revolt as demonstrated by Proposition 13 in California and similar referenda in other states. The combination of these related events can strip much of the basic substance of collective bargaining, or force teacher organizations to yield many hard-to-come-by gains in return for softening the impact of administrator reduction-in-force decisions necessitated by severe fiscal limits and declining enrollments.

On the other hand, there is the likelihood of a positive turn of events on the immediate horizon. Several agencies are currently recommending reform in public education, with attendant recommendations of public support for public education. (See National Commission on Excellence in Education 1983 and Education Commission of the States 1982.) Responsible agencies with considerable national prestige are taking postures that could influence public thought in the direction of greater fiscal support for education. Whether such a reversal in public thought is in the offing remains to be seen (Gallup 1983, 36).

But if there is a general return to adequate funding for the public schools of America, many strings are likely to be attached to it—especially where better salaries and fringe benefits for education professionals are concerned. There is a strong possibility that future teacher bargaining will depend on the willingness and ability of teacher organizations to engage in productivity bargaining, with parent-influenced organizations monitoring the way productivity is defined.

Some writers hold that there is potential compatibility between accountability models like Planning, Programming, and Budgeting systems (PPBS) or management-by-objectives (MBO) and collective bargaining (see Hartley and Richards 1973). In any event, parent-dominated organizations are likely to insist on rigidly defined quantifiable achievement outcomes (for children) as a condition of teacher organization gains in collective bargaining. Despite many teacher organization protestations against quantifiable child achievement as the sine qua non of teacher evaluation, it is likely that back-to-basics adherents will have their say. And it *is* possible to make statistical adjustments that are fair to teachers subject to such evaluations.

This means it is in the best interests of education professionals — teachers and administrators alike — to adopt a spirit of compromise at the bargaining table. If not, public opinion is likely to mandate compromise, often, unfortunately, with simplistic approaches to accountability.

As for collective bargaining in public education in a general sense, there is evidence that certain basic options and tactics are changing. The strike as a weapon seems far more favorable to teachers. This is likely to catalyze more state laws that *require* arbitration of some kind. An alternate possibility, of course, is general public resentment of teacher strikes unless teacher organizations have presented the merits of their case(s) to the public in advance. In any case, the overall outcomes of job actions of any kind will be influenced in great measure by the overall public perception — a point that returns us to one of the central premises of this book, that public opinion is the ticket to successful bargaining.

One more significant trend deserves mention. The family-choice-in-education or "voucher plan" movement promises to temporarily — or permanently — disrupt the essence of collective bargaining. Although the movement is currently dormant, whenever and wherever it is activated there is the strong possibility that overnight entrepreneurs and quick-buck artists will start "schools" quickly, with promises of heightened achievement, while hiring poorly-qualified, low-salaried teachers to maximize profits. Whether voucher plans will become a reality in America remains to be seen.

All signs point to the reality that teacher organizations must modify their overall conceptions of and approaches to collective bargaining. Many aspects of the private sector model — especially certain "winner-take-all" dimensions — must be modified to accomodate compromise because of the developments mentioned above. The demonstrations of raw power by teacher organizations — the rule rather than the exception during the past decade — will have to be replaced by problem-solving approaches that put commensurate accountability on school administrations and teacher organizations alike.

GLOSSARY

COLLECTIVE BARGAINING is relatively new to public education. Because of its recency and unique language, some readers may benefit from an explanation of certain terms. Many definitions of collective bargaining terms are found in the literature of that subject. They vary considerably, according to whether the bargaining referred to is private sector, public sector in general, or public education in particular.

The definitions that follow are oriented to collective bargaining in public education, elementary and secondary levels. The Glossary contain a few new terms that define new developments or emerging trends in public education collective bargaining.

Agency: A political jurisdiction or controlling body, such as a school board or school district.

Agency shop: A provision in a collective bargaining agreement that requires teachers covered by the agreement who do not belong to the teacher organization with exclusive rights to pay a service fee to the organization nevertheless.

Arbitration: A method of settling disputes whereby both parties submit their positions and differences to a third party for a final decision that may or may not be binding. Arbitration may be advisory or compulsory, depending on whether the findings are nonbinding or binding and whether it was entered into voluntarily or by the order of a judicial body or law. Arbitration is used in two separate situations: in the resolution of impasse (interest arbitration) or in the resolution of grievances (rights arbitration).

Arbitrator: A neutal third party who awards a decision after reviewing the positions and differences of both sides in either interest or rights arbitration.

Authorization card: A card signed by an employee authorizing the soliciting organization to be her or his collective bargaining agent.

Bargaining agent: The organization legally recognized to represent employees in a bargaining unit.

Bargaining rights: A legally recognized right to represent employees in bargaining with employers.

Bargaining unit: This definition usually comes into play after a dispute about which employees belong in a certain bargaining organization. The decision is usually rendered by a third party after a hearing. Most laws on collective bargaining hold "community of interest" as the important criterion for determining who belongs in a certain bargaining unit.

Boycott: An effort by a teacher organization to discourage business with the employer with whom the teacher organization has a dispute. This is sometimes directed against a business operated or owned by a board member. When the boycott action is extended to another business doing business with the first, it becomes a *secondary* boycott.

Bumping: The practice wherein seniority operates to displace a junior teacher or other employee from a job during reduction in force or layoff.

Card check: This is a check of authorization cards.

Certification: Formal recognition by the state agency designated by collective bargaining laws of the organization selected by the majority of teachers in a supervised election. This formal recognition makes the organization selected the exclusive representative for all teachers in the bargaining unit.

Checkoff: An arrangement that authorizes the employer to deduct dues from the pay of teachers in the amount of teacher organization dues and assessments. The employer turns the proceeds over to the treasurer of the teacher organization.

Closed shop: A collective bargaining provision whereby all teachers must belong to the bargaining unit *before* they are hired. New teachers are hired through the teacher organization.

Collective bargaining: Execution of the legal requirement of both the school board and the exclusive representative of teachers to meet, confer, and bargain in good faith and to execute a written agreement incorporating agreements reached, except that under no circumstances is either party compelled to agree.

Collective bargaining contract: A formal, written agreement detailing all agreements reached between the school board and the exclusive representative of teachers.

Conciliation: The efforts of a third-party neutral aimed at finding compromise between opposite viewpoints in a labor dispute so that a voluntary settlement results.

Confidential employee: An employee who has access to information that could affect employee-employer relations in a school district. The superintendent's secretary is often a confidential employee.

Contract bar: The time period during which an existing agreement will bar a representation election sought by a competing teacher organization attempting to unseat the organization that has rights of exclusive representation.

Credited service: The years of employment counted toward retirement and seniority.

Crisis bargaining: Collective bargaining that occurs under the pressure of a strike deadline. The opposite of crisis bargaining is the more typical situation where there is ample time to discuss and review proposals and counterproposals.

Cross-check: A check by the public employment relations board (or other appropriate agency) of the employer's payroll to determine whether a teacher organization has a majority. This is sometimes done to certify an organization without going through formal hearings and elections.

Decertification: Withdrawal of organization status as exclusive bargaining unit after a vote by teachers that indicates that they no longer wish to be represented by that teacher organization.

Dispute: Any disagreement between school boards and teacher organizations that requires resolution.

Escalator clause: A provision in a collective bargaining agreement that salaries will be automatically increased periodically commensurate with some prespecified index or criterion. Criteria may be cost-of-living indices, other economic indicators, or salary standards in other school districts.

Exclusive bargaining rights: The right of the organization designated as exclusive representative to bargain collectively for all teachers, including nonmembers, in the bargaining unit.

Fact-finding: An impasse resolution procedure that involves analysis of all issues and facts germane to a dispute. Fact-finding may be performed by an individual or a panel and ends in recommendations for settlement of the dispute.

Final offer arbitration: Binding arbitration wherein the arbitrator is required to select the best of the last offers submitted by each party. This is sometimes called "last best offer" arbitration.

Fringe benefits: These are supplements to wages. They vary from school district to district, but they usually encompass items such as holidays, vacations, insurance, medical benefits, leaves, pensions given to teachers under their conditions of employment.

Good faith bargaining: The qualitative aspect of the bargaining that must take place under collective bargaining laws. Both parties are required to meet at reasonable times and to bargain in good faith on matters within the scope of bargaining, but neither party is forced to agree.

Grievance: An allegation by a teacher that a collective bargaining contract has been violated.

Grievance procedure: A plan specified in a collective bargaining agreement that provides for adjustment of grievances through successively higher levels of administrative authority. The procedure should end with resolution somewhere in the hierarchy; if not, the grievance procedure ends in (rights) arbitration.

Impasse: Failure of both parties to achieve agreement during bargaining, ending in stalemate.

Injunction: An order issued by a court to cease or perform a certain activity because the other party is liable to sustain irreparable injury from the (unlawful) activity.

Labor relations board: A quasi-judicial agency set up under the collective bargaining laws of certain states to adjudicate complaints that allege unfair labor practices, resolve unit determination disputes, certify bargaining agents, and in general monitor the implementation of collective bargaining laws.

Leave of absence: Time off without loss of seniority and with the right to reinstatement; permission to engage in teacher organization business on a full or part-time basis without pay by the school board.

Lockout: Closing down or limiting access of teachers to the schools during strikes or work stoppages.

Mainstreaming: A popular term referring to the legal requirements of Public Law 94-142, namely that handicapped students must be included in regular educational programs to the fullest extent possible, in the least restrictive environments possible.

Maintenance of membership clauses: Organizational security provisions in collective bargaining agreements requiring that teachers who are teacher organization members as of a certain date (or thereafter) remain members in good standing during the term of the contract as a condition of employment.

Management prerogatives: This refers to the right of the school board to make decisions and run the school district without consultation with, notification to, or bargaining with the teacher organization.

Management employee: An employee with significant responsibilities for formulating and administering school district programs.

Mediation: Intervention by a third party during impasse. It is usually nonbinding, noncompulsory, and is the first "tier" of the three-tiered impasse resolution machinery of most collective bargaining laws. The third party attempts to facilitate reconciliation of a dispute between teacher organizations and school boards.

Merit pay: A salary increase given to individual teachers on the basis of more effective teaching, however that criterion is defined.

Negotiating team: The teacher organization team or the school board team selected to negotiate a collective bargaining contract.

No-strike, no-lockout clause: A provision in a collective bargaining agreement in which the teacher organization agrees not to strike during the term of the agreement and the school board agrees that there will be no lockouts.

Open end agreement: A collective bargaining agreement with no specific termination date. Bargaining can be opened by either party at any time, provided the other party is given sufficient notice.

Package settlement: The total money value of a change in salaries and supplementary benefits bargained. Usually, a package settlement is an alternative to item-by-item bargaining on salary-related items.

Past practice clause: A provision in a collective bargaining agreement that seeks to maintain or retain those practices not specifically covered by the agreement but which have attained desirable status because of repeated use and acceptance.

Pattern bargaining: A practice through which teacher organizations and school boards base the collective bargaining agreements on those by other prominent or well-known organizations.

Petition for a representation election: A document filed with the state employment relations board stating that an organization has shown enough interest to meet the requirements for a representation election. State collective bargaining laws differ on how many members are necessary.

Recognition: An agreement by the school board to accept and treat a teacher organization as the collective bargaining agent for designated employees.

Reopener clause: A provision that requires reopening of bargaining of certain contract provisions at a certain time. Usually, those provisions must be modified periodically (wages, pension plans, and fringe benefits).

Representation election: A vote conducted by appropriate agencies to determine which organization in a school district will be selected by the teachers to serve as exclusive bargaining agent.

Rights dispute: A dispute about the interpretation of the provisions of an agreement or other school board rules and regulations.

Rights arbitration: Grievance arbitration.

Scab: A teacher who continues to work during a strike.

Scope of bargaining: The universe of issues included in collective bargaining procedures.

Seniority: The status of a teacher in relation to other teachers, with respect to determining order of promotion, lay-off, vacations, job preferences, and other considerations. Seniority is always based on longevity on the job. Seniority may be *districtwide* seniority, *school-site* seniority, or *qualified* seniority (permitting other factors as considerations which disrupt the order of straight seniority under certain circumstances).

Service fee: An assessment (dues) for all teachers in a bargaining unit to pay the costs of services rendered by the exclusive representative in bargaining and contract implementation.

Strike: A temporary stoppage of work by a group of teachers (not necessarily the teacher organization) for purposes of expressing grievances, enforcing demands for changes in employment conditions, obtaining recognition, or resolving a dispute with the school board. Strikes may be *"quickie"* strikes (spontaneous and unannounced), slowdowns (deliberate reductions of output), sympathy strikes (for support of other organizations), sit-down strikes (remaining on the job) or general strikes, which involve all teachers.

Strike authorization: A strike vote that gives teacher organization leaders the authority to call a strike.

Sunshine bargaining: Bargaining that involves the public, either as participants or observers of all aspects of bargaining.

Unfair practices: A school board or teacher organization practice forbidden by law.

Union security: Bargained contract clauses that require the establishment and maintenance of a union shop, agency shop, maintenance of membership, payroll deduction of teacher organization dues, or other similar provisions intended to guarantee the status of the teacher organization during the term of a collective bargaining agreement.

Unit: The organization consisting of all teachers entitled to select a single teacher organization to represent them in collective bargaining.

Zipper clause: A provision in a contract that precludes further bargaining during the life of a contract.

REFERENCES

Academic Collective Bargaining Information Service. 1977. *Special Report 25, Update: Scope of Collective Bargaining in 14 States.* Washington, D.C.: Academic Collective Bargaining Information Service.

Ackerly, Robert L., and Johnson, W. Stanfield. 1969. Critical Issues in Negotiations Legislation. Professional Negotiations Pamphlets 3. Washington: National Association of Secondary School Principals.

Adam, Roy. 1983. "The Future of Teacher Unions," *Comparative Education* 18(2):197–203.

Adams, Bert K.; Hill, Quentin M.; Lichtenberger, Allan R.; Perkins, Joseph A., Jr.; and Shaw, Philip S. 1967. *Principles of Public School Accounting.* State Educational Records and Reports Series Handbook II-B. Washington, D.C.: U.S. Government Printing Office.

Allen, David. 1977. *Fringe Benefits: The Not-So-Invisible Cost.* U.S., Educational Resources Information Center, ERIC Document ED 137 973.

Alutto, Joseph A., and Belasco, James. 1974. "Determinants of Attitudinal Militancy Among Nurses and Teachers." *Industrial and Labor Relations Review* 27 (2):216–27.

American Association of School Administrators. 1968. *The School Administrator and Negotiation.* Washington: The Association.

Andree, Robert G. 1972. *The Art of Negotiation.* Lexington, Mass.: D. C. Heath, Lexington Books.

Becker, Harry A. 1976. "Mechanisms for Resolving Collective Bargaining Impasses in Public Education." *Journal of Collective Negotiations* 5(4):319–29.

Benson, Gregory. 1979. *The Principal and Contract Management.* U.S., Educational Resources Information Center, ERIC Document Ed 175 151.

Berlo, David K. 1970. *The Process of Communication.* New York: Holt, Rinehart and Winston.

Blumberg, Arthur; Brannigan, Marilyn; and Nason, David. 1981. "Administrative Power and Collective Bargaining in the Schools." *Journal of Collective Negotiations* 10(4):327–35.

Borich, Gary D. 1977. *The Appraisal of Teaching: Concepts and Process.* Menlo Park, Calif.: Addison-Wesley.

Botan, Carl H., and Frey, Lawrence R. 1979. *Trust in the Union: The Effects of Affiliation and Gender on Message Reception.* U.S., Educational Resources Information Center, ERIC Document ED 175 129.

Bowen, David J., and Bogue, Bonnie G. 1980. "PERB: New Directives on Strikes, Post-Impasse Conduct." *California Public Employee Relations Magazine* (June).

Braun, Robert J. 1972. *Teachers and Power.* New York: Simon and Schuster.

Brooks, Richard S. 1975. "Seven Ways To Get Better Press for Your District." *American School Board Journal* 162(11):54.

Brown, Oliver. 1978. "Pages and Pages on How to Cut School Costs—Wisely." *American School Board Journal* 165(10):32–45.

Brown, Thomas A. 1975. "Have Collective Negotiations Increased Teachers' Salaries? A Comparison of Teachers' Salaries in States with and without Collective Bargaining Laws for Public School Personnel, 1961–1971." *Journal of Collective Negotiations* 4(1):53–65.

Byrnes, Joseph F. 1978. "Mediator-Generated Pressure Tactics." *Journal of Collective Negotiations* 7(2):103–9.

Cahen, Leonard, and Filby, Nikola N. 1979. "The Class Size/Achievement Issue: New Evidence and a Research Plan." *Phi Delta Kappan* 60(7).

Caldwell, William E., and Houser, M. Kenneth. 1978. *The Significance of Informal Bargaining Procedures to the Level of Collective Bargaining Conflict.* Paper presented at American Educational Research Association, March 27–31, 1978. Washington, D.C.: U.S. Department of Health, Education and Welfare, National Institute of Education.

Callahan, John J., and Wilken, William H., eds. 1976. *School Finance Reform: A Legislators' Handbook.* Washington, D.C.: National Conference of State Legislatures.

Carlton, Patrick W. 1967. *The Attitudes of Certificated Instructional Personnel Toward Professional Negotiations and Sanctions.* Bureau of Research, U.S. Office of Education, Department of Health, Education and Welfare, Project 6–8267. Washington, D.C.: U.S. Government Printing Office.

Carlton, Patrick, and Goodwin, Harold I., eds. 1969. *The Collective Dilemma: Negotiations in Education.* Worthington, Ohio: Jones.

Carlton, Patrick W., and Johnson, Richard T. 1979. "When Collective Negotiation Is Unconstitutional: Virginia Teachers View the Future." *Journal of Collective Negotiations.* 8(1):83–90.

Chambers, Jay G. 1976. *The Impact of Collective Bargaining for Teachers on Resource Allocation in Public School Districts.* U.S., Educational Resources Information Center, ERIC Document ED 123 719.

Cheng, Charles W. 1978. *Teacher Negotiations: Implications for Citizen Participation in the Schools and the Making of Educational Policy.* U.S., Educational Resources Information Center, ERIC Document ED 159 814.

Clark, R. Theodore, Jr. 1981. "Labor Relations in the Decade Ahead: A Management Perspective." *Journal of Law and Education* 10(3).

Cochran, George C. 1975. "If You Plan, Most Schools Can Operate during a Teacher Strike." *American School Board Journal.* 162(11):38–39.

Coombs, Philip H., and Hallak, Jacques. 1972. *Managing Educational Costs.* New York: Oxford Univ. Press.

Coons, John E.; Clune, William H. III; and Sugarman, Stephen D. 1970. *Private Wealth and Public Education.* Cambridge, Mass: Belknap Press of Harvard Univ. Press.

Counts, George S. 1927. *The Social Composition of Boards of Education.* Chicago: Univ. of Chicago Press.

Craft, James A. 1982. "Post-Recession Bargaining: Mutualism or Adversarial Relations?" *Labor Law Journal* (July).

Cresswell, Anthony M., and Murphy, Michael J., with Kerchner, Charles T. 1980. *Teachers, Unions, and Collective Bargaining in Public Education.* Berkeley: McCutchan.

Cronin, Joseph M., and Crocker, Julian D. 1969. "Principals Under Pressure." *Urban Review* 3(June):25, 34–37.

Cunningham, Luvern L. "Collective Negotiations and the Principalship." *Theory into Practice* 7(Apr.): 62–70.

_____. 1967. "Implications of Collective Negotiations for the Role of the Principal." In *Readings on Collective Negotiations in Public Education,* ed. Stanley Elam, Myron Lieberman, and Michael Moskow. Chicago: Rand McNally, 298–313.

Dahl, Robert A. 1961. *Who Governs? Democracy and Power in an American City.* New Haven: Yale Univ. Press.

Doherty, Robert E., and Oberer, Walter E. 1967. *Teachers, School Boards and Collective Bargaining: A Changing of the Guard.* Ithaca: New York State School of Industrial and Labor Relations.

Donley, Marshall O. 1977. *The Future of Teacher Power in America—Fastback 98.* Bloomington, Ind.: Phi Delta Kappa Educational Foundation.

Downey, Gregg W., and Mullins, Carolyn. 1976. "Where School Boards Do Everything—Even Bargain—in Full Public View." *American School Board Journal* 163(9):31–35.

Drucker, P. F. 1973. *Management.* New York: Harper and Row.

Dubel, Robert Y. 1977. *Mediation, Fact-Finding and Impasse.* U.S., Educational Resources Information Center, ERIC Document ED 137 970.

Dunlap, John F. 1978. "California's Chicken-Or-Egg Question: Statewide Union or Statewide Bargaining First?" *Phi Delta Kappan* 59(7):458–61.

Dunn, Frank, and Bailey, C. Thomas. 1973. "Identifiable Trends in Teacher Attitudes toward Collective Negotiations." *Journal of Collective Negotiations* 2(2):113–23.

Education Commission of the States. 1982. *Action for Excellence.* Denver: Education Commission of the States.

Educational Research Service. 1980. "Class Size Research: A Critique of Recent Meta-Analyses." *Phi Delta Kappan* 62(4).

Edwards, Clifford H., and Burnett, Keith R. 1970. "The Principal's Role in Negotiations." *Contemporary Education* 41(May):311–13.

Eisenhower, R. Warren. 1976. *Grievance Procedures.* U.S., Educational Resources Information Center, ERIC Document ED 123 774.

Elam, Stanley; Lieberman, Myron; and Moskow, Michael H. 1967. *Readings on Collective Negotiatons in Public Education.* Chicago: Rand McNally.

Epstein, Benjamin. 1969. *The Principal's Role in Collective Negotiations.* Professional Negotiations Pamphlets 1. Washington, D.C.: National Association of Secondary School Principals.

Evans, Max W.; Knox, Donald M.; and Wiedenman, Charles F. 1978. *Trends in Collective Bargaining in Public Education.* Seven Hills, Ohio: American Association of School Personnel Administrators.

Fay, Michael J. 1976. *Changing the Power Balance.* U.S., Educational Resources Information Center, ERIC Document ED 123 803.

Feyerherm, Ann E., and Muchinsky, Paul M. 1978. "Structural and Attitudinal Factors Related to Collective Negotiations in Public School Systems." *Journal of Collective Negotiations* 7(1):73–83.

Flango, Victor E. 1976. "The Impact of Collective Negotiations on Educational Policies." *Journal of Collective Negotiations* 5(2):133–55.

Fletcher, Richard K., Jr.; Brimm, Jack L.; Tollett, Daniel; and Stewart, O. C. 1976. *Tennessee Educators' Viewpoints Regarding Professional Negotiations.* U.S., Educational Resources Information Center, ERIC Document ED 144 233.

Flygare, Thomas J. 1977. *Collective Bargaining in the Public Schools—Fastback 99.* U.S., Educational Resources Information Center, ERIC Document ED 145 572.

Fratkin, S. 1975. "Collective Bargaining and Affirmative Action." *Journal of College and University Personnel Association* 26:53–62.

Fris, Joe. 1979. *Teachers' Attitudes toward the Use of Strikes, Mass Resignations,*

Arbitrators and So On. U.S., Educational Resources Information Center, ERIC Document ED 175 129.

Furniss, W. T. 1974. "Retrenchment, Layoff and Termination." *Educational Record* 55:159–70.

Gallup, George H. 1976. "Eighth Annual Gallup Poll of the Public's Attitudes toward the Public Schools." *Phi Delta Kappan* 58(2):191–98.

_____. 1980. "Twelfth Annual Gallup Poll of the Public's Attitudes toward the Public Schools." *Phi Delta Kappan* 62(1):33–46.

_____. 1982. "Fourteenth Annual Gallup Poll of the Public's Attitudes toward the Public Schools." *Phi Delta Kappan* 64(1):37–50.

_____. 1983. "The Fifteenth Annual Gallup Poll of the Public's Attitudes toward the Public Schools. *Phi Delta Kappan* 65(1):33–47.

Gilroy, Thomas P.; Sinicropi, Anthony V.; Stone, Franklin D.; and Ulrich, Theodore R. 1969. *Educator's Guide to Collective Negotiation.* Columbus: Charles E. Merrill.

Gibson, Thomas Q., and Ramos, Elias T. 1982. "Public School Teacher Attitudes toward Unionization." *Journal of Collective Negotiations* 11(2):145–53.

Gittell, Marilyn. 1969. "Urban School Reforms in the 70's." In *Confrontation at Ocean-Hill Brownsville,* ed. Maurice R. Berube and Marilyn Gittell. New York: Praeger, 327–34.

Glass, Gene V., and Smith, Mary Lee. 1978. *Meta-Analysis of Research on the Relationship of Class Size and Achievement.* The Class Size and Instruction Project, Leonard S. Cahen, principal investigator. San Francisco: Far West Laboratory for Educational Research and Development.

_____. 1979. *Relationship of Class Size to Classroom Processes, Teacher Satisfaction, and Pupil Affect: A Meta-Analysis.* The Class Size and Instruction Project, Leonard S. Cahen, principal investigator. San Francisco: Far West Laboratory for Educational Research and Development.

Glime, Raymond G. 1978. "How to Use Collective Bargaining to Increase Your Board's Authority." *American School Board Journal* 165(3):46–48.

Golladay, Mary A. 1976. *The Condition of Education, 1976 Edition.* Department of Health, Education and Welfare. Washington, D.C.: U.S. Government Printing Office.

Greenfield, Daniel. 1982. "Resist the Urge to Tie Teacher Salaries to the Consumer Price Index." *American School Board Journal,* July.

Hagburg, Eugene C. 1966. *Problems Confronting Union Organizations in Public Employment.* Columbus: Labor and Research Service, Ohio State University.

Haggart, Sue A. 1972. *Program Budgeting for School District Planning.* Educational Technology Publications. Englewood Cliffs, N.J.: Rand.

Hartley, Harry J., and Richards, James J. 1973. "Collective Negotiations with P.P.B.S.: An Accountability Model for Education." *Journal of Collective Negotiations* 2(2):147.

Haney, Walt, and Madaus, George F. 1978. "Making Sense of the Competency Testing Movement." *Harvard Educational Review* 48(4).

Hatch, Terrence E. 1971. "The Principal's Role in Collective Negotiations." *National Association of Secondary School Principals Bulletin* 55(359).

Hazard, William R. 1975. "Tenure Laws in Theory and Practice." *Phi Delta Kappan* 61(7):451–54.

_____. 1978. *Education and the Law.* New York: Free Press.

Hennessy, Mary L., and Warner, Kenneth O. 1967. *Public Management at the Bargaining Table.* Chicago: Public Personnel Association.

Hickcox, Edward S. 1967. *Power Structures, School Boards and Administrative Style.* U.S., Educational Resources Information Center, ERIC Document ED 012 510.

Hicks, Jean Lois Hefner. 1973. "An Attitudinal Study of Potential Areas of Conflict in Professional Schools Employee Negotiations in Kansas." Ph.D. diss., Kansas State Univ., Manhattan.

Higginbotham, Richard L. 1975. *Preparation for Bargaining: Negotiation and Administration of the Contract.* U.S., Educational Resources Information Center, ERIC Document ED 108 351.

Hill, Barbara Jane Fauskin. 1973. "An Analysis of Factors Associated with Grievance Binding Arbitration in the Public Schools and Possible Implications for California." Ph.D. diss., Univ. of Southern California, Los Angeles.

Hollander, E. P. 1958. "Conformity, Status and Idiosyncrasy Credit." *Psychological Review* 65(2).

Holley, William H., Jr.; Scerba, J. Boyd; and Rector, William. 1976. "Perceptions of the Role of the Principal in Professional Negotiations." *Journal of Collective Negotiations* 5(4):361–69.

Howe, Nancy J., and McCarthy, Harold. 1982. *Participative Management: A Practice for Meeting the Demands of the Eighties.* U.S., Educational Resources Information Center, ERIC Document ED 216 435.

Iannaccone, Laurence, and Lutz, Frank. 1970. *Politics, Power and Policy: The Governing of Local School Districts.* Columbus, Ohio: Merrill.

James, H. Thomas; Kelly, James A.; and Garms, Walter I. 1966. *Determinants of Educational Expenditures in Large Cities of the United States.* Stanford: School of Education.

James, Tom. 1976. "Teachers, State Politics and the Making of Educational Policy." *Phi Delta Kappan* 58(2):165–68.

Jensen, Vernon H. 1963. "The Process of Collective Bargaining and the Question of Its Obsolescence." *Industrial and Labor Review* (July):546–56.

Jones, William R., Jr. 1969. "Changes in Relationships among Various Segments of the Educational Community as They Relate to the Adoption of Collective Negotiation Agreements." Ph.D. diss., Univ. of Colorado, Boulder.

Karlitz, Howard. 1979. "Unionization of Educational Administrators in the USA." *International Review of Education* 25(1):95–96.

Katz, Ellis. 1982. *Educational Policymaking. A View from the States.* U.S., Educational Resources Information Center, ERIC Document ED 226 403.

Kerchner, Charles T. 1979. "The Process Costs of Collective Bargaining in California School Districts." *Journal of Collective Negotiations* 8(1):39–50.

Kerlinger, Fred N. 1973. *Foundations of Behavioral Research.* New York: Holt, Rinehart and Winston.

Kirst, Michael W., ed. 1970. *The Politics of Education.* Berkeley: McCutchan.

Knezevich, Stephen J., and Fowlkes, John G. 1960. *Business Management of Local School Systems.* New York: Harper and Row.

Knoester, William P. 1978. "Administrative Unionization: What Kind of Solution?" *Phi Delta Kappan* 59(6):419–20.

Kowalski, Theodore J. 1978. "Are You Pushing Your Administrators Into Collective Bargaining?" *American School Board Journal* (July):35.

Kramer, Louis I. 1969. *Principals and Grievance Procedures.* Professional Negotiations Pamphlets 2. Worthington, Ohio: National Association of Secondary School Principals.

LaNoue, George R., ed. 1976. *Educational Vouchers: Concepts and Controversies.* New York: Teachers College Press.

Levin, Dan. 1982. "Teacher Unions Grapple with the Crisis Facing Organized Labor." *American School Board Journal* 169(7).

Lieberman, Myron. 1975. *Neglected Issues in Federal Public Employee Collective Bargaining Legislation.* U.S., Educational Resources Information Center, ERIC Document ED 105 615.

———. 1976. "Must You Bargain With Your Teachers?" *American School Board Journal* 163 (9):19–21.

———. 1978. What to Expect From Your Teacher Union When Your Board is Under the Financial Ax." *American School Board Journal* 165(9):39.

Lieberman, Myron, and Moskow, Michael. 1966. *Collective Negotiations for Teachers.* Chicago: Rand McNally.

Likert, Rensis, and Likert, Jane Gibson. 1976. *New Ways of Managing Conflict.* New York: McGraw-Hill.

Lindman, Erick L. 1975. *Dilemmas of School Finance.* Arlington, Va: Educational Research Service.

Lipsky, David B., and Drotning, John E. 1977. "The Relation Between Teacher Salaries and the Use of Impasse Procedures Under New York's Taylor Law: 1968–1972." *Journal of Collective Negotiations* 6(3):229–44.

Long, Gary, and Feuille, Peter. 1974. "Final-Offer Arbitration: 'Sudden Death' in Eugene." *Industrial and Labor Relations Review* 27(2):186–203.

Lundberg, Larry. 1976. *Preparing for Negotiations.* U.S., Educational Resources Information Center, ERIC Document ED 123 762.

Lussier, V. L. 1975. "Collective Bargaining and Affirmative Action." Paper presented at the First Annual Meeting of the American Association of Affirmative Action, Austin, Texas.

McCarty, Donald J., and Ramsey, Charles E. 1967. *A Study of Community Factors Related to the Turnover of Superintendents—Community Power, School Board Structure, and the Role of the Chief School Administrator.* U.S., Educational Resources Information Center, ERIC Document ED 014 130.

McCarty, Donald J., and Ramsey, Charles E. 1971. *The School Managers: Power and Conflict in American Education.* Westport, Conn.: Greenwood Press.

McDonnell, Lorraine M., and Pascal, Anthony H. 1979. "National Trends in Teacher Collective Bargaining." *Education and Urban Society* 11(2).

McKersie, Robert B. 1965. *A Behavioral Theory of Labor Negotiations.* New York: McGraw-Hill.

Marx, Herbert L., ed. 1969. *Collective Bargaining for Public Employees.* New York: H. W. Wilson.

Maslow, Abraham H. 1954. *Motivation and Personality.* New York: Harper and Row.

Masters, W. Frank. 1975. "Teacher Job Security Under Collective Bargaining Contracts." *Phi Delta Kappan* 56(7):455–58.

Miller, William C., and Newbury, David H. 1970. *Teacher Negotiation: A Guide for the Bargaining Team.* West Nyack, N.Y.: Parker.

Minar, David. 1967. "Community Politics and School Boards." *American School Board Journal* (Mar.):33–37.

Mitchell, Douglas E. 1976. *A Collective Bargaining Research Agenda: Hypotheses and Methods.* Paper presented at symposium, Organization, Collective Bargaining and Work. Annual meeting, California Educational Research Association, Burlingame, California. Washington, D.C.: National Institute of Education.

Modesto Bee. 24 Apr. 1981, a-16.

Moore, William J., and Newman, Robert. 1976. "The Influence of Legal and Nonlegal Factors on the Bargaining Status of Public School Teachers." *Journal of Collective Negotiations* 5(2):97–111.

Morphet, Edgar L., and Jesser, David L., eds. 1968. *Emerging Designs for Education:*

Programs, Organization, Operation and Finance. Denver: Designing Education for the Future.

Nasstrom, Roy R., and Brelsford, Robert L. 1976. "Some Characteristics of Militant Teachers: A Reassessment Based on an Indiana Study." *Journal of Collective Negotiations* 5(3):247–55.

National Association of Elementary School Principals. 1982. *Negotiating and Administering Contracts – July. School Management Handbook 6.* U.S., Educational Resources Information Center, ERIC Document ED 222 992.

National Commission on Excellence in Education. 1983. *A Nation at Risk.* Washington, D.C.: U.S. Government Printing Office.

National Commission on Teacher Education and Professional Standards. 1968. *Negotiating for Professionalization.* Washington, D.C.: National Education Association.

National Education Association. 1968. *Guidelines for Professional Negotiation.* Washington, D.C.: The Association.

Newby, Kenneth A. 1977. *Collective Bargaining: Practices and Attitudes of School Management, Research Report 1977–2.* U.S., Educational Resources Information Center, ERIC Document ED 146 711.

Newman, Harold R. 1979. "Mediator Pressures: High and Low." *Journal of Collective Negotiations* 8(1):77–80.

Newport, M. Gene. 1969. "Grappling With Grievances." *Supervisory Management* 14(9):6–9.

Nierenberg, Gerald. 1968. *The Art of Negotiating.* New York: Hawthorne.

O'Connell, James F., and Heller, Robert W. 1976. *Factors Leading to Impasse in Teacher-School Board Collective Bargaining.* U.S., Educational Resources Information Center, ERIC Document ED 120 936.

Ornstein, Allan. 1981. "The Trend Toward Increased Professionalism for Teachers." *Phi Delta Kappan* 63(3):196–98.

Ostrander, Kenneth J. 1981. *A Grievance Arbitration Guide for Educators.* Boston: Allyn and Bacon.

Parker, Hyman; Repas, Bob; and Schmidt, Charles. 1967. *A Guide to Collective Negotiations in Education.* East Lansing, Michigan: Social Science Research Bureau.

Perry, Charles R., and Wildman, Wesley A. 1970. *The Impact of Negotiations in Public Education.* Worthington, Ohio: Jones.

Peterson, Richard B. 1976. "A Cross-Cultural Study of Secondary School Teachers' Attitudes Regarding Job Satisfaction, Professionalism, and Collective Negotiations (Sweden and State of Washington)." *Journal of Collective Negotiations* 5(2):113–124.

Peterson, Richard B., and Smith, H. Dean. 1974. "Making Sense Out of Teacher Professionalism, Job Satisfaction, and Attitudes toward Collective Negotiations." *Journal of Collective Negotiations* 3(3):227–39.

Phi Delta Kappan. 1979. 60(6):472–73.

Pierce, Douglas R. 1976. *Teachers' Association Impacts upon Governance of a School System.* U.S., Educational Resources Information Center, ERIC Document ED 123 800.

Pisapia, John R. 1976. "Does Teacher Unionism Affect Professional Commitment?" *Journal of Collective Negotiations* 5(2):167–74.

———. 1979. "Trilateral Practices and the Public Sector Bargaining Model." *Phi Delta Kappan* 60(6):424–27.

Powell, Edward M. 1976. *The Teachers' Right to Strike Versus the Students' Right to an Education.* U.S., Educational Resources Information Center, ERIC Document ED 123 714.

Pulliam, Mark S. 1982. "Union Security Clauses in Public Sector Labor Contracts and

Abood v. *Detroit Board of Education:* A Dissent." *Labor Law Journal,* Sept.

Reed, Donald B. 1976. *Teachers and Collective Bargaining.* U.S., Educational Resources Information Center, ERIC Document ED 140 411.

Reed, Vincent E. 1977. "The Do's and Don'ts of Living with a Teachers' Contract," *NASSP Bulletin* (May):80–84.

Richardson, Bruce A. 1975. "Listen, Mr. Shanker, It's Not Quite as Simple as You Make It Sound," *American School Board Journal* 162(5):49–65.

Rogers, Carl R. 1965. "The Interpersonal Relationship: The Core of Guidance." In *Guidance: An Examination,* ed. Ralph L. Mosher, Richard F. Carle, and Chris D. Kehas. New York: Harcourt, Brace and World.

Ross, Doris. 1978. *Cuebook: State Collective Bargaining Laws.* Denver: Education Commission of the States.

Rubin, Louis. 1979. "Educational Achievement and Public Satisfaction." *Educational Leadership* 36(8):537–40.

Sabghir, Irving. 1970. *The Scope of Bargaining in Public Sector Collective Bargaining.* New York: Public Employment Relations Board.

Salisbury, Robert H. 1967. "Schools and Politics in the Big City." *Harvard Educational Review.* 37(3):408–24.

Sarthory, Joseph A. 1971. "Structural Characteristics and the Outcomes of Collective Negotiations." *Educational Administration Quarterly* 7(3):77–89.

Schnaufer, Pete. 1966. *The Uses of Teacher Power.* Chicago: American Federation of Teachers.

Schofield, Dee. 1976. *Collective Negotiations and the Principal.* U.S., Educational Resources Information Center, ERIC Document ED 123 738.

Schramm, Le Roy H. 1977. "Is Teacher Tenure Negotiable: A Review of Court Decisions." *Journal of Collective Negotiations* 6(3):245–57.

Selden, David. 1967. *Winning Collective Bargaining.* Chicago: American Federation of Teachers.

Sexton, Michael J.; Fox, Milden J., Jr.; and Potter, Danny R. 1978. "The Scope of Teacher Collective Bargaining." *Journal of Collective Negotiations* 7(2):145–65.

Sinclair, John E. 1977. "Separate Bargaining Units for Principals: The Wrong Solution." *NASSP Bulletin* (May):52–56.

Shils, Edward B., and Whittier, C. Taylor. 1968. *Teachers, Administrators, and Collective Bargaining.* New York: Thomas Y. Crowell.

Spiess, John A. 1970. *Community Power and Influence Studies: Two Positions.* U.S., Educational Resources Information Center, ERIC Document ED 051 550.

————. 1971. *Community Power Study Applications to Educational Administration.* U.S., Educational Resources Information Center, ERIC Document ED 057 488.

Sosnowsky, William P.; Simpkins, Edward; and LaPlante, Frances M. 1976. *Teacher Unions on Mainstreaming.* Washington, D.C.: U.S. Department of Health, Education and Welfare, National Institute of Education.

Stern, David; Bagley, Kate; Larnders, Roy; Spaeth, Nancy; and Wolfe, Marian. 1978. *From Both Sides: How California Teachers and School District Representatives View Collective Bargaining under SB 160 of 1975.* Final Report to the School Finance Equalization Project, California State Department of Education. Berkeley: Field Service Center, School of Education.

Stinnet, T. N; Kleinmann, Jack; and Ware, Martha L. 1966. *Professional Negotiations in Public Education.* New York: Macmillan.

Stoops, Emery; Rafferty, Max; and Johnson, Russell. 1975. *Handbook of Educational Administration.* Boston: Allyn and Bacon.

Thayer, Lee O. 1968. *Communication and Communications Systems.* Homewood, Ill.: Irwin.

Thomas, J. M., and Bennis, W. G., eds. 1972. *Management of Change and Conflict.* Baltimore: Penguin Books.

Tomkiewicz, Joseph. 1979. "Determinants of Teacher Militancy: Factors Affecting the Decision to Strike." *Journal of Collective Negotiations* 8(1):91–96.

Tracy, Lane. 1974. "The Influence of Noneconomic Factors on Negotiators." *Industrial and Labor Relations Review* 27(2):204–15.

Underwood, Kenneth E.; McCluskey, Lawrence; and Umberger, George R. 1978a. "A Profile of the School Board Member." *American School Board Journal* 165(10):23–24.

_____. 1978b. "Male and Female Board Members Think Alike—And Think Conservatively." *American School Board Journal* 165(10):27.

U.S. Congress. House. Committee on Education and Labor. *Oversight Hearings on Elementary and Secondary Education.* 92d Cong., 2d sess., 1972. H.R. 12695.

U.S. Department of Health, Education and Welfare. 1960. *Financial Accounting for Local and State School Systems.* Washington, D.C.: U.S. Government Printing Office.

Walton, Richard E, and McKersie, Robert. 1965. *A Behavioral Theory of Labor Negotiations.* New York: McGraw-Hill.

Walworth, William. 1978. "Does Your Board Need a Labor Relations Consultant?" *American School Board Journal* 165(7):38–39.

Weintraub, Andrew, and Thornton, Robert J. 1976. "Why Teachers Strike: The Economic and Legal Determinants." *Journal of Collective Negotiations* 5(3):193–206.

Wildavasky, Aaron. 1974. *The Politics of the Budgetary Process.* Boston: Little, Brown.

Wirt, Frederick M., and Kirst, Michael W. 1975. *Political and Social Foundations of Education.* Berkeley: McCutchan.

Woodworth, Robert T., and Peterson, Richard B. 1969. *Collective Negotiations for Public and Professional Employees.* Glenview, Ill.: Scott, Foresman.

Wortman, Max, and Randle, Wilson C. 1966. *Collective Bargaining Principles and Practices.* Boston: Houghton Mifflin.

Zachary, Peter T. 1976. *Mediation, Arbitration, Fact-Finding, and Impasse.* U.S., Educational Resources Information Center, ERIC Document ED 123 713.

Zack, Arnold. 1974. *Understanding Grievance Arbitration in the Public Sector.* Report submitted to the Division of Public Employee Relations, U.S. Department of Labor. Washington, D.C.: U.S. Government Printing Office.

Zeigler, L. Harmon; Tucker, Harvey J.; and Wilson, L. A. 1976. "School Boards and Community Power: The Irony of Professionalism." *Intellect* (Sept.–Oct.): 90–92.

Zuelke, Dennis C., and Frohreich, Lloyd E. 1977. "The Impact of Collective Negotiations on Teachers' Salaries: Some Evidence from Wisconsin." *Journal of Collective Negotiations* 6(1):81–88.

INDEX

DATE DUE

DEMCO 38-297